The Hundredth Monkey

ACTIVITIES THAT INSPIRE PLAYFUL LEARNING

Nate Folan and Friends

Nate Folan • Ryan McCormick • Larry Childs
Renee Cavaluzzi • Paul Radcliffe • Michelle Wilson
Angel Krimm • Suze Collinson-Runnells • Peter Aubry

Project Adventure
Advancing Active Learning

Book interior design by:
SYP Design & Production, Inc.

Photos by:
Nate Folan and Andrew Siems

Cover design by:
Greg Clarke with Nate Folan,
Andrew Siems, and everyone
else who added their two cents!

Illustrations by:
Nate Folan, enhanced by Greg Clarke
and Sara Day, and inspired by the work
of Colin Cramm, Illustratie and Animatie

Printed by:
Walch Printing

Table of Contents

Introduction 1

Foundational Concepts 7

Activities 20

Activities Sequences 258

Appendix 290

Activity Index 311

Dedication

This activity guide is dedicated to
the "peter pans" of the world,
especially my brother-in-law, Keith Wilson
and great friend and mentor, Tony Calcia,
whose playful spirits and passion for life
flow through this book and the child in all of us.

Gratitude

The Hundredth Monkey represents the art and contributions of many creative minds, moving bodies, loving hearts, and playful spirits of people affiliated with Project Adventure during the past five years. The original idea was that many trainers would contribute activities to PA's newest activity book instead of having an activity book attributed to any one trainer, or author. While the original concept changed throughout the project, I did my best to represent every aspect of every person involved. The result is a collection of super fun activities, sequences and other ideas intended to inspire playful learning. It has been an adventure – joyful, challenging, surprising, and gratifying – to work and play with everyone who helped bring forth the creation of this activity guide.

My deepest gratitude to:

- Ryan McCormick whose playful tinkering, wildly creative mind, and collaborative spirit brought forth many of the activities included in this activity guide. Without Ryan, *The Hundredth Monkey* would not exist as it does. I am grateful to have joined Ryan in playful collaboration of many of these activities and to have shared many insightful conversations about our work with him. Most of all, I am grateful to call Ryan a close friend.

- Larry Childs whose continued dedication to this project and perspective and support throughout the process has been invaluable. Larry contributed many activities geared toward the classroom and perhaps found his voice best in the activity "Sneak Attack." I am grateful to have Larry as a supervisor, idea bouncer, and especially a friend.

- Rene Cavaluzzi, Paul Radcliffe, Angel Krimm, Michelle Wilson, Suze Collinson-Runnells, and Peter Aubry who, in addition to Larry, Ryan, and I, are the authors of this book. The contributions of these six people could easily be summarized in one word – selfless. They have given of themselves not only while contributing to this book, but also in every task and service they deliver for Project Adventure and PA clients. I am grateful for the diversity, criticism, and commitment they have offered.

- Lisa Howard, Andrew Siems, Ethan Doss, Suze Collinson-Runnells, Aaron Nicholson, MB Buckner, and Chris Damboise whose willingness to play with the activities after only reading the descriptions and provide necessary feedback on our ability to convey enough information to get the activities to jump off the page and hopefully into the program of many practitioners around the world. I am grateful for their honesty, attention to detail, and enthusiasm.

- Laura McDonald, Joe Karr, Liz Penman, Jeff Frigon and the many Project Adventure facilitators and trainers for sharing activities and ideas they have discovered along the way. I am grateful for their dedication to the field of experiential education and their continued efforts to be a part of Project Adventure in the best way that they are able – by being themselves.

- The many youth and adult participants who accepted the invitation to play and were game to "try something new." Their participation, playfulness, and perspective were significant in shaping the contents of this book. I am grateful for everyone who has been willing to step out of, or maybe into, themselves and play.

- Dick Prouty for answering the "hard" questions and sharing his perspective. I am grateful for Dick's insights and willingness to listen to my rants and rambles.

- Abbie Bruett whose dedication to Project Adventure's product and catalog service over the years provided valuable feedback, criticism, and insight that helped shaped the contents of the book. I am grateful for Abbie driving a deadline and "speaking her truth" while being open to my questions and concerns.
- Greg Clarke for his patience, steadiness, and masterful use of the tools necessary to bring the design of the cover to life. I am grateful for Greg's friendship and consistent "don't overthink it" or "don't worry about it too much" reminders.
- Sara Day whose expertise in design provided critical feedback and pulled it all together in the end. I am grateful for Sara's openness and incorporation of our ideas with her own.
- Mark Collard, Bart Crawford, and Kristen Okura for their value adding conversations and support. Mark and Bart have been consistent consultants, coaches, and inspiration throughout the process and beyond. Kristen (with a penguin's spirit) offered insights that significantly shaped the afterword. I am grateful for the collegial relationships and friendships I share with all 3 of these passionate people.
- Karl Rohnke for sharing himself and his stories, especially the story found in the introduction. I am grateful to have crossed paths with Karl, a living legend, and to have found him down-to-earth, humble, and generous.
- Peter Aubry whose flexibility and understanding, as project manager, allowed for this project to emerge as it did. Peter stepped in or out when he felt necessary and made decisions that demonstrated his value for the greater good. I am grateful for Peter's patience, openness, and support.
- Rufus Collinson for staring at the screen for days editing and trying to make sense of what I had written. Thanks to Rufus's questions, edits, and deep caring that helped me to more effectively say what I had to share. I am grateful for the poem that is Rufus Collinson and the unconditional love she shares with everyone.
- Tony Calcia who, many years ago, took the time to listen to a young 16 year old (me) struggling to find his place in the world and in doing so significantly influence who I am and what I do today. I am grateful for Tony's friendship, mentoring, and passion for life.
- My family, especially my parents Pam and John Folan, whose understanding and support has consistently empowered me to pursue a life a bit different than the norm. I am grateful to all family members for their love.
- My loving wife, Michelle Wilson, whose patience, conversation, criticism, support, and playfulness inspire me every day, especially throughout the writing of this book. I am especially grateful for Michelle's constant love and openness. These attributes seemingly allowed her to understand why (at times) I wrote without sleep through the night, accept when I was not present with her (or anyone and anything else for that matter), and encourage me to stay positive while finishing this project.

After reading this message of gratitude I hope it is clear that many, many, people, including anyone I inadvertently forgot to mention, helped shape the content and presentation of this book. And thank YOU for picking it up! May all the ideas, love, energy, and spirit poured into this book flow through you when you present the activities and play, learn, and grow!

— Nate Folan, 2012

The Hundredth Monkey

The Japanese monkey has been observed in the wild for more than 30 years. In 1952, on the island of Koshima, scientists were providing monkeys with sweet potatoes dropped in the sand. The monkeys liked the taste of the raw sweet potatoes, but found the dirt unpleasant. An 18-month old female named Imo found that she could solve the problem by washing the potatoes in a nearby stream. She taught this trick to her mother. Her playmates also learned this new way and taught their mothers, too.

This cultural innovation was gradually adopted by various monkeys before the eyes of the scientists. Between 1952 and 1958, all the young monkeys learned to wash the sandy sweet potatoes to make them more palatable. Only the adults that imitated their children benefitted from this social improvement. Other adults kept eating the dirty potatoes.

Then something startling took place. In the autumn of 1958, a certain number of Koshima monkeys were washing sweet potatoes – the exact number is not known. Let us suppose that when the sun rose one morning there were 99 monkeys on Koshima Island who had learned to wash their sweet potatoes. Let's further suppose that later that morning, the hundredth monkey learned to wash potatoes.

THEN IT HAPPENED!

By that evening, almost everyone in the tribe was washing sweet potatoes before eating them. The added energy of this hundredth monkey somehow created an ideological breakthrough!

But notice. A most surprising thing observed by these scientists was that the habit of washing sweet potatoes then jumped over the sea. Colonies of monkeys on other islands and the mainland troop of monkeys from Takasakiyama began washing their sweet potatoes!

Thus, when a certain critical number achieves an awareness, this new awareness may be communicated from mind to mind. Although the exact number may vary, this Hundredth Monkey Phenomenon means that when only a limited number of people know of a new way, it may remain the conscious property of these people. But there is a point at which if only one more person tunes in to a new awareness, a field is strengthened so that this awareness is picked up by almost everyone!

The Hundredth Monkey by Ken Keyes, Jr.

Why The 100th Monkey?

By Dick Prouty

The 100th Monkey phenomenon is really the story of the change process. As the new learning of washing sweet potatoes began to be noticed by some monkeys, at some point now commonly referred to as the "tipping point," the learning spread throughout the whole group. And then, seemingly miraculously, it spread to other islands of monkeys who suddenly began washing their potatoes too.

We know that the change process in nature is not even and steady. For example, as water cools from 40° to 33°, it is a liquid; then at 32 degrees, ice forms. In physics, this is called a phase transition and there are laws for these changes. Similarly, in groups, from classes of students to cohorts of teachers to a camp of 200 campers, the positive behavior and cultural change promoted by adventure activities is not steady and linear, but really comes in fits and starts. Then, suddenly there is real progress. Malcolm Gladwell has given us the "tipping point" language, and it is a common term used to describe that time when change spreads rapidly in a human organization.

Whether or not there is scientific evidence that the remote jumping of behavior is possible (try Googling Bell's Theorem), the 100th monkey story is a great metaphor for the way that the change process can work slowly and steadily for a time and then rapidly.

The activities in this book are wonderful tools to use in any curricula involving learning and change. The wonderful thing about these activities is that the end users and the facilitators of them do not have to fully understand the theory behind the parable of the 100th monkey. If one immerses in the activity, using all of one's gifts, and simply plays and has fun, learning happens.

Of course, for the full power of these activities and maximum learning to occur, the right framing and processing, in the context of the right curricula, all are necessary. But many of you know this already, and others can easily learn that through our other PA trainings and offerings. As we process our activities with the experiential learning cycle, and use our Full Value methods, these activities can be part of a change or learning process that is powerful indeed.

And, the best thing about using these activities is that you will be doing what brain research has said is even more powerfully appealing to us than eating – playing. We have evolved through actively collaborating and "playing" together. And here we are...Enjoy!

Introduction

Introduction

Something magical happens when we play. It's hard to explain, but easy to experience. There's a sense of lightness, timelessness, and pure joy. Regardless of age, playing enables us to be ourselves and feel fully alive. In the book *Play*, Stuart Brown explains this concept by stating, "When we play, we are engaged in the purest expression of our humanity, the truest expression of our individuality. Is it any wonder that often the times we feel most alive, those that make up our best memories, are moments of play?" Recall for a moment the last time you played. Were you alone or with other people? Were you inside or out? Was your play structured or unstructured? Whatever or wherever it was, recall how you felt. Recall the memories. Run through the images, dance with the sounds. Smile.

Play has been the foundation of Project Adventure programming since it began, sort of... According to Karl Rohnke, one of PA's founders, it wasn't always that way. I had the great fortune to speak with Karl, after meeting him for the first time at PA's 40th Anniversary event. Karl explained that when he and others first started implementing Outward Bound concepts at Hamilton-Wenham Regional High School, the concept we now call Project Adventure was not initially received with enthusiasm. The PA founders (ex-Outward Bound instructors) were pushing expedition-inspired scenarios in a non-expedition setting and expecting the group to take on an expedition mentality. "The Project", as Project Adventure was initially called, wasn't working. It wasn't until an attempt was made to add fun and play to the traditional physical education curriculum that the students began to respond positively.

One example that Karl shared was inflating a truck inner tube and kicking it around as though he were playing soccer. As Karl told the story, he laughed and exclaimed, "The activity was boldly unique and more than fulfilled the physical aspects of the physical education curriculum while engaging even the most reluctant students. Students recognized that something different was going on and wanted a piece of the action. It seemed as though this serendipitous introduction of fun and play was enough to engage the most disinclined students." Karl went on to say, "As success built on success, the encouraged staff became widely creative, audaciously changing and adapting the rules to make childhood games less competitive, yet more inclusive", and that's when it (PA) began to work. Project Adventure has been inspiring change in individuals, groups, educational settings and beyond for more than 40 years.

Play offers an experience unlike any other. Providing a space where playful adventures can be experienced by students, educators, as well as many others, has been significant in the success of Project Adventure. These experiences prepare people for the adventure they are about to embark on, whatever and where ever that may be. In many ways, play and adventure are synonymous, resulting in a magical way of being. This is perhaps best highlighted again by Stuart Brown: "Stepping out of a normal routine, finding novelty, being open to serendipity, enjoying the unexpected, embracing a little risk, and finding pleasure in the heightened vividness of life. These are all qualities of a state of play." This could also be said for adventure. For anyone who has experienced Project Adventure, it is clear that PA is a step out of the normal routine. Project Adventure is a community of innovative people, who passionately guide participants of all ages through moments of laughter, surprise, uncertainty, awe-inspiring chance, and choices. Vivid, yes... intense, glowing, present, brilliant, vibrant, connected, inspired...this is how we feel when we experience adventure – when we play.

— Nate Folan
with Karl Rohnke

About This Activity Guide

The Hundredth Monkey is a resourceful collection of more than 100 new and adapted activities accompanied by many variation ideas. It was designed for a wide range of practitioners in a variety of settings. With a fresh look into Project Adventure's foundational concepts, multiple framing and debriefing ideas, and a special sequencing chapter, there is plenty to inspire anyone who hopes to advance the human condition. If you wish to empower people to play, laugh, connect, learn, reflect, grow, heal, achieve, perform and live fully, this activity guide is for YOU! *The Hundredth Monkey* is an inspirational and practical offering to those of you who hope to spread the joy of adventure and the boundless potential for learning and growth.

Just so you know...

Throughout this guide, we refer to the participants as participants, players, or people. These words could refer to all potential participants including but not limited to campers, students, residents, patients, and clients. Likewise, we refer to the people leading the activities as practitioners or facilitators. The words practitioners or facilitators could refer to all potential users of this book including but not limited to challenge course facilitators, camp counselors, classroom teachers, physical education teachers, professors, youth workers, youth ministers, orientation leaders, counselors, therapists, administrators, corporate trainers, organizational development professionals, and human resource professionals.

How to use this activity guide

The book is organized into three sections in addition to this Introduction. Section 1 reinforces the use of adventure as a learning methodology. The scope of activities can be found in Section 2 and Section 3 features activity sequences.

In Section 1, Project Adventure's foundational concepts are presented with new perspectives. This provides you with a frame work and initial understanding to help with leading the activities. If you are familiar with PA's foundational concepts and theory, we hope another view will give you something to play with, ponder and eventually inspire your practice and the prac-

tice of others. While adventure activities are effective, it is the people, both the practitioners and the participants, who make the activity what it is. Collectively we create what is experienced and ultimately determine the outcomes. In other words, the activities don't work unless we do. And, the activities won't play unless we do! Use an activity at a time, link a series of activities together in a sequence, or drop them into the curriculum you are developing or delivering. Above all else, play and have fun!

One consistent challenge with experiential education and adventure learning is that it doesn't live in the books we publish; it lives within the experience, the interactions and reactions of our participants with activities, other aspects of adventure, and you! In other words, it is important for all of us to continually develop our selves and our practice. To learn this and fully "get" what adventure learning is, we recommend that you experience it. We do recommend that you read the Introduction and become familiar with some of the theory upon which adventure teaching and learning is based, yet understand that it will only bring you so far. What we truly hope for is that you experience adventure learning first hand with us at Project Adventure. Our immersion approach to training allows an opportunity for you to experience the activities and the adventure process in the same way your participants will. This experience not only provides significant insight, but greatly enhances your ability and outcomes. For some, it could even be life changing!

Section 2 contains the individual activity descriptions. The activity descriptions have been organized in alphabetical order based on the name of the activity. Each activity description is intentionally designed to guide a practitioner through the facilitation of an activity in an adventurous way – framing, playing, debriefing. Also, most activity descriptions include multiple framing and debriefing ideas, along with a host of tips and variations, illuminating the versatility and potential of each activity. We are optimistic that this section will inspire the creative process in everyone who references the book. To support this, we have included a few vignettes, or stories, about the emergence of an activity, which is less about credit and more about building our collective wisdom. We look forward to learning from you when you are in one of our workshops or at a conference how you creatively frame and insightfully debrief an activity, participants' insights that flowed through a space you helped to foster, or any number of variations and new ideas that emerged while playing these activities.

Activities, when facilitated well, are very effective in achieving desired results, be it for fun or other specific outcomes. We chose learning themes to provide focus and also be expansive enough for you, the practitioner, to determine the desired results most appropriate for your group, program, and setting. Assessing your group, program, and curriculum needs inform the selection of the most effective learning theme. Use the learning themes as a guide initially, and as you become more familiar with the activities and their potential, you should be able, with your experience and professional skills, to modify them to fit the specific needs of your group and settings you work in. Ultimately, we hope that participants themselves become experienced and skilled enough to define their own learnings and that you feel confident in offering this opportunity.

In Section 3, you will find a concept new to our activity books. We have listed five activity sequences in a format similar to the activity descriptions and organized them by different class or program time frames. Each sequence flows through a progression of activities that build on one another connected with segues or transitional framing ideas and culminate with a final debrief. The sequences represent the collective creativity of many trainers at Project Adventure who shared their ideas and built upon the concepts of others. The result is an engaging and effective sequence of activities likely to bring participants into a state of flow or optimal experience as described in *Flow*[1] by Mihaly Csikszentmihalyi.

How to use the activity descriptions

Each activity description in Section 2 has a title, information on how to lead the activity, and the materials needed to run it. A brief overview, group size, learning themes, and time frames

provide a snapshot of each activity enabling you to select activities more quickly.

Each activity description includes:
- Overview – A brief description of the activity including the type of activity, a brief explanation, and a lens on potential outcomes.
- Group Size – Recommended group size for the activity to be effective.
- Learning Themes – Subjects chosen to provide learning opportunities for participants. Use these as a guide to selecting activities for meeting your own more specific learning objectives or desired results.
- Estimated Time – An approximate time frame (it is important to note that the length of time for each activity will vary greatly depending on your group's need for processing behaviors and/or feelings that arise during a given activity).
- Materials/Props – What you'll need to facilitate each activity.
- Setup – How and what you'll need to prepare to facilitate each activity.
- Framing – An idea or a few ideas of how you might introduce the activity, peaking the interest of your participants and getting them to consider the relevance of the experience they are about to have (the framing can be used verbatim, but is offered mainly as a guideline as it is important to use framings, including language, length, and details, that best resonate with and engage your groups).
- Procedure – Steps to communicating the rules and guidelines for each activity.
- Reflection/Closure/Discussion – Questions for discussion and/or activities for reflection that will help your participants look at the "What?" "So what?" and "Now what?" of the Experiential Learning Cycle. Some descriptions include several debrief ideas to assist you in selecting what is most appropriate for your group. If there is something that happens during an activity that you need to resolve or explore during the reflection, do so. Don't feel limited to the reflection we've designed. This can't be emphasized enough.

Activity sequences in Section 3 are structured in much the same way – with a few noticeable

---

1 *Flow*, Csikszentmihalyi, Harper and Row, 1990

additions. In addition to the items above, each activity sequence description includes:

- Segue/Transitional Framing – Offers language to aid in a more seamless transition from one activity to the next.
- Opening/Next/Culminating Activity – Indicates which activity is being presented next in the sequence followed by related information.

You will also find boxes with facilitation tips, comments, and safety checks as appropriate. Many descriptions also include a number of variations. Some variations may be commonly known; others emerged during the writing process and while playing with the activities. A few variations seem like they should have been a separate activity description all together and some are. Still others simply add value, intensity, and challenge to the ever expanding potential of the activity.

Learning Themes

Adventure Learning has embraced and benefitted from the focus and attention given to the needs of students in the 21st century. The core premise is to not only complement the core subject's content to educate students but also to be integrated within them. Some of the main benefits of Adventure Learning reside in the area of Social Emotional Learning (SEL) and what are now being labeled and defined as 21st Century Skills. In our *Stepping Stones* guide, we state that "SEL is necessary for children to develop into competent caring people who make good decisions and have positive relationships." We would now add to this that SEL skills combined with 21st century skills will prepare people of all ages for what is projected to be required of them in the 21st century even with the future being more unknown than ever. Outcomes unknown – sounds like an adventure, right?!

Two key organizations that have advanced these concepts are CASEL (Collaborative Association for Social Emotional Learning) and The Partnership for 21st Century Skills. Their work in the area of student development has influenced many educational institutions and their subsequent educational programs, curricula and instructions. These are part of what The Partnership for 21st Century Skills call support systems, which influence student outcomes.

Our hope is that if you want to, or are required to build your curriculum based on student outcomes, this section and the following information will be helpful.

We believe that readers and users of this book will sometimes use these activities without being driven by outcomes. Playing these activities for FUNN (Functional Understanding Not Necessary) has pure value with positive non-directed results for participants – without a doubt! However many educators must now have all of their curricula and instructions outcome-driven, and thus their lesson plans and curricula must have identified intentional student outcomes. We have provided a structure to the activity write-ups that assist in this process.

Each activity description includes learning themes related to student outcomes. We have identified seven key Learning Themes and present them in a progressive order commonly associated with the flow of an adventure program. These outcomes have been compiled from a variety of sources but are clearly influenced by the organizations mentioned above and the legacy of Project Adventure's programming. Under each Learning Theme are bulleted points providing further insight into the more general learning theme heading. We invite you, the reader, to define your own specific participant outcomes or connect pre-existing outcomes to these learning themes as you develop your curriculum and instructions. Additionally, we hope that you find this as helpful as we have in being outcome-focused when working with students, groups and teams.

Learning Themes

1. Fun and Play
   - FUNN (A whimsical acronym for Functional Understanding Not Necessary)
   - Playing to Play
2. Physical Activity and Movement
   - Warm-ups and Stretching
   - Movement Concepts and Motor Skills
   - Healthy Lifestyle
3. Building Trust, Relationships, and Community
   - Building the Foundation of Trust
   - Ice Breakers and Getting to Know Each Other

- De-inhibitizers and Energizers
- Establishing Full Value Contracts and Generating Group Norms
4. Self Awareness and Self Management
   - Self Assessment and Self Expression
   - Self Care and Self Love
   - Self Efficacy
   - Goal Setting
   - Flexibility and Adaptability
5. Social Awareness
   - Recognizing and Appreciating Similarities and Differences
   - Empathy and Compassion
6. Relationship Skills
   - Trusting Self and Others
   - Teamwork, Collaboration and Co-creation
   - Effective Communication
   - Leading and Following
   - Care for Self and Others
   - Confronting Others and Conflict Resolution
7. Responsible Decision Making
   - Critical Thinking and Problem Solving
   - Using and Managing Information
   - Risk Taking and Initiative
   - Imagination, Creativity and Innovation

Important Recommendations

Training

The outcomes of the activities and activity sequences in this guide are greatly enhanced through appropriate training. A "well-run adventure program" typically includes staff who are playful, reflective, and passionate, and trained in the use of adventure; including Project Adventure's foundational concepts or similar concepts included in this introductory section . Project Adventure suggests a comprehensive training plan that addresses the following key areas:

- Experiencing adventure activities including warm-ups, ice-breakers and initiatives
- Basic theory of adventure and experiential education
- Facilitation, processing and debriefing skills
- Techniques for goal setting and group development
- Safety and risk management skills appropriate for the activities in this book

Props and Equipment

Each activity includes a list of props that are necessary. Many props are available in your existing equipment rooms or storage closets. Project Adventure offers a Portable Adventure Challenge Kit (PACK Bag) designed specifically to accompany this activity guide as well as individual items for purchase.

While the activities in this guide do not use any high or low challenge course elements, both are significant to an effective adventure program. Low challenge course elements are an excellent tool for group problem solving, conflict resolution and processing. High challenge course elements are used extensively as peak experiences. A well-rounded program, using challenge courses and complementary activities, such as those in this book, provides exhilarating experiences that build trust and competency, and help participants break through perceived limits. Project Adventure is the pioneer in designing, installing, maintaining and providing training in the use of challenge courses. As you develop your adventure program, consider adding these elements to further enhance the value that this type of program affords your students.

Assessment

Assessment is a critical component of any program. It is important to not only assess individual and group goal achievement but also overall program goals. Individual and group assessment frequency varies depending on the population you are working with. However, we advocate that periodic check-ins be done with an outside expert such as those from Project Adventure, who are experienced in helping you build your assessment skills.

Foundational Concepts

The information presented in this section covers the foundational concepts or cornerstones utilized by Project Adventure in our Adventure Programs. The implementation of these concepts, while conducting the activities in this book, will contribute to the success of your program. These concepts promote and support the attributes of Adventure: play, risk taking, fun, challenge and safety!

Challenge by Choice

adapted from *Stepping Stones*
(Project Adventure, 2008)

Since it emerged, Challenge by Choice has had a profound impact on adventure programming, the adventure and experiential education field, and, most importantly, the lives of many people. Challenge by Choice assumes that people know themselves, their bodies, and their goals best and empowers them to make choices associated with this understanding. In doing so, it invites participants to engage without having to opt out of an activity, rather to find a way to participate within the experience that is engaging and challenging for them while adding value

to the group. Choosing how to be within an adventure experience allows a participant to affirm or discover who they are, determine how to act, and ultimately how to be in the world. Challenge by Choice ultimately enables every person to appreciate their comforts and discomforts, choose an appropriate level of challenge for themselves, and grow beyond their fears into the fullest expression of themselves.

A way to understand the concept of Challenge by Choice is by looking at the optimal learning zone. Most of us can recognize three different zones within which we function: comfort, stretch/growth and panic. (See diagram).

Challenge by Choice strives to have people learn how to participate in their stretch zones while learning to move out of their comfort zones and avoid or not choose situations that put them in their panic zones. The core element here is that participants determine how they can add value to an activity while challenging themselves. In doing so, they become less inhibited, scared, or concerned with what others think about them, and become more in touch with who they really are and what they are really capable of. The essence of Challenge

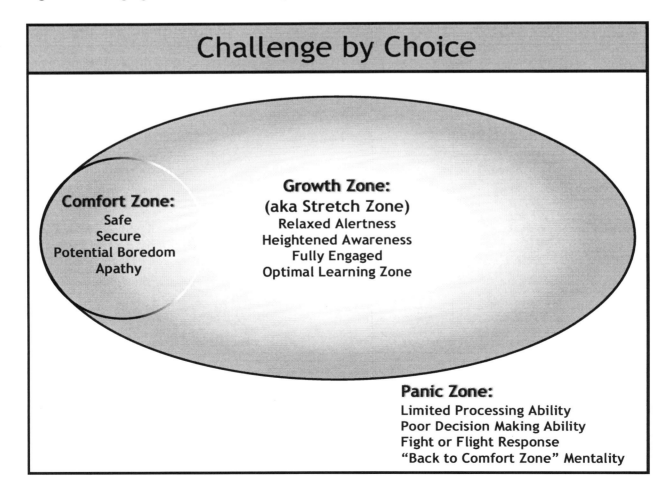

Challenge by Choice

Comfort Zone:
Safe
Secure
Potential Boredom
Apathy

Growth Zone:
(aka Stretch Zone)
Relaxed Alertness
Heightened Awareness
Fully Engaged
Optimal Learning Zone

Panic Zone:
Limited Processing Ability
Poor Decision Making Ability
Fight or Flight Response
"Back to Comfort Zone" Mentality

by Choice is eloquently conveyed in the song "I Choose"[2] by India Arie:

Because you never know where life is gonna take you
and you can't change where you've been.
But today, I have the opportunity to choose.

(And I choose) to be the best that I can be.
(I choose) to be authentic in everything I do.
My past don't dictate who I am. I choose. (Yeah)

Sounds nice, right? So, how do we best support our participants to choose their challenge and be the best they can be? One way is being able to recognize which zone our participants are in during activities (and at other times). When participants are in their comfort zones, they are often bored, not challenged and disengaged. Participants in their panic zones are frequently hyper-vigilant, anxious and will do anything to remove themselves from the anxiety-provoking situation. A participant in the panic zone has a very difficult time learning and processing new information. Therefore it is critical to help participants determine what their stretch zone looks like. Typically, participants in their stretch zones are fully engaged, demonstrate relaxed alertness, and may express when feeling slightly uncomfortable. Once each participant understands what it means to exist in their personal stretch or growth zones, the next step is to assist them in identifying and communicating goals. Furthermore, tools and strategies to support each participant in their stretch zone, e.g., taking a deep breath or three, may also be necessary. This will lead to learning, discovery and feedback that will help them to grow.

As facilitators, we will have much more success if we keep the concept of Challenge by Choice in mind as we conduct the activities in this book and beyond. Remember that while not participating may not be an option in some environments, it is also true that not everyone has to participate in the same way and at the same level to challenge themselves. Participants who appear to be in their comfort zones should be challenged into their stretch zones. Conversely, participants who appear to be in their panic zones should be supported in finding ways to

participate in their stretch zones. Work with your participants using this model to help identify ways that they can work with each other so that they might engage more in their stretch or challenge zones.

A few additional considerations regarding Challenge by Choice:

- Challenge by Choice invites us to be less comfortable being comfortable and become more comfortable being less comfortable.
- Challenge by Choice asks us to choose to function while acknowledging and appreciating our fears.
- Challenge by Choice brings awareness and opportunities for goal setting.

Throughout *The Hundredth Monkey*, there are many activities that subtly or explicitly introduce, reinforce, or utilize the concept of Challenge by Choice exceptionally well, e.g., stepping out of one's comfort zone, taking risks, making mistakes and failing, and being our greatest, most authentic selves. A few examples are:

- Juggle Moves
- Knee Tag
- Stationary Handshakes
- 52 Card Pick-up
- A Mess of Handshakes (activity sequence)

Full Value Contract

When inviting participants to voluntarily challenge themselves, explore aspects of themselves that may cause them to feel vulnerable, and hopefully grow into the best person they can be, it is important to have the committed support of everyone in the group. The Full Value Contract (FVC) is just the tool needed to draw out a true commitment of support from everyone and is a cornerstone of a well-run adventure program. It is critical to the effective use of the activities in this guide and the safety, enjoyment, and growth of everyone involved.

The FVC instills responsibility in everyone (practitioners and participants) for creating an environment where all feel safe enough to take risks and reveal their most authentic selves while developing social emotional skills. The FVC also serves as a structure for creating behavioral norms that everyone agrees to practice and maintain throughout the life of

---

2 Testimony: *Vol. 1, Life & Relationship.* India Arie. Mowtown 2006.

the activity, class, session; and in the case of a full-school or agency implementation, all the time and in all interactions. This norm-setting process establishes an atmosphere of caring, feeling connected and of feeling valued. This atmosphere is critical to participants being able to engage fully in adventure activities.

It is understood that the FVC fits the unique spirit and purpose of the group. However, it has also been viewed as a shared creation developed in words that are understandable to all group members, ultimately establishing a common language. This is not always true as time frames shrink and the pressure to meet certain desired results rise. What we (our groups and us) put into our Full Value Contract determines the effectiveness of its use and the depth of our relationships to it and each other. As facilitators, it is our responsibility to offer the type of Full Value Contract that is most appropriate and effective for each group we work with within the associated context. There are a number of ways to establish a Full Value Contract. To simplify, let's consider three basic categories – pre-determined, co-created, and group-generated.

Pre-determined FVC

The pre-determined FVC is established by someone or something other than the group itself, be it the practitioner, program, curriculum, or institution (school, camp, business, etc.). A pre-determined FVC is typically a set of three to six manageable behaviors communicated with positive language. A few examples of pre-determined FVCs can be found in many of Project Adventure's publications, e.g., *Adventure Curriculum for Physical Education*[3] and *Exploring Islands of Healing*,[4] and *Adventures in Business*.[5] These examples offer a general guideline for appropriately introducing a pre-determined Full Value Contract for each group. Furthermore, each book demonstrates the way in which to bring this type of FVC to life. Simply, stating the terms of a FVC and moving on is not enough.

A pre-determined FVC is most appropriate for, yet not limited to, programs where time is limited or the forming stage of the group[6] must be accompanied by check-ins and celebrations to be effective. While this type of FVC can be efficient and quickly establishes norms, buy-in may be limited due to the lack of ownership in the development of the concepts. It is essential that a group agrees to the behavioral norms and commits to the responsibilities of upholding the FVC. A pre-determined FVC provides the structure for a safe space initially while the group further develops the FVC (see co-created FVC) or generates a new FVC entirely (see Group-generated FVC).

Co-created FVC

A co-created FVC is one where the group members are invited to build upon a pre-determined FVC defining the concepts in their own terms or words. This process empowers the group to have more ownership in creating the Full Value Contract while they work within the safe FVC structure introduced by the facilitator, program, or organization. There are many ways to invite co-creation; some examples are seen in the following activities:

- Pi Charting (*High School ACPE*)
- Full Value ESP (*Creating Healthy Habits*)
- Full Value Speed Rabbit (*Middle School ACPE*)

Once these activities are conducted, the group can put the newly established behavioral norms they identify into practice. As the group works together over time, they can change and modify these norms based on the feedback they give themselves.

Group-generated FVC

A Group-generated FVC represents the essence of the Full Value Process. At its fullest expression, a Group-generated FVC invites participants to engage with one another to reflect and agree upon the norms of the group without any, or limited, structure. It typically engages a group that is ready to care, develop, and own the responsibility of their own Full Value Contract. However, it is also an effective tool for creating buy-in early in a group's development. Most groups fully appreciate the concepts,

3 *Adventure Curriculum for Physical Education*, Panicucci, Jane et. al. Project Adventure, 2003.

4 *Exploring Islands of Healing*, Schoel, Jim and Maizell, Rich.Project Adventure, 2007.

5 *Adventures in Business*, Smolowe, Ann; Butler, Steve; and Murray, Mark. Project Adventure, 2001

6 Stages of Group Development, Tuckman, Bruce. 1965.

behaviors, and values being expressed when they come directly from within the group and its members, and therefore they feel more connected to their FVC. Consequently, they are more motivated to live and maintain the terms expressed by the group. Some examples of a Group-generated FVC are:

- The Being
- FVC Visual Representations
- FVC Cards (See Full Value Stock Market in Section 2 and Full Value Flow in Section 3)

While determining which type of FVC best meets your program needs and group spirit, imagine establishing a whole school- or whole organization-wide FVC. Better yet, imagine what a Full Value Contract might look like on a global scale. It seems that Tracy Chapman has thought about this, given the lyrics to her song "New Beginning". [7]

We need to make new symbols
Make new signs
Make a new language
With these we'll define the world

Establishing a Full Value Contract worldwide would be quite the feat, don't you think! Perhaps all we may need to do though is determine our own personal FVC, support others developing their own, and respect one another's values. Something to dream about and set intentions!

Considerations for Full Value Contracts

Got room for more? Below are a few more considerations regarding group norms and the Full Value Contract:

- The FVC is an opportunity to *practice* healthy behaviors within a group setting to further explore the meaning and effectiveness of each FVC concept or behavior. The focus should be on practice, rather than being perfect. There must be opportunities for failure and mistakes, as well as success for participants to learn which behaviors are most effective and desired in their group. For example, in order for a group to learn how to 'Be Here', both focus and lack of focus and presence and lack of

presence must exist within the group. Likewise, to learn how to 'Be Safe' there may be moments where the experience feels completely safe, while at other times feels less safe. It is the opportunity to process the experience that will determine effective and desired behaviors.

- Norms exist whether they are spoken, written, drawn, or acted out. Norms are the generally accepted behaviors in any group spoken or unspoken, written or unwritten, formal or informal. Be aware of the informal norms and draw attention to them so the group may determine whether or not they are healthy for the group.
- The FVC, regardless of type, is most effective when reinforced through consistent check-ins, celebrations, and goal setting.
- The FVC is intended to support Challenge by Choice – the choices of each individual, risk taking, goal setting, and ultimately participants choosing to be their best selves.
- The FVC is an opportunity to actively experiment, play with, or try on new behaviors.
- The FVC is an opportunity for every individual to reflect on their own value system and behaviors as well as imagine, dream up, and empower their best and most authentic self.

The Hundredth Monkey includes many activities that introduce, reinforce, or utilize the concept of Full Value Contract exceptionally well, e.g., a group's commitment to creating and maintaining a safe environment. A few examples are:

- FVC Stock Market
- Don't Break the Ice
- Sonic 2 (aka Sonic and Tails)
- Traffic Signs
- Full Value Flow (activity sequence)

Experiential Learning and Experiential Learning Cycle (ELC)

This activity guide is experiential and based on the theory of experiential learning. Play is experiential in nature, engages us, and is significant to the way we learn. When we play, we are likely to learn something, whether or not we process or debrief it. However, as facilitators, educators,

---

7 *New Beginning*. Tracy Chapman. Elektra, 1995.

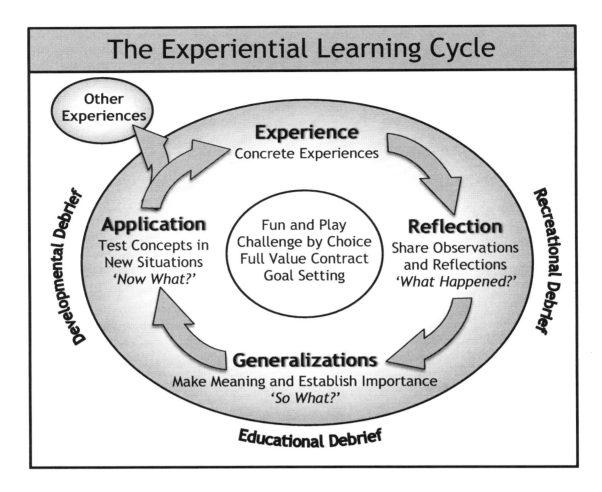

The Experiential Learning Cycle

Other Experiences

Experience
Concrete Experiences

Fun and Play
Challenge by Choice
Full Value Contract
Goal Setting

Application
Test Concepts in
New Situations
'Now What?'

Reflection
Share Observations
and Reflections
'What Happened?'

Generalizations
Make Meaning and Establish Importance
'So What?'

Developmental Debrief

Recreational Debrief

Educational Debrief

counselors or people who play a key role in the development of others, it is our responsibility to provide participants with the opportunity to gain as much from their experience and each other as possible. We may also pursue a specific goal, or desired outcome, or choose to adventurously learn what it is our participants have discovered from their experience. Whatever it may be, the Experiential Learning Cycle (See diagram) is a vehicle for optimal learning and explains the rationale for the activity structure used in this activity guide.

The Experiential Learning Cycle was developed from David Kolb's learning theory model.[8] It tells us that helping participants to experience a seemingly isolated event (the activity) and giving it context (helping them to create meaning from it) provides them with the opportunity to learn, understand, apply and transfer knowledge. Kolb highlights the four phases of

a learning cycle: concrete experience, reflective observation, abstract conceptualization and active experimentation. These phases are inclusive of the diverse learning styles of our participants and provide an effective debriefing structure.

The Experiential Learning Cycle: Meeting Program Goals at Three Levels

Many facilitators are gifted at providing opportunities that meet a range of goals for a variety of program types on a daily basis. To be successful, we must transition from one set of goals to another and determine which level of processing or debrief is most appropriate for the group and associated goals. In any given week, we may be tasked with meeting outcomes that range from the fun of a recreational program to an educational program with specific learning outcomes; to exploring the complex dynamics of a group with the goal of behavioral change in a team or organization. While fun may be at the forefront of all of these programs, determining the level of processing

8 David A. Kolb, *Experiencial Learning: Experience As the Source of Learning and Development.* (Englewood Cliffs, NJ: Prentice Hall, 1984).

depth may be challenging for some facilitators. To better prepare our transitions among different program types and related goals, let's consider three levels of processing depth that reside on a spectrum or continuum associated with the Experiential Learning Cycle. The three levels associated with program type are: recreational, educational, and developmental.

With respect to the base model of the ELC and the Adventure Integrated Model, the three levels of processing can be associated with each phase of the ELC. As you read below, you may notice that the concepts are not very new, however, the goal is to introduce a new language that better supports the appropriate level of processing depth needed to meet the goals of a particular program or setting.

Recreational Debrief

A Recreational Debrief invites the group to simply reflect on their experience. In other words, a debrief, should one occur at all, might ask participants what they remember from the day or to share a highlight from the experience. The recreational level debrief aligns with the "What?" or Reflections and Observations phase of the ELC, during which participants are asked to reflect on their experience or share objective information about the activity or experience. As mentioned previously, not every experience needs to be processed, debriefed or reflected upon. There is value and learning in letting an activity speak for itself.[9] However, without going too deep, there is also value in remembering and sharing vivid moments of awesomeness! Doing so occurs in the realm of a recreational level debrief. This level of debrief aligns with goals that focus on a fun, shared experience, with the opportunity to playfully bond or connect. The purpose of a recreational level debrief is to briefly highlight something special about an activity or experience and bring closure.

A few ideas for facilitating a recreational debrief are:

- One Word Whip – Describe the best part of the activity or experience in only one word.

- Celebration Circle – A debrief variation of the classic activity 'Have You Ever?', participants acknowledge people or events with a special celebratory clapping sequence.
- Dundie Awards (As seen on the TV show, 'The Office') – Participants present a special, custom-tailored, and often humorous award to others in the group.

Questions for the recreational level:
- What happened?
- What was your favorite part?
- What will you remember most?

Educational Debrief

The next level, the Educational Debrief appropriately meets program goals that seek more depth and cognitive learning. This level aligns with the "So What?" or Generalization phase of the ELC. Participants at this phase are invited or guided to analyze their experience and make meaning that may be abstract in nature. It is here that we as facilitators might ask our participants, "What did you learn from this activity or from your experience?" or "What worked well? What might you improve?" The participants are now invited to analyze their experience and form conclusions about what they learned. The goal at this level is for participants to build more knowledge or awareness around a particular topic.

A few ideas for facilitating an educational debrief are:

- World Wisdom Cards – A set of cards consisting of insightful generalizations from around the world.
- Keepers/Changers – The group indicates what behaviors or learning they would like to keep or change.
- Key/Significant Learning – Participants share a key or significant learning.

A couple of simple questions a facilitator might ask his or her group at this level:
- What did you learn from this experience?
- What does this information (reflections and observations) tell us?

9 *Effective Leadership in Adventure Programming*. Priest, S., & Gass, M. Human Kinetics, 1997.

Developmental Debrief

The third and final level, the Developmental Debrief, provides the most depth and moves the debrief beyond words. While many facilitators understand that this level of debrief is to be associated with the "Now What?" or Transfer and Application phase of the ELC, the concept of active experimentation conveyed in Kolb's ELC model often seems misunderstood. Transfer, Application, and active experimentation all imply action. And so this level of debrief should prepare participants for action by focusing on, "What are we going to do with what we learned?" Have participants set goals, stated, or even written down, related to what they are going to try to do during the next activity or some other area of their lives. This way there is something more tangible to check-in on during a subsequent debrief. A simple way to look at this is to acknowledge and appreciate the learning and then go play with it!

Spinning through all phases of the ELC provides the fullest depth a learning experience can offer. The result is a change or reinforcement in behaviors associated with the growth and development of an individual or team; hence the term developmental. Likewise, processing at this level could also be considered therapeutic, where experimenting with new behaviors and behavior change is also the goal. A developmental debrief prepares the participants to experiment, to stretch themselves according to Challenge by Choice, and ultimately try something new in either a familiar or unfamiliar context.

A few ideas for facilitating a developmental debrief are:

- Goal Setting – STAR Goals, SMART Goals, GPS-E, etc. (see Goal Setting below)
- Letter to Self – Participants write a letter to themselves (to be sent and opened at a future date) indicating who or how they hope to be in the months or year ahead.
- Group-Generated FVC – The group generates their own Full Value Contract based on their experience with each other. (see Full Value Contract section)

Some sample questions for processing at the developmental level:

- What from this experience will you use immediately in your life, as in tomorrow?

- Based on what you learned, what would be an appropriate goal for you to set?
- Given what you learned from this experience, what is one behavior you would be willing to experiment with during the next activity?

Goal Setting

The process of goal setting is a significant element in an adventure program and an opportunity to strive for and practice being our truest selves. It fosters engagement, resiliency, and growth among participants, and ultimately determines their motivation. According to *Drive* by Dan Pink, research has shown that autonomy, mastery, and purpose, which includes being able to personally set and attain goals, is significant to the motivation of an individual, and consequently a group.[10] Helping participants and groups to set and attain goals is one of the fundamental skills for success in an adventure program. This is encouraged through Challenge by Choice, explored and refined through the flow of the Experiential Learning Cycle, and supported with a Full Value Contract. These foundational concepts are where goal setting and personal or group growth occurs.

Goal setting requires the ability to understand: what is desired or needed; see what needs to be accomplished to attain a goal; and plan a series of steps following those steps to goal attainment. At Project Adventure, we believe this process is best supported in a group setting. Making positive choices - according to Challenge by Choice - and then pursuing them is the action of goal setting. Challenge by Choice invites participants to establish a goal that is a step out of their comfort zone, taking a risk to try something new - less familiar and less comfortable - with the focus on developing a new skill or habit. Similarly, through the lens of the Experiential Learning Cycle, participants put their goals in action during the transfer and application or active experimentation phase. Therefore, spinning through the ELC, they experience these actions, reflect on them, and receive feedback from peers. Lastly, they assess progress toward their goal and make adjustments as needed, all within the context of a supportive group.

---

10 *Drive*. Pink, Dan. Riverhead Books, 2009.

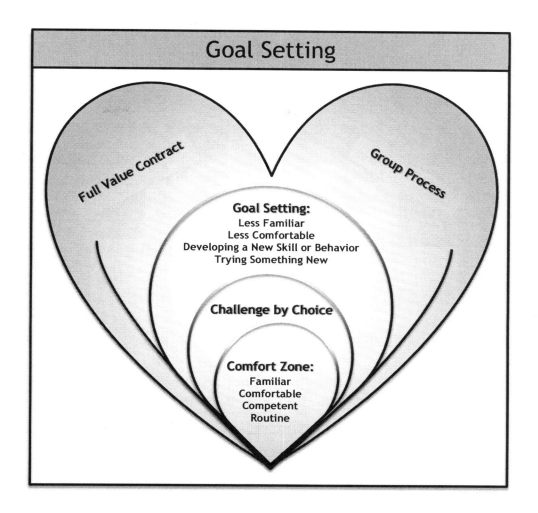

Goal Setting

Full Value Contract

Group Process

Goal Setting:
Less Familiar
Less Comfortable
Developing a New Skill or Behavior
Trying Something New

Challenge by Choice

Comfort Zone:
Familiar
Comfortable
Competent
Routine

Experiential learning and the goal setting process are more likely to be successful when supported by a Full Value Contract. In other words, participants are more likely to set their own goals and feel safe stepping out of their comfort zones to try something new when a Full Value Contract is present and effectively used. Ultimately, the effective facilitation of adventure activities provides safe opportunities for practicing and reflecting on goal setting and goal attainment.

To help participants be as successful as possible with goal work, Project Adventure has traditionally utilized SMART[11] or STAR[12] Goals as tools. Similarly, *The Hundredth Monkey* offers an additional goal setting tool called GPS-E and offers a host of activities perfect for goal setting, exploring old or new behaviors, and growing into our greatest selves.

---

11 *Stepping Stones.* Aubry, Peter. Project Adventure, 2008.
12 *Achieving Fitness.* Panicucci, Jane et al. Project Adventure, 2007.

GPS-E

Goals, like GPS devices, are used to get us where we want to go. They are a guide for when we get lost, yet sometimes may even cause us to get confused or lost. They help us to grow and provide a reference if we feel off track or desire positive affirmation. GPS-E is a four-part goal setting process that can stand alone or be combined with SMART and STAR goals to create the most advanced goal setting system around!

G-Goals   Invites participants to communicate an individual or group goal, by simply answering the question, "What is your goal?"

P-Plan   Asks participants to determine a plan, or series of action steps, that will enable them to achieve the goal. "How do you plan to achieve your goal?" "How will you accomplish it?" "What action are you willing to take to achieve your goal?"

S-Support	Acknowledges that goals are more likely achieved with the support of others. "What support do you need from others in the group to achieve your goal?" "What resources are available to you?"
E-Evaluation	Reminds participants to track the progress of their goal and make adjustments and/or refinements as needed. "How will you know whether you have achieved your goal?" "What will you use for measuring and tracking your goal?"

The Hundredth Monkey offers many activities that explore and reinforce goal-setting practices. A few examples are:

- Tollbooth Boogie
- The Longest Shadow
- Merge
- Community Celebration
- Building Blocks (activity sequence)

Sequencing and GRABBSS

How do you decide which activities to use? It's easy, right? Choose the right activity at the right time. Simple! For the magicians among us, unconsciously, it is seemingly that easy. However, there are many other aspiring magicians and plenty of practicing technicians in the field who desire a bit more in this area. The following are two models to support you in this endeavor. Learn them, practice them, tuck them away, then be present and go with what you sense is right! Sure, you might try and fail, but isn't that where the learning happens?

Project Adventure has conveyed the importance and practice of both sequencing and the GRABBSS model in many of its publications. A few that may be of interest to you are highlighted here. Most significantly, Mark Collard's take on sequencing in both, *No Props* and *Count Me In*, have been expressed in a way not found in any prior PA publication. This has quickly become an insightful way to introduce the mystifying topic of sequencing in many of our trainings and guide for our practice. Likewise, GRABBSS as it appears in *Islands of Healing*, refined in *Exploring Islands of Healing*, and adapted in the *Adventure Curriculum for Physical Education* has stood the

test of time. See these PA publications for more information.

Sequencing – The Right Activity at the Right Time

Sequencing is a critical ingredient to the success of your adventure program. Understanding that "sequencing is about preparing your group – mentally, physically, and emotionally for what's coming up"[13] requires the ability to plan ahead and then be adaptable. An effective practice is to develop an activity sequence based on the needs or goals of the group prior to their arrival. Once your participants arrive, however, learning to read your group and preparing to let go of what you had planned may be necessary. Your activity sequence should use some 'lead up' activities that will help you gauge what is appropriate for your group. This on-the-run assessment, using the group's reaction and level of participation in these lead-up activities, will influence your activity selection and sequence of activities. Looking at their: behaviors – readiness to participate, body language, affect – will assist you in determining what to do next. An appropriate sequence can lead your group to success, and can help you create a fun, positive experience in which everyone feels valued, and can pursue their individual and group goals. As a result, you stand a better chance of meeting your program goals.

Basically, participants, especially those who are new to one another, need to crawl before they walk, walk before they run, and run before they fly. While the goal is flying, being our truest selves, appropriate steps must be taken as we emerge. Again, how we do this; how we prepare our group is critical. Go too fast and we may scare our participants. Go too slow, we are likely to bore them. Finding the sweet spot requires your presence, awareness, attunement, and understanding.

The simple and effective sequencing model offered by Mark Collard progresses through three stages – ice-breakers, de-inhibitizers, and peak experiences – and continually builds trust. The model has more to do with how and when an activity is introduced and less about what type of activity, e.g., warm-up, energizer, communication, trust, cooperation, etc. Simply put, sequencing is about meeting the group where

13 *Count Me In*. Mark Collard. Project Adventure, 2008.

they are at and building trust, along with other skills, within the group. The foundations of trust are established the moment you or your participants walk through the door, arrive on your site or you on theirs. Trust grows or diminishes with every interaction in every moment whether you are programming or not. The result often has to do with how prepared you are to prepare your group for what's to come and how authentically you interact with your group.

For a more elaborate description of sequencing and perspectives on trust, check out *No Props* and *Count Me In* by Mark Collard.

GRABBSS – Choosing the Right Activity

GRABBSS has popped up in most every PA publication and training manual since it was published. While there are many other options for helping you choose activities, this one seems unmatched. GRABBSS is a series of questions associated with seven key focus areas that are observable during your program, yet helpful to knowing prior to your group's arrival. GRABBSS will help you develop your program or choose an activity, but is only effective with strong awareness and observation skills.

Goals

How does this activity relate to the goals of the group and overall program, or those that you see emerging? Basically, why are you doing the activity?

Readiness

Is the group ready (mentally, emotionally, physically) to do the activity? What needs to change before the group has the ability to undertake the next stage of the program?

Affect

What is the feeling of the group? What sensations are they experiencing – boredom, excitement, apathy, resistance, etc?

Behavior

How are the group members or individuals acting? Are the interactions among members positive or negative for the group? How cooperative are they? Will their behavior be appropriate for the activity?

Body

What are the physical abilities of the group? What physical characteristics of the group will impact the program? Are the individuals tired, do they substance abuse, do any individuals have a disability, are they hot or cold, etc?

Stage

What stage of development is the group in? Using Tuckman's popular rhyming schema to describe the varying levels, are they Forming, Storming, Norming, Performing or Transforming? Does the group need additional skills to function at a higher level (stage) of development?

Setting

What is the physical setting of the program, and the 'cultural' background of the participants? Are you inside or outside, secluded or likely to be disturbed? Is the space limited? How long have the people known / worked with each other?

Basically you are asking "Where is my group at, based on what they are showing or telling me and what do they need?" and "How does this play into the big picture goals of the program?" This is followed by making clear and conscious decisions on what you will do, particularly as it relates to the selection of an activity within the sequence of activities.

For a more detailed description of GRABBSS, check out *Islands of Healing* by Dick Prouty, Paul Radcliffe, and Jim Schoel and *Exploring Islands of Healing* by Jim Schoel and Richard Maizell.

A Deep Look into a Mystifying Question – Which Came First…?

Which came first, the rubber chicken or the egg? If you have engaged in a playful adventure experience, it is obviously clear what came first – the rubber chicken and the fun that comes with it! Without the rubber chicken, which represents play and fun in this case, would there be any engagement from the participants and an egg filled with opportunities for reflection, learning, and growing? When I think of this analogy, I laugh. Did you? I hope so. Laugh again! All right, let's move on.

Often times, the concepts of Challenge by Choice, Full Value Contract, and the Experiential Learning Cycle are depicted as a sturdy foundation on which the house of adventure stands. For a house to be built and a foundation to be set, it should be clear that something else came first – the earth. The earth is what the house is truly built on and where all of the materials to build the house come from. In other words, the earth in all its beauty and splendor is necessary for the foundation and the house to exist. Likewise, if a house of adventure is to exist on a solid foundation of Challenge by Choice, Full Value Contract, and the Experiential Learning Cycle, then what in the case of this analogy is the earth? What does the earth represent? What is necessary for the entire adventure to exist?

I have been pondering this question since I began with Project Adventure. I have explored this idea by observing others and reflecting on my own practice as well as engaging in many intriguing dialogs with other trainers and facilitators. What I have come to believe and understand is that something must exist before the foundation is laid and the adventure is built. What is necessary seems organic, dynamic, and pure. It is something that may be challenging to understand. It is perhaps what makes an adventure experience magical. It is playing. It is relating. It is reflecting. It is loving. It is YOU!

Disregard thoughts of being arrogant, conceited or egocentric. Really, get over yourself so you can hear this! While it's not all about you and never should be, you do have the power to make a significant impact on the adventure experience you introduce then co-create with your groups. Developing yourself as a practitioner and as a human being is essential and necessary. To do so, practice playing, relating, reflecting and loving. Practicing these four critical behaviors will breathe life and authenticity into Project Adventure's foundational concepts and greatly enhance the effectiveness of a fun adventure experience or likelihood that an adventure will exist at all. Easier said than done, right? This is why the focus is on the practice of these behaviors, not necessarily perfecting them.

Playing

Play has already been communicated as significant, magical even, to adventure programming and life in general. Play engages us with the lure of being fun. It allows us to be present with ourselves, the people and space around us, and the experience itself. Play enables us to connect and build relationships with other people by exploring and discovering boundaries. Play empowers the child within all of us to purely present itself without inhibition, fear, prejudice, or judgment. According to Ryan McCormick, "Much of what we do is simply reconnecting people with this part of their lives; where everything is new, where we are willing to try, to say silly things, laugh a LOT, and truly believe anything is possible." Play allows us to be the purest expression of our being while being present with everyone and everything around us.

In all aspects of facilitation, practice:

- Playing often.
- Playing differently than you typically play using new techniques, props, and style.
- Playing for no other reason than to play and for fun, but that's a given!

Relating

Relationships are significant to an adventure experience as they foster trust, motivation, and allow people to feel connected and safe. Relating to another person is essential to being human. Relating an activity to other aspects of life is necessary for learning. It is the relationships with the people and with the experience that makes this type of learning so powerful. The opportunity to play a game with other people and connect it with meaningful implications to the world around us allows us to better empathize and have compassion for others. The more we engage in authentic relationships with our participants, the more likely they are to trust us, engage playfully in the experience, trust each other, and openly share their personal experiences and learning with the rest of the group.

In all aspects of facilitating, practice:

- Being present with yourself, with others, and the space around you.
- Relating to others, especially those who are least like you.
- Relating activities to other areas of life and helping others to do the same.

Reflecting

Reflection enables us to assess our experience and further develop our self-awareness. Through reflection we are able to more accurately identify our emotions and how they affect ourselves and others. We learn to better express ourselves and communicate with others. Finally, reflection empowers us to identify personal attributes while building our self confidence and self love. It is the culmination of these aspects of self awareness gained through reflection that inform or reveal our unique aptitude and passion, or what Sir Ken Robinson refers to as our "element."[14] In other words, self awareness helps us to discover what we love.

In all aspects of facilitating, practice:

- Reflecting on the adventure experience and the outcomes; be it an hour-long activity session or a semester-long course and everything in between.
- Reflecting independently and with others on your facilitation.
- Reflecting on participants and the interactions among people – among participants, you and participants, you and co-facilitators.

Loving

Love is complicated and often misunderstood. It seems clear, however, when we love something and when we don't; when we care for someone and when we don't. Sharing what we love and loving others is an amazing experience. Self-love – caring for oneself, taking responsibility for, respecting, and knowing oneself (e.g., being realistic and honest about our strengths and weaknesses)[15] – helps us to feel confident sharing what we love. Love or the lack of love, like fear, can be sensed by most anyone. By facilitating from a loving place, your words, actions and gestures will be perceived as genuine and trustworthy. Your belief in the activities and principles will be evident. Simply, if you do not love what you are doing, neither will your participants. If presenting from a loving, passionate place, your participants will most likely love the experience, even when it becomes difficult, and learn to love and accept one another.

In all aspects of facilitating, practice:

- Loving what you do and why you do what you do.
- Loving the people you play and work with

from all aspects of who you are – mind, body, heart, and soul, especially those who are most difficult to love.
- Loving the experience that emerges through co-creation and the lessons it offers.

Closing

All that has been described in the Introduction and in Section 1– the necessary practice of playing, relating, reflecting, and loving, PA's foundational concepts and YOU – brings forth the ultimate essence of adventure and perhaps that of living life here on Earth. It is to live the fullest, most integrated and complete expression of our being. We have a great potential to unlock this essence as suggested in this quote by Marianne Williamson made famous by Nelson Mandela:

"Our deepest fear is not that we are inadequate. Our deepest fear is that we are powerful beyond measure. It is our light, not our darkness, that most frightens us...as we let our light shine, we consciously give other people the ability to do the same. As we are liberated from our own fear, our presence automatically liberates others."[16]

When we invite participants to engage in an adventure experience, we are inviting them to discover, affirm, acknowledge, and appreciate themselves in their truest, most authentic selves. In doing so, we are inviting everyone to acknowledge and appreciate his or her fears, to move beyond individual comfort zones, risking failure and embarrassment on a journey towards existing fully. Through the practice and development of ever-stronger collective skills, we have the ultimate potential to exist in the fullest expression of our collective being, as a global community, and address the daunting challenge that our institutions and the wider world face.

Project Adventure is a catalyst for adventure experiences that bring out the best in each individual and each group. A Project Adventure experience is a way of playing, reflecting, learning and growing. Ultimately a PA experience is a way of being. Let your light shine and consciously choose to be yourself – your most authentic self – whether you are participating in an adventure experience, facilitating an adventure group, or carrying your adventure learning forward to life beyond.

14 *The Element*. Robinson, Sir Ken. Viking Adult, 2009..

15 *The Art of Living*. Fromm, Erich. Harper and Row, 1956..

16 *A Return to Love: Reflections on the Principles of A Course in Miracles*. Marianne Williamson. Harper Collins, 1992.

Activities

5 Handshakes, 5 Minutes

Overview

A quick, interactive, and playful icebreaker/energizer of creatively quirky handshakes. Participants attempt to perform each of the 5 handshakes introduced with as many people as possible. 5 Handshakes, 5 Minutes is an excellent choice for engaging large groups and a great alternative to Crosstown Connections.

Group Size	12 or more
Learning Themes	• Fun and Play • Physical Activity and Movement • Building Trust, Relationships, and Community
Materials / Props	None

Setup

Begin with the group in a circle in an open space.

Framing

Say to participants:

"There can be such joy in sharing handshakes. I'd love to share some with you. Specifically, five handshakes in five minutes. Here's how it works."

Or:

"An adventure is a chance to try something different. When we greet someone, we often use a standard handshake. Let's explore five new handshakes!"

SAMPLE HANDSHAKES

Wild Turkey (a.k.a Turkey Handshake)

- Inspired by a community of wild friends residing on Moraine Farm (PA's headquarters in Beverly, MA)
- Two people set up as if to give each other a High 5
- However, one person spreads his or her fingers wide, making the feathers of the turkey, while the other makes a fist and extends the thumb, making the body and head of the turkey.
- They then connect these turkey parts, making a whole turkey complete with commonly associated turkey noises… "gobble, gobble, gobble…"

Suffern Shuffle

- The handshake for pro-athletes to non-athletes
- Introduced by a group of PE Teachers from Suffern, NY
- Slap right hand to right hand, left to left, and then repeat right to right, and left to left.

- Turn to the side, jump, and gently – gently – bump shoulders.
- Including a fun sound like, "ding," when bumping shoulders adds to the fun. Encourage unique sounds.

Happy Salmon (a.k.a. Ice Fishing)

- Happy What? Happy Salmon, a favorite for ice fishing fanatics!
- Two participants face one another and extend arms and hands as if to perform a regular handshake.
- Rather than shaking hands, they slap each other's forearms like fish tails and say, "ey, ey, ey…"

Wind-up Toy Handshake
A greeting of unpredictable wound-up wonder

- Two people face one another, hold hands, and wind-up three times.
- The wind-up is performed by simultaneously moving arms and bending legs. While arms and hands roll down toward the ground, participants move towards a squatting position. As arms roll up towards the head, participants stand tall.
- After three wind-ups, participants detach from their partners and move in their most inspired and unique wind-up toy fashion!
- Encourage a variety of unique and fun wind-up toys. Some ideas, if participants are stuck, might be:
    - The Energizer Bunny
    - The Cymbal Clanging Monkey
    - The Penguin
    - The Hopper
    - The Forward Roller
    - The Spinner
    - The Robot
    - The Break Dancer
    - The Curly Shuffle
    - The Chattering Teeth

Logger (a.k.a. The Lumberjack)

- Create a thumb-on-thumb stack.
- One person extends the "thumbs up" gesture.
- The other person grabs the partner's thumb and extends his or her thumb.
- Repeat until all four hands are stacked on top of one another.
- Participants move this handshake with a push and pull motion, back and forth, with the deep repetitive sound of "hey, hey, hey…" that gets louder and louder and faster and faster.

Procedure

Say to participants:

1. "I will ask for a volunteer, demonstrate a handshake and say, 'Go!'"

2. "When I say, "Go!", try to do the handshake with as many people as possible."

3. "When I raise my hand (gesturing a circle), return to a circle."

4. "I will then ask for another volunteer, demonstrate another handshake, and say, 'Go!'"

5. "We will experience five handshakes in five minutes."

6. "I need a volunteer."

Reflection/Closure/Discussion

None needed

Tips and Comments

- When asking for volunteers, you don't need to choose just one. If many group members volunteer, invite them into the center of the circle. Ask them to pair up, and they can demonstrate with you as they learn. This could lead to more volunteering and risk taking in the future and reduces the "I didn't get chosen" feeling that could occur.

- Consider a sequence of handshakes that progresses from familiar to less familiar, gently guiding participants through a 'stretch' experience. This will subtly introduce or reinforce the idea of moving out of one's stretch zone to experience something new and, in this scenario, something fun! It also becomes a quick assessment of how playful your group might be.

- This activity usually inspires participants to share handshakes they know. Sometimes it happens in the moment and you can choose to roll with it or not. Otherwise, consider having participants partner with each other at the end to create or share handshakes.

___

Safety

Read your group and read the cards to be sure all of the tasks are appropriate. If you have any concerns, you can select the cards that would work best for your group at this time. Choose an appropriate play space based on your group and their ability to move with awareness of their surroundings.

52 Card Pickup

Overview

A fun and active mingling activity perfect for ice breaking and getting to know one another. 52 Pickup also introduces the idea of working together with the option of using the activity as a timed initiative. Participants pick up cards with particular tasks on them from the ground or floor. They then choose to perform the tasks or return the cards in an effort for the entire group to pick up all cards from the ground and consequently complete all tasks.

Group Size	12 or more
Learning Themes	• Building Trust, Relationships, and Community • Self Awareness and Self Management • Social Awareness
Variation 1 Materials / Props	52 Card Pickup Deck (Remove the "challenge cards" from the deck)
Variation 2 Additional Materials	• Stop watch • All Cards ('task' and 'challenge')

Setup

Lay the cards out face down on the floor and spread them out (or on table tops). Prepare the space for people to be up and mingling and gathering together.

Variation 1: 52 Card Pickup Mixer

Framing

Say to the group:

"Your challenge as a group is to complete all of the tasks on the cards ending with all of the cards in your possession."

Or:

"So, there are all these cards on the ground. Our goal will be to pick them up. However, there is a little more information regarding how we will do this that I need to share."

Or:

"Have you all heard of 52 Card Pickup? Well, that's what we are about to do only there's a twist to how we go about picking up the cards."

Procedure

1. Each person may only pick up one card at a time. Everyone in the group can simultaneously pick up cards versus waiting turns.

2. Upon reading the card you may either choose to complete the task, find someone else who is willing to do the task or return that card to the ground and choose another.

3. Once you complete the task written on the card, keep that card in your possession and choose a new one.

4. You can expect there to be simultaneous activity. For example your task may be to give everyone in your group a handshake or to gather everyone in your group to do the wave.

Reflection / Closure / Discussion

Ask the group:

1. What cards were the most fun or interesting? Did you like this activity? Why or why not?

2. What did you learn about your group members or yourself?

3. What were all the different ways people were involved in the activity?

4. Can you think of any examples of how you or someone else practiced Challenge by Choice?

5. Were there any examples of leadership that arose in this activity?

Variation 2: 52 Card Pickup "The Challenge"

Estimated Time

25 minutes for initiative version (52 Card Pick-up "The Challenge")

Framing

Say to the group:

"Your challenge as a group is to complete all of the tasks on the cards as quickly as possible and end the activity with all of the cards in your possession. You will have two or three rounds to work toward your best time."

Procedure

1. The first round will set a baseline time. (In the first round, the facilitator might choose not tell the group that they are being timed, allowing them to get more familiar with the activity and to enjoy the mingling aspect without pressure. Before round 2, the facilitator could announce the baseline time and have the group work to beat it.)

2. Each person may only pick up one card at a time. Everyone in the group can simultaneously pick up cards rather than waiting turns.

3. If a participant picks up a task card, he or she may either choose to complete the task or return that card to the ground and choose another.

4. If a participant picks up a "challenge card", e.g., "Return one card to the ground," he or she must follow the directions on that card.

5. Once a player completes the task or challenge written on the card, he or she may keep that card in their possession and choose a new one.

6. Expect simultaneous activity. For example, one task may be to give everyone in the group a handshake or to gather everyone in the group to do the wave.

Reflection / Closure / Discussion

Ask the group:

1. How did the time pressure impact your group?
2. Were you able to bring your time down – why or why not?
3. What were the obstacles that arose – how did you overcome them?

Tips and Comments

52 Card Pickup is a great activity for introducing Challenge by Choice and allows the facilitator to assess their group in terms of a group or individual's willingness to take a risk and act silly, the participants' desire to interact with each other beyond familiar relationships, and the overall feel and energy of a group.

Altershake

Overview

A mystifying problem-solving activity that will test any group's persistence and perception. Participants attempt to shake hands with everyone in the group once and only once, while alternating the hand they shake with each time, e.g., right, then left, then right, then left and so on. Altershake invites the necessity of determination and the exploration of effective communication, efficient decision making and innovation.

Group Size	8 – 16
Learning Themes	• Relationship Skills • Responsible Decision Making
Materials / Props	None

Setup

Provide enough space for participants to move around at a walking pace.

Framing

Say to group:

"There are many ways to solve a problem. One way is through trial and error. A group may try a solution to the problem only to learn that it doesn't work. The effort is not all lost, however, as the group may have learned something that could be used for the next attempt."

Or:

Estimated Time

20 minutes

Safety

Given that this activity requires people to alternately shake hands, determine if it is appropriate for your group especially if there are participants with one arm or no arms at all or religious or cultural restrictions on touching.

"This activity is sure to test your persistence, communication, and perception. It requires you to communicate effectively, make decisions efficiently, and be persistent and innovative in the midst of a baffling challenge."

Procedure

1. Inform your group that the goal of the activity is to shake hands with everyone in the group.

2. Explain that while this may appear to be a simple goal, the challenge is to do so while observing the following rules:

   a. Each person may shake hands with another person once and only once.
   b. Each person must alternate hands with each handshake. This means that if someone uses their right hand to shake one person's hand they must then use their left hand to shake the next person's hand, then their right, their left again and so on. A handshake is defined as one person gripping and shaking the hand of another person.
   c. Each person is responsible for ensuring that they comply with the two rules described above – alternating hands each time they shake hands and shaking hands, as defined, with each person once and only once.

3. Check for understanding of the goal and rules, and then direct the group to begin.

Reflection/Closure/Discussion

Reflection 1: Relationship Skills

1. How would you describe your teamwork and communication?

2. Would you consider what you described as an example of an effective or ineffective team, or both?

3. What are the qualities that make for an effective team?

4. Is there anyone you would like to celebrate for demonstrating any of the qualities you described?

Reflection 2: Responsible Decision Making

1. What were some of the potential solutions you tried? How was it decided that you would try these solutions?

2. Did all attempts move you closer to the actual solution?

3. How would you describe your group's problem-solving process? Were you innovative?

4. (If the ABCDE Model of Problem Solving was introduced) Was the ABCDE model of problem-solving used? Why or why not? (See next page Tips and Comments.)

5. How is this similar to or different from your problem-solving process with past activities?

6. What is one important thing to remember when solving problems in the future?

Reflection 3: Use the 'Simple Six' technique.

1. What happened?

2. Has it happened before?

3. Are you satisfied with the results? Why or why not?

4. Is it similar to or different from other times in your life?

5. Does it tell you anything about your group or yourself?

6. What would you like to do about _____ for the next attempt or when you return to _____ ?

Tips and Comments

- Altershake is a challenging problem-solving activity that has sometimes resulted in groups shutting down, losing interest, or yearning to be doing something else. That said, it isn't for everyone, yet for the right group, the experience and discoveries can be profound.

- Most groups have successfully solved the problem by accepting a truly alternate handshake. That handshake being a right hand of one person shaking the left hand of another person, thumbs oriented in opposing directions; one up, one down.

- To date, we are aware of only one group, eight participants in a Debriefing Tools workshop (January 2010), who solved the activity by exclusively using traditional handshakes, i.e., right hand to right hand both thumbs oriented up and left hand to left hand both thumbs oriented up. Curious souls may then ask, "Is this possible with any group, with any number of participants?" and, "Is there a pattern, or mathematical reason, that explains or verifies the solution to this problem?" If you find out, let us know!

Variations

- **ABCDE Model of Problem Solving** – Consider offering your group the ABCDE model of problem-solving as a tool for practicing effective communication and making decisions more efficiently.

    - **Ask** questions to understand the problem.
    - **Brainstorm** solutions openly.
    - **Choose** a solution to try.
    - **Do** it.
    - **Evaluate** the solution – adapt or discard it.

- **Time It!** – Adding a time element to the activity tends to add urgency to finding a solution. One way to do this is to time the activity inviting multiple trials from the start. Another approach would be to time multiple trials once the group has decided on a solution that works in accordance to the rules outlined above.

Armada

Overview

A frantic flotilla of fun for larger groups. Teams play an ever intensifying variation of dodge ball flinging fleece balls, acquiring teammates, and jumping ship. When playing Armada, it doesn't matter which team you are on as long as you were on the team – i.e., everyone playing – that created an epic experience for all! There are many potential outcomes so gather your large group and go!

Group Size	40 – 80
Learning Themes	• Fun and Play • Physical Activity and Movement • Building Trust, Relationships, and Community • Self Awareness and Self Management • Social Awareness • Relationship Skills • Responsible Decision Making (It's all here if you want it to be!)
Materials / Props	• At least 4 120-foot ropes • Fleece balls (1 per person) • At least 4 hula hoops • At least 4 half noodles or boffers • Foam rectangles (i.e., Stepping Stones)

Setup

- Shape each rope into a triangle and arrange so that top points face each other.
- Place a hula hoop and boffer in the back third of each triangle.
- Scatter fleece balls along the ropes in the spaces between the triangles. Fleece balls should be "reachable."
- See diagram.

Safety

There are many safety and facilitation tips woven into the procedure above. Please review those and consider what they offer to create a safe, playful learning environment. Beyond these tips, consider reviewing general considerations when throwing soft objects at each other. For example, participants should not aim at another player's head. The tagging zone is below the shoulders. Also, some participants may find creative ways to retrieve fleece balls that are just out of reach for an individual by relying on the counter balance or spotting of other players. This is acceptable – just be aware and ready to "spot" verbally and physically as needed. Finally, as each level increases in intensity, be prepared to check in regarding the Full Value Contract, especially about safe and fun play.

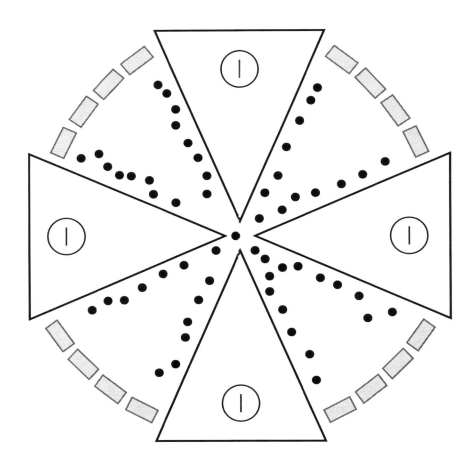

Initial Setup

Additional Setup
for Level Five

Creatively divide your group into four teams. (See page 299.)

Framing

Say to participants:

"Has anyone heard of the Spanish Armada? Specifically, it is a historical reference to the great fleet of ships sent by Phillip II of Spain against the English in 1588. It refers to a large group of war ships or a large group of moving things (thefreedictionary. com). This does not mean that we are going to war with each other, but we are going to play a game inspired by this historic fleet of ships and, hopefully it gets us all moving around a lot."

Procedure

1. Once the teams have been created and the players populate their triangle, invite the group to kneel or sit as the rules are explained, especially if it is a large group of very excited players!

2. Explain the setup. Point out the rope boundaries, fleece balls, hula hoops, and boffers, and assign any metaphors that have meaning for your group.

3. Explain and demonstrate the rules of the game.

   a. Each team will have one minute to identify a "captain or medic" immediately after the rules have been stated.
   b. All fleece balls must remain on the ground, or floor, until the game starts.
   c. Everyone begins with their foot on or in the hula hoop.

    d. Players will be retrieving and throwing fleece balls at one another.

    e. Everyone must remain within their triangle during the duration of play.

    f. Players, including the "captain and medic," must kneel where they are if:

        i.   They step out of their triangle.

       ii.   They have been hit by a fleece ball before it hits the ground.

      iii.   A fleece ball that they threw is caught by a player on another team before it hits the ground.

    g. If kneeling, a player may continue to catch and throw fleece balls, but may not move.

    h. The role of the "captain or medic" is to revive his or her teammates by tagging them with the boffer. A player who is tagged by his or her "captain or medic," may stand and move again.

    i. The "captain or medic" only may use the hula hoop as a safe zone. This means that if the "captain or medic" is hit while standing with at least one foot in the hula hoop, he or she does not have to kneel.

    j. The game may end if:

        i.   The "captain or medic" has been hit.

       ii.   A predetermined amount of time, e.g., five minutes, has expired.

      iii.   All of the players, including the "captain or medic," on one team are kneeling.

4. Check for understanding of the rules, and then play!

5. It may be helpful to play a few games at this level before advancing to other levels, if the group has not played this game before or is getting re-acquainted with the rules. Remember to have the participants return the fleece balls to the reachable space between triangles before starting a new game.

6. When the group seems ready, advance through the levels or additional variations described in the Tips and Comments section below.

Reflection/Closure/Discussion

There is much to reflect on, process, review, and debrief throughout the entire course of this game. Rather than providing specific debrief questions, we are including a few debrief techniques that may be appropriate for this activity and large groups.

- **Take a Stand Debrief** – Take a Stand is a common activity used for a variety of reasons, but mostly as a way for a group to get to know one another. It can also be used as a technique for debriefing or processing an experience. To do this, consider pre-recording statements that participants could respond to by choosing: Agree, Not Sure, Disagree or All the Time, Most of the Time, Some of the Time, or None of the Time. Identify triangles to represent one response from the set of either three or four responses. Read a statement and ask participants to move toward a triangle that indicates their response to the statement. For example, a statement could read "I played safe." You could then ask the participants to move to the triangle that best indicates their response – All the Time, Most of the Time, Some of the Time, or None of the Time. This technique provides a nice quantitative visual display of responses while being somewhat active. Also, you never know when it will spark a quality conversation...but it's bound to happen.

- **Traffic Light/Take a Stand Debrief** – Combining Take a Stand and Traffic Light Debrief using red, yellow, and green fleece balls creates a moment of quick, interactive reflection that brings awareness but keeps participants in the game.

To facilitate this, let the fleece balls be where they are at the end of a game. Invite participants to think about how they and others were playing the game. Specifically, ask them to note a behavior that was:

- **Red** – something that should stop.
- **Yellow** – was concerning or prompted a question.
- **Green** – something that should continue.

Have participants move to a red, yellow, or green fleece ball that matches their response. Ask a few people to share responses or invite either homogenous groups (same color fleece ball) or heterogeneous groups (one of each color fleece ball) to meet and discuss their responses.

- **Remote Control (aka Play, Pause, Reverse, Fast Forward, etc.)** – Create small groups of four by grouping one participant from each team, or reconnecting a group from the original group-splitting activity used before the game began. Ask each of these small groups to re-enact a highlight from the game. Each group should discuss their favorite moments or experiences, choose one, and practice the re-enactment. After five to ten minutes of practice, bring the small groups together. Invite groups to share their re-enactments and allow one person, or the whole group to "click" Play, Pause, Reverse, Fast Forward, etc. on an imaginary or mock remote control. Watch your favorite highlights in reverse, fast forward or even super slow motion. It's like watching your favorite video clips over and over again!

Tips and Comments

Level Variations

Level Two – No Safe Zone

1. Play Armada as described above with one simple change – remove the hula hoops. Now the safe zone no longer exists for the "captain or medic," which means that each team will need to strategize ways to "protect" their "captain or medic" from being hit by a fleece ball.

2. Provide adequate time for each team to develop this strategy.

3. Play a few games at this level, allowing the players the opportunity to reflect on their strategies and make adjustments as needed.

4. When the group seems ready, play at the next level or skip to the fourth level.

Level Three – In Hiding

1. Continue playing Armada with yet another simple change – remove the boffer. In this level, the hula hoop, aka the "safe zone," and now the boffer, no longer exist. A "captain or medic" still exists on each team. Players now have an added goal of determining who the "captain or medic" on each team is. This provides each team with more opportunities to strategize, communicate, and problem solve en route to discovering who the "captain or medic" is on each team, while trying to protect the identity of their own.

Tips and Comments *(continued)*

2. Provide adequate time for each team to develop multiple strategies:

   a. Discovering the "captain or medic" on each team.
   b. Protecting the identity of their own "captain or medic."
   c. Preventing their "captain or medic" from being hit by fleece balls.
   d. Keeping as many players up and moving for as long as possible.

3. Play a few games at this level, allowing players the opportunity to reflect on their strategies and make adjustments as needed.

4. It might also be beneficial at this point to process the experience. This level provides a great opportunity to explore fairness, communication, execution of a plan, and effective teamwork.

5. When ready, move on to the fourth level.

Level Four – Winning Teammates

1. Hang in there, two more levels to go! Are you asking yourself, "What's with all the levels?" Levels allow the game to become progressively more complex and interesting at a pace that is not overwhelming for your groups. Make sure that your group is ready for additional rules before moving forward, as more rules can result in more fun or, at times, more confusion or unneccesary conflict.

2. At this point, all rules apply, or if you or your group prefer, add rules from this level to any of the three previous levels.

3. At this level, the facilitator may, at any time, call "toe on the line." When "toe on the line" is called, play stops immediately and every player runs to the nearest side of their triangle facing the player of another team.

4. Once everyone has paired off with someone from another team – on your call – they will play one game of Rock, Paper, Scissors (RPS). Provide a quick reminder of RPS rules as needed. Those who win stay within their triangle. Those who match stay where they are as well. Those who do not win (aka lose) change teams, joining the team of the person they lost to.

5. This variation starts to move people around a bit which may result in interesting dynamics. Some players who lose in RPS have no problem with this and continue playing hard as if they were always a part of their new team. Others love playing against their former team. Others still seem challenged to play for another team or against their former team. Be on the lookout for this and process as needed.

6. Play a few games at this level, allowing players the opportunity to reflect on their experiences. This level provides great opportunities to explore commitment, loyalty, abandonment, name calling, acceptance and letting go and moving on. Also, it is usually a wonderful time to check in regarding Challenge by Choice and/or the Full Value Contract. Use debriefing tools and techniques as needed to reach desired results or discover what is resonating with your participants.

7. And again, when the time seems right, move on to the fifth level.

Level Five – Jumping Ship

1. By now, you have realized that there is a lot to this game – a lot of fun, a lot to process, a lot to learn. The fifth level frees up the fun, and controlled chaos, even more. It requires a quick addition to the original setup. Place three or four foam rectangles (aka stepping stones) within the wider distance between each triangle. See diagram.

2. To play, maintain the rules you have been playing with until this point and add these additional rules:

   a. Anyone, at any time, may jump from one triangle to another, as long as he or she can make it without contacting the space between triangles or being struck by a fleece ball.

      i. If players land between triangles or are hit by a fleece ball while in the act of transition, they must kneel and remain where they are until tagged by their "captain or medic."

      ii. If they make it onto another triangle, a couple of things may occur.
      They may get hit with a fleece ball. If this happens, players must kneel and hope that the "captain or medic" will revive them by tagging them with the boffer or a hand if a boffer is not being used.

      They may challenge a player on that team to a game of Thumb Wrestling or Finger Fencing. Play a quick game or two of either game to introduce or re-mind participants how to play. If an opposing player accepts the challenge and wins, the challenger remains. However, if an opposing player accepts and loses, they must return, with the challenger, to the challenger's team. The opposing player may also choose to decline the challenge altogether. Now, if the challenging player is hit with a fleece ball while engaged in a game of Thumb Wrestling or Finger Fencing, the hit does not count.

   b. Players may also use the foam rectangles (aka stepping stones) as a way to cross from triangle to triangle without touching the space between triangles. If a player who is crossing on the foam rectangles encounters a player from another team, each player must stop and play a quick game of RPS to deter-mine who moves forward or goes back to their triangle. Once a player makes it to another triangle, the goal and rules stated above apply.

3. One fun thing during this level is to randomly stop play and ask participants from each team to identify themselves, one team at a time. Doing so brings awareness of how much a particular team has scattered and affirms that you do not need to be with your "team" – your people – to have a good time!

4. This variation increases the action dramatically and moves players around even more. This seems to lead, mostly, to more fun! Because there is so much going on, be prepared to stop the game at any time to check in especially around fun, fair-ness, and safety.

5. Continue playing at the level that seems to be most fun for the group and most effective for reaching desired results. This level provides a look at risk taking, independent action, taking initiative, awareness, and independently resolving conflicts. As stated before, this level is also a wonderful time to check in regard-ing Challenge by Choice and/or the Full Value Contract. Continue to use debrief-ing tools and techniques as needed to reach desired results or discover what is resonating with your participants.

Additional Variations

- Hey, isn't this Medic? Yes! If it didn't jump out at you or you were unaware, Armada is an enhanced version of a classic dodge ball game called Medic (aka Star Wars). Use any Medic variations to further enhance Armada, essentially a four-way version of Medic.

- Add or remove rope triangles depending on your group size. Doing so will help to monitor the intensity of play, number of teams, and overall participation.

- There are many ways to convey the framing and rules of a particular activity to your group. One technique that has worked well with games such as Armada, in which there are many rules especially as the levels and game intensify, is to disseminate the information via one representative from each team, i.e., the captains or medics. Invite the representatives *only* to meet with you in the center of the playing area requiring the other players to have their feet in the hula hoop. If playing within the context of a nautically-based theme (aka pirate-themed) feel free to throw a few pirate-inspired reminders to keep the other players in their places. Provide the representatives with the details – framing and rules – needed to play the game. Check for understanding, and then send them on their way. Representatives are then responsible for communicating the details of the game, as they understand them, to their team. Of course there may be misinformation and some confusion, but that's all part of the game. Roll with it and process as needed. Continue with this format to communicate additional rules, offer feedback, or provide any other relevant information. Encourage teams to switch their representatives as needed. Disseminating information this way is an effective technique for creating an adventurous environment, engaging groups, and exploring leadership and communication.

- If framing with a nautical theme, consider the following metaphors. The rope triangle is the bow of the boat. The hula hoop is the helm. The boffer, or half pool noodle, is a healing stick. The fleece balls are cannon balls. The foam rectangles, introduced during level 5, can represent either debris of a damaged boat or a rickety make-shift bridge between boats.

Game Story

Armada emerged in the Fall of 2006 during a week-long program for 5th graders. Suze Collinson was the lead facilitator, joined by Vince Canziani, Topaz Terry Murphy, Ryan McCormick, and me. Each year the program was given a theme and this year's theme was nautical. We called it Seadogs in Training, to be more inclusive and minimize the glorification of pirates, sort of. After a little convincing, Suze got us to dress up as pirates and began planning activities with the nautical theme. Some of us morphed deeper and deeper into character as the planning and program went on.

One night we were sitting around a table, gamestorming a culminating peak experience. We envisioned a game that would be super fun, engage everyone, and go on for as long as our group wanted to play. We drew pictures, played with props, and bounced ideas back and forth while using our best pirate voices and newly acquired pirate jargon, "arrrrrrrgh!" Then it came. "What if we played a game like Medic or Star Wars…" "…but made it bigger." "Big enough for our whole group (approximately 60 participants) to play." The group was synergizing. "Yes, ooh, this is exciting...but what will it look like?"

We sketched it out. Four wedge-like triangles pointed at each other. "Ah, yes, those are the bows of the boats." "Right!" Circles and a line in each. "What are those?" "Shiver me timbers, that thar is the helm and the line, that's the captain's sword, of course. No messing, or you'll be walking the plank." "Belay your tongue!" We were in full character now. "What? What does belay your tongue mean?" "To hold it. Stop talking. I read it in some pirate book." "I can't wait to use that when I am teaching belay in a challenge course training." "Arrrrrgh, focus up, you scallywags." The pirate jeering continued. "And the dots?" "Them be cannon balls. We gonna shoot them at other ships – for fun." "Yeah, yeah, for fun!" "Quiet!" There was a moment of reality creeping in.

"Um, I don't think we can be playing games inspired by wartime tactics. Do you?" "Well, there are many games in our field referred to as soft war games." "Can you believe that? It seems weird given the work we do and the hopes for learning we have." We went on for a while listing the number of games inspired by war and then convinced ourselves that regardless, the games are fun and, when processed well, lead to significant learning and growth. We were convinced that we could make this work. Besides we really wanted to play this new game, or enhanced version of other games we loved. "I've got it. This is not a war. We are just practicing. That's why we called this week 'Seadogs in Training.' We will introduce the group to the Spanish Armada's favorite training game." "That's it!" "What's it?" "Armada, that's what we'll call it" "Yargh, Armada." We all "Yargh-d" and pounded our fists on the table and did other pirate stuff, running around our cabin like we were Max from Maurice Sendak's *Where the Wild Things Are!* It's so fun to be able to tap into your own 5th grade energy once in a while!

And that we did. After a few very successful days, we prepared for our biggest day of the week, loaded with what could be referred to as major events. One of those events was introducing and playing Armada, for the first time ever! It was awesome! We couldn't stop playing! Suze did a tremendous job of remembering the rules, creatively introducing new ones on the spot, and managing the group as if she had played this game more than a hundred times. Armada was a huge success. Not only was the game a success, it reminded us that gamestorming with creative people, passionate for playful experiences can lead to activities that have a significant impact on a person who chooses to engage and play for fun. We will never know the full impact, but we did witness a group of 5th graders and their teachers willing to risk being silly, pushing their physical limits, and having fun! Because of this, we co-created an experience that still holds a place in my heart and hopefully in the heart of everyone else who was part of that program.

If you couldn't tell, this 5th-grade program was a very special event. Armada was one of the many fun, hilarious, and significant moments we shared. It was a moment that inspires the affirmation, "I can't believe this is what we do for work. It is such a gift to work with playfully passionate people who care about others."

Balloon Tag

Overview

A fast-paced blooper of a tag game! Participants swat balloons around with the grand hope that one will make contact with another person. Balloon Tag is infused with ridiculous fun and the opportunity to explore and express group norms. Simply put, it brings out the best in people!

Group Size	10 or more
Learning Themes	• Fun and Play • Physical Activity and Movement • Building Trust, Relationships, and Community • Self Awareness and Self Management
Materials / Props	• 1 balloon per person • Extra balloons for popping potential or simply adding more fun!

Safety

Participants should be made aware of the potential of bumping heads and bodies as they retrieve balloons from the ground.

Setup

Gather the group in a clear, open space, preferably without wind…although, a massive open field with a slight wind would make for an adventurous experience, so, if you have the opportunity, give it a try!

Framing

Say to participants:

"Have you heard of the concepts of qi (chi), prana, mana, the force, or simply…vital energy? These concepts are often associated with an invisible life force, and may be interpreted as 'the stuff magic is made of' or the substance that souls are made of. In life, there are times when we feel distracted, distant from ourselves and others, and need to gather our qi. Consider this activity an opportunity to practice gathering your qi or your balloon which represents your invisible life force!"

Procedure

1. Distribute one or two balloons to each person to inflate and tie off. If the balloons move the group to play informally, which most often occurs, encourage that and play along. Allow for creative and humorous moments to occur, and then re-gain your group's attention.

2. If your read is that balloons will distract participants from hearing and understanding the rules, have a container or bag to prevent the balloons from going too far. Otherwise, roll with the kinesthetic learners learning in their way.

3. State the objective to the group, "Your goal is to get as many 'tags' as you can during each two-minute round."

4. Explain and demonstrate the rules.

    a. Everybody's It.

     b. Participants attempt to "tag" other participants with their balloons and may only hit their balloons with an open hand.

     c. Participants may not hold the balloons in their hands, nor can they tag another person while holding the balloon.

     d. In order to move, participants must "dribble" their balloons by bumping them with an open hand, keeping them in the air.

     e. Participants must track and use the balloon(s) they started with and may not interfere with other participants' balloons.

5. Play three to five rounds, providing opportunities to share personal bests, humorous moments, or Full Value check-ins between each round as needed.

Reflection/Closure/Discussion

Static Cling Affirmations – Have your group use the classic technique of rubbing a balloon in their hair to create static cling. Have each participant attach his or her balloon to another person while sharing an affirmation regarding how they interacted with the group during Balloon Tag. Affirmations can be general or specifically related to the group's Full Value Contract. Balloons can be taken off one person to be re-energized and recycled, allowing for many affirmations to be shared. Having many balloons available provides the group with the opportunity to adorn their group mates with multiple balloons and affirmations.

Balloon Propulsions Debrief

1. Have each participant find a partner and face one another.

2. Demonstrate the Balloon Propulsion technique (described below) and have partners attempt to have their balloons collide from a balloon propulsion release.

3. As balloons connect, participants move further and further apart, attempting to connect from greater distances.

4. Introduce an opportunity to reflect and share. If balloons collide (or connect), partners should take a moment to share something they liked about how the group played Balloon Tag. If balloons miss or do not collide, participants should take a moment to share something that they didn't like about how the group played the game.

5. Take the reflection one step further by continuing the balloon propulsion technique and introducing these opportunities to share. If balloons collide or connect, have participants share a moment outside of the game when they feel connected to the group. If balloons miss or do not connect, have participants share a moment outside of the game when they felt disconnected to the group.

6. If there is time or, for a journal assignment, have participants consider what it means to feel connected to or disconnected from their group. Have them express what they or others do to create that situation.

Variations

- **Balloon Tracking Off** – This slight adjustment to rule "e" above allows participants to use any balloon they can find! Participants may not interfere with other participants' balloons while they are dribbling; however, once a balloon touches the ground, it may be picked up and used by anyone.

- **Balloon Propulsion Tag** – Instead of dribbling the balloon and hitting the balloon with an open hand to attempt a tag, try moving and making a tag by using balloon propulsion. Balloon propulsion is achieved by holding the balloon in one hand and pulling back on the tied end with the other hand, then letting go. The force will propel the balloon forward, at least hopefully, a short distance. In this variation, participants are required to propel their balloons in order to move and make a tag. They may not run with a balloon in hand.

- **Tandem Balloon Tag** – Play either Balloon Tag or Balloon Propulsion Tag with the simple twist of being connected to a partner, by linking arms or holding hands. Now every partnership is It. Have fun!

Behavioral Settings

Estimated Time ◑

20 minutes

Overview

An unexpected and insightful reflection on behaviors. Participants brainstorm behaviors associated with particular settings. When the settings are switched, conversation is sparked. Behavior Settings builds Self Awareness while providing the opportunity for self-reflection and Self Management.

Group Size	10 – 15
Learning Themes	• Self Awareness and Self Management • Social Awareness
Materials / Props	• Index cards • Markers

Setup

Consider 6-8 settings to be explored and write each setting on an individual index card. Place the cards in front of the group in a straight line. For example:

School	Friend's House	Home	Party	Concert	Work

Framing

Say to the group:

> "We are going to explore our behaviors as they relate to particular settings. The goal is to spark quality conversations about how we behave."

Procedure

1. Ask participants to:
   a. Brainstorm behaviors associated with each displayed setting.
   b. Write each behavior on an individual index card.
   c. Place each index card under the appropriate setting.

2. Allow enough time to have a sufficient number of behaviors to discuss. As participants begin to share behavior cards or place them under the related settings, other participants may be inspired to record a few more behaviors.

3. Review the behaviors displayed with their corresponding settings. Provide time and space for participants to share their perspectives and listen to the perspectives of others.

4. Once there has been sufficient conversation, switch some of the setting cards so that the "list" of behaviors below seem unrelated to the new settings. For example, switch "a friend's house" with "work" and "party" with "school." This is where it gets interesting and hopefully engages your participants further. Prepare for a variety of reactions and responses from the participants.

5. Discuss the reactions and responses.

Reflection/Closure/Discussion

1. What were your reactions when the settings switched?

2. What was it about the behaviors and the settings they are listed under that caused you to react the way you did?

3. What might this tell us about our behaviors in particular settings?

4. Could we say that certain behaviors are acceptable in certain settings? Are there some behaviors that seem acceptable in many settings? Are there any behaviors that may not be acceptable at all?

5. How do we determine which behaviors are acceptable and which are not? What influences your behaviors in the settings that you find yourself in?

Game Story

(Co-created by Nate Folan and Wilderness Therapy Guide, Anson McNulty. Anson is currently the Assistant Program Director at Summit Achievement, Stow, Maine where he has worked since 2002.)

Behavioral Settings was inspired by a group of adolescents at Summit Achievement, a residential treatment center with a strong wilderness component based in Stow, Maine. The program structure provided lots of practice transitioning from one setting to another. Participants in the program spend time in classroom, residential, and wilderness settings and reflect on their behaviors, along with the impact of their behaviors, in each of these settings. Each group of adolescents was considered a team and typically guided by three Wilderness Therapy Guides, who allied with the participants and supported their group function and goal setting.

Individuals in one particular group were struggling to demonstrate acceptable behaviors in the classroom, even after multiple discussions with their guides. It was one of those moments when what was being taught, or more specifically *how* it was being taught, was not transferring. The leaders weren't connecting with the team. And the behaviors were not changing. That's when the guide team whom Nate was working with realized that they needed to make a change. They discussed different ideas and activities, but nothing seemed fitting. At that point, they decided that they needed to make it up! The concept of behavioral settings, described above, began to take form.

Building on one another's ideas, they came up with something new. They had an outcome in mind, that of communicating in a way that would engage the team in a discussion providing discoveries of significant insights and ultimately better choices regarding behaviors. As with any adventure, outcomes were unknown. They were amazed by the reaction of the participants when the behavioral setting cards were changed and laughter and authentic conversation ensued. The team was prepared to set goals and chose to demonstrate behaviors better suited for learning.

Block Party

Overview

A collaborative problem-solving activity with creative solutions. An entire group attempts to lift as many blocks as possible. Block Party is a great activity for exploring teamwork, collaboration, and problem solving.

Group Size	4 – 12
Learning Themes	• Building Trust, Relationships, and Community • Relationship Skills • Responsible Decision Making
Materials / Props	• Plastic or wooden blocks – 10 blocks per person **1 or 2 inch cubes work best.**

Setup

Open space

Framing

Say to participants:

"Has everyone heard of a block party? A block party is a large public party in which many community members of a single neighborhood gather to celebrate their connectedness. Block parties can be challenging to get off the ground and typically improve with time as they require lots of idea sharing, collaboration, and application of learning from previous attempts."

Or:

"What does it take for a group of people or a team to really get an idea or project off the ground? Consider this as you collaborate to literally lift these blocks off the ground."

Procedure

Say to the group:

1. As a group, attempt to lift or suspend as many blocks as you can.

2. Each person may use one (or both) index fingers only.

3. All blocks must be connected to each other in a single plane. Blocks may not be lifted in separate disconnected sections.

4. Blocks must be on the ground and then lifted to standing height for an attempt to be considered successful.

Reflection/Closure/Discussion

1. Would you agree that your progress improved over time? What allowed for that to happen?

2. What was your contribution? What role did you play?

3. Can you recall a time when an individual or group goal was revised? What would you consider the benefits of this activity?

4. What might this experience have been like without the social support that was demonstrated? What might that tell us regarding the significance of social support contributing to sustaining a healthy lifestyle?

Tips and Comments

Variations

- **No on Rule 3** – Omit rule 3 and allow participants to lift as many blocks as possible with a wider range of possibilities. Ideas may include stacking in multiple planes or lifting in separate disconnected sections.

- **Distant Connections** – Consider connecting and lifting blocks using the end of chopsticks or long wooden dowels. Connect one end of the chopsticks or wooden dowel directly to the blocks and the other end to the tip of the participant's index fingers.

Brain Buckets

Overview

A fairly challenging small group activity during which participants are asked to pass objects from one cup to another. The cups, however, are somewhat attached to their heads. Brain Buckets is a great activity for exploring communication, particularly how we convey ideas to one another, understand the ideas of others, and what happens in between.

Group Size	4 – 12
Learning Themes	• Fun and Play • Self Awareness and Self Management • Social Awareness • Relationship Skills
Materials / Props	• 1 large plastic cup or container per person • Two 12 – 15 inch lengths of string per person • 1 ping pong ball (or similar light object) per person

Estimated Time

15– 30 minutes

Safety

Caution participants not to pull too hard on their strings. The cups could slide off their heads and onto their noses.

Setup

You will need to create the Brain Buckets by attaching the two lengths of string to the base of each cup. The best method for attaching the string is to poke two opposing holes in the sides of a cup. Be sure the holes are small and close to the bottom of the cup – the higher up the holes are, the more challenging the activity. Pass one end of string through the newly-created opening and tie a knot big enough to prevent the string from pulling through. Do this for both lengths of string. In the end, you should have a cup hat that sits on your head and can be held in place with the two attached strings. The bottom of the cup should be against your head. Using a variety of cups and bowls makes this activity more exciting. Use caution when cutting or drilling holes.

Framing

Ask participants:

"Have you ever struggled to get an idea across, to share your thoughts? Have you ever felt that no one understood you? Well, getting your ideas across can be challenging and today you're going to be invited to share your ideas with others, but it's going to look a little different than what you may be used to."

Procedure

1. Distribute a Brain Bucket to each participant and explain its use.
2. The objective is to pass an object (ping-pong ball) from one cup to another without dropping it on the floor.
3. Cups must sit atop the head.
4. Participants may not make contact with the cups. Participants may use the strings only to steady the cups, not to tie the cups to their heads, or anything for that matter.
5. Provide a brief opportunity for participants to practice moving about while wearing the Brain Buckets. Provide advice when appropriate.
6. When the group is ready to move on, remind participants of the difficult challenges associated with sharing ideas and place ping pong balls in the Brain Buckets of about half the group.
7. Invite participants with ping-pong balls to attempt transferring them into the empty Brain Buckets of other participants.
8. Participants may not touch the cups or ping-pong balls.

Reflection / Closure / Discussion

1. What was most challenging?
2. How did you communicate with others? Was it effective? Challenging?
3. What strategies worked? Will those strategies help us when we are struggling to get our own ideas across?

Tips and Comments

It may be helpful to appropriately divide the group into smaller groups of three. Two participants attempt an object transfer while the third provides direction and assistance.

Bridging the Gap

Overview

A problem solving activity for pairs. Two people try to lift as many blocks between them as they can. Bridging the Gap is a great activity for exploring teamwork, collaboration, and especially, goal setting.

Group Size	2 or more
Learning Themes	• Building Trust, Relationships, and Community • Self Awareness and Self Management • Relationship Skills
Materials / Props	• Plastic or wooden blocks – 10 blocks per person 1 – 2 inch cubes work best.

Setup

Open space or between furniture

Framing

Say to the group:

"What are some building blocks for reaching a goal? Great! You are going to have the opportunity to explore these ideas with a partner. We'll check in in a little while."

Or:

"Exploration of our limits helps to identify a goal that truly stretches us. Communication is essential when exploring our limits. Be aware of how and what you communicate as you bridge the gap between you and a partner."

Or:

"Bridges connect people, communities, even countries. Connections can be strengthened when working toward a common goal. A common goal is essential for bridging the gap among people – individuals, communities, nations."

Or:

"A bridge reduces the distance between two places, people, or things. While the goal in this activity is to create greater and greater distance between you and a partner, you may discover that it brings you closer and closer."

Procedure

Say to the group:

1. Find someone who has the same or similar block as you. (Find a partner)
2. Attempt to suspend as many blocks between you as possible.
3. Each person may use one index finger on one hand.
4. Blocks must be in a straight line and single plane.

5. Blocks must start on the ground and be lifted to standing height for a successful bridging of the gap.

6. Be aware of how others are doing and what their goals are while continuing to work toward your personal best.

Reflection/Closure/Discussion

1. What are some building blocks for reaching a goal? Do these ideas apply to the goals you have set?

2. What did you notice about your communication? Did your feelings have any effect on how you were communicating? What might we learn from that? Where could you use what you learned? Is there a goal you could set to improve your communication in the future?

3. Did you and your partner discover a common goal? Were you committed to that goal? How did you work toward that goal? What might that tell us about goal setting in general? What common goal would you be willing to work toward that might connect our community?

4. What was required to bridge the gap between you and your partner? What is a "bridge" that brings people or communities closer? What are you willing to do to strengthen the bridges, or connections, in your community?

Tips and Comments

Variations

- **3D** – Allow participants to lift as many blocks as possible, without the requirement of having to be in a single plane, straight line. Blocks may be configured in three dimensions during the lifting attempt.

- **Three's a Crowd & Connect 4** – If progressing to Block Party, an activity challenging the entire group to lift as many blocks as possible, or exploring cooperative/collaborative learning in small groups, consider the following intermediate challenge. Invite three or four participants to lift as many blocks as possible. Blocks must be in a single plane, yet may extend in multiple directions.

- **Academic Link** – Bridge Knowledge – Use this activity to inspire inquiry into bridges built around the world, from the biggest successes to the biggest failures. Encourage participants to identify their favorite bridges and explore who built them and what they connect.

Bust a Move

Overview

An exploration of movement with a partner. In addition, participants playfully explore the limits of their imaginations and creativity as well as the magic of co-creation. Bust a Move gets people moving in ways they didn't think possible and moving on more quickly than they thought they could.

Group Size	2 or more
Learning Themes	• Fun and Play • Physical Activity and Movement • Relationship Skills • Responsible Decision Making
Materials / Props	• Plastic or wooden blocks – at least 2 blocks per person 1 – 2 inch cubes work best.

Setup

1. Clear an open space.
2. Have participants find partners.

Framing

Say to participants:

"You've heard the saying, 'There is no use crying over spilled milk.' What do you think it means? We've got a chance to practice that."

Or:

"This is an opportunity to explore movement, communicate with a partner, and make mistakes."

Or:

"It's time to bust a move!"

Procedure

1. Tell participants to suspend four blocks in a straight horizontal line between them using only the tips of their index fingers. In other words, participants position two blocks on the tips of their index fingers and connect their two blocks directly to their partners' in a straight horizontal line – to start anyway!

2. Invite participants to then play and explore moving creatively with their partners. Encourage participants to discover different ways of moving together while challenging themselves to move beyond their comfort zones which will be evidenced by blocks crashing to the floor! At this point, participants should know what to do – pick 'em up and play on! If not, a little gentle coaching should get people and blocks up and moving again.

3. Consider introducing additional movement ideas from the list of Block Stunts below.

Reflection/Closure/Discussion

If Bust a Move was used to develop skills for a block tag activity or in an entire block sequence, a debrief or reflection may not be needed. If it was used as a single activity, consider the following:

1. Does anyone have any favorite moves aka Block Stunts to share?
2. How did you respond when blocks fell to the floor?
3. Were there any challenges when moving with a partner? What were the challenges associated with communication, moving, etc.?
4. What are some strategies for moving with a partner (learned during the activity)?
5. Could these strategies be used anywhere else in your life?

Tips and Comments

- Demonstrations and participation by the facilitator are highly recommended.
- **Block Stunts** – If not discovered as participants are exploring, offer some of the following:

  Step Over – Step over the blocks of another pair while your and their blocks remained suspended.

  Under – Move under the blocks of another pair while your and their blocks remained suspended.

  Twist – Step over your own blocks while they are suspended between two partners.

  Twirl – One partner twirls/spins under his/her own blocks while remaining connected to his/her partner.

  Upside Down – Partners attempt to turn their blocks from horizontal to vertical.

  Busta Move – Partners attempt their best dance moves while maintaining an appropriate connection.

  Jump – Partners attempt to jump while maintaining an appropriate connection.

  Toss and Catch – Originally connected partners attempt to toss their blocks in the air and catch them all...in their hands, their shirts, on their feet, etc.

  Disconnect to Re-connect/Release and Catch – Originally connected partners attempt to release their blocks and then re-attempt to connect as if they were always suspended. If successful, partners can measure how far they allow their blocks to drop before connecting!

  Block Stunt Club – How many block stunts can your group create? Take pictures and post each new and different stunt.

Circle Call

Overview

A quick energizer or warm-up in which participants playfully form three types of circles called by the facilitator, or another participant. Circle Call is a great way to get your group into a circle and playfully introduce a setting in which to plan, check in, and celebrate.

Estimated Time

10 minutes

Group Size	8 or more
Learning Themes	• Fun and Play • Physical Activity and Movement • Building Trust, Relationships, and Community
Materials / Props	None

Setup

None

Framing

Say to the group:

"Circles can be significant and helpful to our experience. We may need different-sized circles for different occasions. Let's practice a few."

Procedure

1. Direct participants to create a Super Hero Circle by placing their fists on their hips so that their elbows are touching the elbows of their neighbors. Once the entire circle is connected, direct them to make a sound associated or representative of a super hero. The sound could also be a theme song of a particular super hero. Practice a few times.

2. Next, direct participants to create an Airplane Circle by taking a few giant steps back creating a large circle. The circle will be complete when each participant is just barely touching the finger tips of their neighbors, leaning forward, and balancing on one foot while making the sound of an airplane. Again, practice a few times.

3. Now, make alternate calls between Super Hero Circles and Airplane Circles. The group should respond accordingly by forming each type of circle called.

4. Finally, add a third circle type called a Velcro Circle, by directing participants to make the circle smaller and smaller until they are standing shoulder to shoulder. Once everyone's shoulders are touching, the group should make a sound representative of Velcro coming together.

5. After establishing all three circles (Super Hero, Airplane, and Velcro) and their associated sounds, randomly call different types of circles for the group to quickly form.

Reflection/Closure/Discussion

1. Given the nature of this activity, it may be appropriate to simply play, laugh, and move on to the next activity.

2. Speaking for the experience might also be a beneficial consideration. For example, you might say, "As I mentioned before we played, circles can be significant and helpful to our experience. Feel free to call a circle any time to plan, check in, or celebrate."

3. If you desire to process the experience further, consider the following:

   a. (Fist to Five) How was your response time? Were there times when you were better able to follow? Were there times when you led? What was that like?

   b. Given our experience so far, what is the value of being in a circle when sharing information (i.e., discussing ideas, expressing feelings, confronting others, and celebrating each other and our experience)?

   c. Have you noticed any down side to being in a circle?

   d. Can you think or imagine a time in the near future when calling a circle may be beneficial? What might some of those scenarios be?

   e. Who would you say should be responsible for calling circles in the future?

Tips and Comments

- Circle Call is a playful and effective way to introduce the Calling Group process. Calling Group is a behavior management technique described in *Exploring Islands of Healing* (Schoel & Maizell, 2002) and Project Adventure's Behavior Management through Adventure (BMTA) model. It has the potential to make Calling Group more enjoyable and fun!

Variations

- There are many people in the field of experiential education who playfully prefer different names for the same or similar activities. For example:

  – Ethan Doss, Youth and College Program Specialist and Trainer with Project Adventure, likes to use Magnetic Circle instead of Velcro Circle.

  – Chris Ortiz, Lead Trainer and Program Design Coordinator with High 5 Adventure Learning Center, uses three different calls all together. Chris plays this game with calls such as Chowder, Chicken Wing, and Flamingo. Can you guess which is which? Chowder is the same as Velcro, Chicken Wing replaces Super Hero, and Flamingo is an Airplane Circle.

  – Lastly, Sam Sikes, Founder of DoingWorks and author of many activity books, published a similar activity, called the Great Round-up, in the book *Raptor and Other Teambuilding Activities* (Sikes, 2003).

  Play with all of the variations above independently, and then combine them for fun and playfully test your group's reaction time!

- Create additional circle types to be called by varying height levels, i.e. standing on toes, kneeling, sitting, laying, etc. What would you call a circle that gets people to stand on their toes or sit on the floor or ground?

- Have participants create other circle forms, or types, to be called. For example, a group may come up with the idea of a Redwood Forest circle. To create this circle, a participant may have directed the group to stand close enough to reach the shoulders of their neighbors with their hands. Once the entire group is connected, they may balance on one foot while lifting the other foot and placing it on the inner thigh, lower leg, or near the ankle as in Tree Pose, a common posture from yoga. Participants should be discouraged from placing their feet directly on their knees. This circle represents a redwood forest because redwood trees are interconnected throughout their root system, which enables them to stand so tall. They hold each other up!

- Invite participants to practice calling the different circle types for the group to form. This helps to develop the voice of your participants and increase the likelihood of them calling and feeling comfortable to call a circle in the future.

___

Safety

Remind participants that, as the game progresses, they should be aware of players who have taken a knee, as well as other players who may be crossing more erratically through the general area of play.

Circle Tag

Overview

A tag game that sends everyone running in circles. When the game begins, players quickly leave their spots trying feverishly to tag as many people in subsequent order, starting with their immediate neighbors, before they themselves are tagged. Circle Tag presents itself as an energizing game that instigates communication as confusion sets in; great as a warm-up or perhaps something more!

Group Size	10 or more
Learning Themes	• Fun and Play • Physical Activity and Movement • Building Trust, Relationships, and Community
Materials / Props	None

Setup

1. Form a circle so that if everyone were to spread their arms, they would touch just the tips of their neighbors' fingers. Everyone should be facing the inside of the circle. (Create an Airplane Circle as described in Circle Call.)

2. Ask participants to introduce themselves to their neighbors, the participants to their immediate right and left. They may also wave to the people who are almost their neighbors – those close to them on the right and left

Framing

Say to the group:

"Has anyone had the experience of being so focused on a task that, once completed, they lost sight of the bigger picture or what to do next? What might you do if that were to happen to you? Consider those responses as we play the next game!"

Or:

"Developing an awareness of the people in your community is important. There may be moments of confusion or misunderstanding today (throughout the school year, etc.). Being willing to ask each other questions when confused and to provide answers when possible may be helpful."

Procedure

1. Explain that everyone's goal is the same — to stay in the game as long as possible.

2. On the Start signal, everyone attempts to tag the person to their immediate right and avoid being tagged by the person to their immediate left.

3. If a participant is tagged, he or she must get down on one knee (take a knee).

4. Once a participant has tagged the person to their immediate right, he or she will continue pursuing the next person sequentially to the right who has not been tagged and not taken a knee. Because much of the group will have been tagged

within the first moments of play, the next person to be tagged may be someone who was, from the start, only two people to the right, six to the right, or more!

5. While confusion is part of the game and will most likely make it fun, it's what participants do with the confusion that may provide significant learning. Participants may communicate with others to determine whom they should tag next or whom they need to avoid.

6. Feel free to stop the game at any point or continue playing until only one player remains.

7. Return to a circle and play again, only this time to the left!

Reflection/Closure/Discussion

1. Describe your experience.

2. Was anyone confused while playing this game?

3. How did you handle that confusion?

4. Did anyone help anyone else? How?

5. What did we learn from this game that might help us today, through the school year, with the next activity, etc.?

Tips and Comments

- Consider playing Circle Tag with a large group of twenty or thirty or more. If you do, please note that there is much more action to monitor for safety. Be diligent and stop the game as necessary.

Variations

- **That's One!** – For smaller groups, of about ten people, each player is allowed to be tagged two or three times before being eliminated.

- **Circle Tag with Ankle Biters** – Participants who have been tagged and are taking a knee can tag anyone they can reach without scooting.

- **Circle Tag Squared** – Same rules as Circle Tag yet played in pairs who are connected by linked arms.

- **Ga-Circle Tag** – Introduce a ball or balls to the game. Participants who have been tagged and have taken a knee attempt to tag anyone they can with the ball. Players may pass the ball and tag others with it by striking it with an open hand only. Facilitators may help keep the ball in play as needed.

- **Meteor Shower Tag** – Before the game begins, provide everyone with one or two fleece balls. Play Circle Tag as described above. Once players have been tagged and taken a knee, they must remain on their knees, but may attempt to throw their fleece balls at anyone who is still up and moving around. If a fleece ball, while in the air, comes into contact with a player who is up and moving, he or she must take a knee. Players who are taking a knee may throw as many fleece balls as they can reach without leaving their spots and with the use of one pivot foot. Players who are up and moving around may retrieve fleece balls, but may not throw them at other players. They can, however, pass them to players who are on their knees with the grand hope that these people will help them.

Safety

Circle Up is intended to be a fun and interactive way to create community and establish a safe space for people to check in. Facilitators may need to help participants distinguish when a playful and fun Circle Up or a more serious and respectful Circle Up is needed.

Circle Up (aka Perfect Circle)

Overview

A variation on the classic warm-up activity that places the facilitator among the participants in a circle rather than in the center of a square. Circle Up playfully introduces the circle as a significant tool for developing a plan, addressing an issue, and celebrating others or an event.

Group Size	12 or more
Learning Themes	• Fun and Play • Physical Activity and Movement • Building Trust, Relationships, and Community
Materials / Props	None

Setup

None

Framing

Say to the group:

"Developing your voice is essential to being a part of this community. Having a structure in which to share your voice is necessary to being heard. A circle represents community and provides the space to be heard. Let's play with this."

Or:

"As we move forward in our time together, it may be necessary to establish a setting in which your ideas can be heard. We are going to playfully practice establishing and re-establishing this setting in the form of a circle."

Procedure

1. Begin with everyone, including your self as the facilitator, standing in a circle.

2. Direct participants to acknowledge and remember the people to their immediate left and right.

3. Say to the group, "Whenever you hear me or anyone else call "Circle up", our task is to re-establish this circle exactly as it is right now, standing next to the same people we are standing next to in this moment."

4. Once the circle is accurately re-established, participants yell, "We're all here!"

5. Practice, then play for a while with the facilitator calling, "Circle up!" Run to random spots and playfully change directions just before the circle has been re-established to generate excitement and fun!

6. After playing for a bit under your direction, invite participants to call and continue playing!

Reflection/Closure/Discussion

1. Explain that a perfect circle can be called by anyone at any time to develop a plan, address an issue, or celebrate a person or event.

2. What is it about a circle that might provide an appropriate setting for planning, discussing issues, celebrating, etc.?

3. When might you call a perfect circle in the future?

As the group develops, consider checking in to see how the perfect circle is working out.

1. Let's take a minute to check in on the use of our perfect circle.

2. Have there been times when we could have used our perfect circle?

3. Have we been using our perfect circle effectively?

4. What do we need to do to continue using our perfect circle effectively or use our perfect circle more effectively?

5. What simple guidelines could we add to help us better communicate during our perfect circle?

Tips and Comments

- When participants are encouraged to practice using their voices, they are more likely to use their voices when it is necessary e.g., when developing plans, resolving conflicts, or affirming the choice of another person.

- Circle Up works well in a sequence after activities in which part of the activity requires the group to reorganize themselves alphabetically.

- Circle Up is a variation of the activity Quick Line Up (*QuickSilver*, p.182)

___

Safety

No special safety procedures are required for this activity in its stationary version. For the moving 'change up' version, alert the group to potential obstacles and restrict running if needed.

Collaborative Numbers (aka Key Punch Jr.)

Overview

An engaging, timed activity for multiple small groups. The challenge involves participants collaborating in small teams to touch numbers randomly printed on a large sheet of paper in sequence. In successive rounds, groups capitalize on learning from previous attempts with a goal of continuous improvement. Collaborative Numbers is ideal for indoor settings where space may be limited.

Group Size	2 or more
Learning Themes	• Self Awareness and Self Management • Relationship Skills • Responsible Decision Making
Materials / Props	• One sheet of paper for each student with the numbers 1 – 60 scattered randomly on the page • Page dimensions: 8 ½ x 11 (works) or 11 x 17 (ideal)

Setup

Participants are seated at desks, tables or even on the floor in groups of three or four. Students can help with the math. Hand out one number sheet, face down, to each group. Remind them, 'No peeking!'

Framing

Say to the group:

"Imagine that you are an air traffic controller. To safely land planes, you need to touch a screen, which will alert the correct planes to land in the designated locations and order. To achieve the task accurately, you need to touch your screen in the proper manner with speed and accuracy. Remember, we have a lot of passengers wanting to arrive at their destinations yesterday!"

Procedure

1. Tell participants that when you say, "Go", they are to turn their papers over and try to touch with their fingers as many numbers in sequential order from least to greatest as they can in 60 seconds. They are not allowed to write on their paper or tear it in any way. After the time is up, they are to turn their papers over.

2. Next, direct the participants to form small groups of three or four.

3. Tell participants that they now have one to three minutes to plan how, as a team, they will touch as many numbers as possible, again in sequential order from least to greatest. Speed is of the essence. How many numbers can they touch drawing on their collective effort? Numbers must be touched just once by any group member – every member need not touch each number.

4. Do two to four more rounds, asking them between rounds to discuss ways to improve their score, each time trying to set a goal for how many they believe they can get based on their strategy discussions. If the group gets to 60, they can continue their count by resuming from 1.

5. Do a round and ask the groups to think about how they did and if they want to change anything. Consider having them share strategies across groups. Chart results and set goals by team and/or set a collective goal by adding each group's goals. This fosters an interesting tension between competition and collaboration.

6. Give the groups three to five rounds depending on time and interest. Throughout the activity, the central theme is pursuit of continuous improvement.

Reflection / Closure / Discussion

Ask students:

1. What was different about working by yourself versus working in a small group? Were you able to accomplish more as a small group? Why or why not?

2. Were you able to be here, be safe, and be honest during this activity? Was it easier to practice these skills when you worked alone or when you worked in a group? Why or why not?

3. How does this activity support skills for working in groups on other tasks we will face as a class/team?

Tips and Comments

- Adapted from "Collaborative Numbers" in Laurie Frank's book, *Journey Toward the Caring Classroom* (Wood 'n' Barnes, 2004)

Variations

- Require that each team member touch at least one number during each round.

- Instead of asking students to touch the numbers in sequential order, have them do factors of 60 or the multiples of five.

- After a couple of stationary rounds, place number sheets all around the room, building and/or grounds. When the facilitator shouts, 'Change Up!', each group must seek another sheet – one they have not yet visited. Upon arrival, they continue counting where they stopped on the previous sheet. Let the activity run for three to five minutes and monitor engagement to determine a stopping point.

- Modify the sheet if it seems too challenging for your group. For instance, reduce the range from 60 to 20 for younger children.

- Use letters, words or dates for content review in a specific content area.

- If appropriate, tape number sheets to the ceiling of an indoor space. Ask participants to refrain from viewing the number sheets as the instructions are being given and between each round. Now there are a couple of options to consider – a lifting or non-lifting. For a non-lifting variation, provide each small group with a stick long enough to reach the ceiling while standing on the ground, e.g., a broom handle or tent pole. Another option may be to provide a few wooden dowels or the like for the group to assemble. In this case, players would need to contact each number using the stick, tent pole, or whatever has been provided. If choosing to facilitate the lifting option, we recommend that proper spotting and lifting techniques be introduced or reviewed. For this variation, create groups of eight to ten and require participants to touch the numbers with their hands.

Safety

Participants should be aware of each other, especially their heads, as they bend down to pick up name cards and turn to deliver to the matching person.

Community Celebration

Overview

A two-part, problem-solving initiative. After celebrating their coming together, the group forms a circle and each member, one by one, says his or her name aloud as quickly as possible. After that, group members simultaneously pick up name cards, return them to the matching person, quickly re-form the circle alphabetically, and say all of the names alphabetically. Community Celebration is a great way to reinforce names while exploring problem solving, goal setting, and acceptance.

Group Size	10 or more
Learning Themes	• Building Trust, Relationships, and Community • Relationship Skills • Responsible Decision Making
Materials / Props	• Index cards • Markers • Stop watch

Setup

1. Create a large open space.

2. Ask each participant to write his or her name on a blank index card. Collect all name cards from participants.

3. Ask participants to form a circle inside the open space so that you can explain the task.

Framing

Say to the group:

"In order for our group to become a community, it is important that we share a few things – our names, where we fit in, and solutions to problems. In this way, we will continually celebrate each individual member of our community."

Procedure

1. Direct participants to greet their neighbors – the people to their immediate left and right. They will need to remember these people as the group will eventually recreate the circle exactly as it is.

2. Tell the group that the objective is to solve the challenge you are about to give them in the shortest time possible.

3. Explain that after celebrating their coming together, the group will say their names aloud going around the circle as quickly as they can. They will simultaneously pick up name cards, return them to the matching persons, and re-form the circle alphabetically. Once this circle is formed, participants will say all of the names aloud alphabetically.

4. Invite a participant to lead the group in a celebration by tossing the name cards (confetti) as high into the air as they can.

5. Time starts when the last card lands on the ground as this is when the challenge begins.

6. Participants say their names around the circle as quickly as they can.

7. Once the last person has said his or her name, participants pick up the name cards, return them to the matching persons, and attempt to re-organize themselves in a circle in alphabetical order. Participants can pick up as many or as few cards as they wish.

8. Once they have re-arranged themselves alphabetically, the group repeats their names in alphabetical order starting with the individual whose name is closest to A and ending with the individual whose name is closest to Z.

9. Time stops when the last person has said his or her name and says, "Stop." The group has a responsibility to remind this person to say "Stop."

10. At the end of each round, briefly explore strategies for improvement.

11. Have the group re-form the original circle.

12. Repeat 2-4 times.

Reflection/Closure/Discussion

After each round:

1. Encourage the group to explore what they did, what they learned, and what they will do next round.

2. Or encourage them to explore what worked and what didn't work.

At the end of the activity:

1. Ask the participants to identify ways in which they communicated that helped them to improve each round.

2. Ask participants to identify what behaviors were helpful and which were not helpful.

3. Finally, ask the group members to identify how it felt to celebrate their success and ultimately their community.

Tips and Comments

- Community Celebration is adapted from the activity Name Time in *Creating Healthy Habits* by Dr. Katie Kilty (Project Adventure, 2006).

Variations

- Challenge the group to hand any card to any person so that individuals line up or circle up according to their name card not their actual name.

- Consider playing with the format and have groups line up or create other geometric shapes instead of forming a circle.

- Consider forming and re-forming circles in the opposite order. First, the group simultaneously picks up name cards, lines up alphabetically, and says all of the names out loud alphabetically; then the group quickly reforms in the original circle and repeats the names again in sequential order.

- If the order described above is used, an additional variation could challenge the group to say their names alphabetically during both parts of the task, once when they are in alphabetical order as well as when they return to the original circle.

Safety

Bottoms Up: If one or more of your participants have had a recent tailbone or wrist injury, play a more appropriate activity from the list on page 62 instead.

Concentric Circles

Overview

A nicely structured icebreaker with moments of spontaneous laughter and exchanges. Beginning with two circles facing one another, two players (one from each circle) engage in a partner activity. Before each new partner activity, the circles rotate and participants discover new partners. Concentric Circles is an ideal large group opener that provides a few personal connections among the mass of a larger whole.

Group Size	10 or more
Learning Themes	• Building Trust, Relationships, and Community • Self Awareness and Self Management • Social Awareness • Relationship Skills
Materials / Props	None

Setup

- Provide enough open space for a large circle with some additional space to move around.
- Be prepared to deliver clear and concise instructions.
- Be prepared with a means for getting the group's attention as this activity flows in and out of paired activities.

Framing

Say to the group:

"We are going to create a giant wheel of people and play several different games in the next ten minutes, with the intention of giving and receiving support."

Procedure

1. Begin in a large circle.
2. Instruct every other person to take a giant step forward. Help players to do this quickly and effectively by walking around the inside of the circle and coaching every other person to consecutively step in.
3. Ask each circle to begin walking quickly in opposite directions listening for your instructions. After ten or fifteen seconds, shout "Freeze" then "Change directions and walk quickly again". This has a musical chairs quality. Again, after an interval of time shout, "Freeze!"
4. Now the inside ring of the circle turns to face the outside ring of the circle, and everyone shakes hands with their first partner (whoever is standing directly in front of him/her).
5. The facilitator must help confused pairs to match up and may choose to partner with someone if there are an odd number of players.

6. Game One: **Shoelace Tie**

    a. Greet your partner. Learn each other's names.

    b. Choose one shoe between the two of you. The shoe must have laces. Untie the shoelace.

    c. Each of you must place one hand behind your backs and keep it there as you cooperatively try to re-tie the untied shoelace.

    d. If successful, try using only your non-dominant hands to cooperatively re-tie another shoelace, or see how many times you can tie and untie the shoelace.

    e. Say goodbye to your partner.

    f. The outer circle now shifts two people to the right by taking two giant steps to the right. You are facing your new partner.

7. Game Two: **Off Kilter Sculpture**

    a. Greet your partners. Learn each others' names.

    b. Create a unique balancing shape with your partner by giving and receiving weight so that if your partner wasn't there, you wouldn't be able to make that shape (you would fall over).

    c. Hints: Try holding wrists, leaning into each other's backs, or pressing palms together. The facilitator can offer a quick demonstration.

    d. Keep trying until you've made a shape that is different from the pairs around you, then try copying some of the other shapes you see.

    e. Thank your partner and say, "Goodbye."

    f. The outer circle now shifts two people to the right by taking two giant steps to the right. You are facing your new partner.

8. Game Three: **Bottoms Up**

    a. Greet your partner. Learn each other's names.

    b. Sit on the ground facing your partner.

    c. Place your hands on the floor and the soles of your feet together.

    d. Try to lift your bottoms off the ground at the same time, while keeping your feet connected! Let the giggling begin!

    e. Variation: Try keeping one foot on the floor.

    f. Safety note: If you or your partner has had a recent tailbone or wrist injury, play Shoelace Tie instead.

Debrief (discuss with your last partner)

1. Did the size or strength of your partner make it easier or harder to lift their bottoms off the ground?

2. What kinds of assumptions did you make about your partner's strength, weight or balance? Were they valid?

3. How did you adjust to your partner's unique qualities? If you were not successful, did you still make a good effort?

4. What could you have done differently?

5. How can the partnering skills you practiced apply in the classroom, social settings, workplace, etc.?

Tips and Comments

- Visually demonstrate each activity in addition to providing verbal instructions.
- Adjust facilitation of the circling motion to attain the desired level of physical exertion, group coordination, safety and fun.
- Throw "get-to-know-you" questions into the mix by alternating between physical challenges and questions. For example:
  - What was your most recent adventure?
  - If you could travel anywhere in the world, where would you go and why?
  - Who is someone you admire most in your life and why?
  - If you could support any one person with a challenge in his or her life, who would you support and how?
- Consider introducing the following partner activities, as well as others, to add more variety, fun, and meaning:
  - **Finger Fencing** (*No Props*, p.78)
  - **Snoopy and the Red Baron** (*No Props*, p.79)
  - **Stationary Foot Tag (aka Top It)** (Found in *The Hundredth Monkey*)
  - **Wiggle Waggle** (*No Props*, p.42)
  - **Tiny Teach, aka Tiny Teaching** (*A Small Book About Large Group Games*, p.48)

Estimated Time

5 minutes

Copy Claps

Overview

A wonderfully engaging attention-getter. Without saying a word, a leader engages the group with a series of claps – each one more complex than the preceding – inviting the group to follow.

Group Size	12 or more - best suited for groups of 20 or more
Learning Themes	• Fun and Play • Building Trust, Relationships, and Community
Materials / Props	None

Setup

None, although the activity works best with a group that is engaged in rich conversation or a particular task

Framing

None

Procedure

1. Without saying a word, step out into the group and clap once. You can expect a response of one or two claps, or none at all.

2. If anyone claps, give an affirming head nod or eyebrow raise. If not, no problem!

3. Clap twice and allow for a response from most of the group.

4. Clap three times, followed by a response from the entire group.

5. Now that you have the group's attention, play with 'em a bit. Present a series of progressively more complex patterns leading the group to joyful perplexity!

6. End with a final series of claps that evolves into a courteous round of applause, thanking everyone for playing along.

7. Now you have your group's attention and they will be ready to hear what you have to say.

Reflection/Closure/Discussion

None needed

Tips and Comments

- This is a great non-verbal alternative to "If you can hear me, clap once, if you can hear me, clap twice…"

- See Clapping Game in *Count Me In: Large Group Activities That Work* (p. 86) for another excellent energizer that is guaranteed to raise the energy of your group and make 'em laugh!

Variations

- Incorporate a variety of sounds, whistles, snaps, stomps, jump-claps and different body movements. Have fun with it and keep the energy flowing!

- Culminate the activity by seamlessly flowing into the series of snaps, claps, and sounds expressed in the activity Coming and Going of the Rain (*Silver Bullets*, p.92)

Cross the Line (Team Activity)

Overview

A surprising activity instigating ridiculous behaviors that eventually lead to profound insights. One half of a divided group attempts to get the other half of their team to their side of the line in any way they can. Cross the Line seems to bring out a plethora of behaviors that many participants might like to deny or ignore. This leads to many rich learning opportunities as indicated in the debrief section. Check it out!

Group Size	12 or more
Learning Themes	• Self Awareness and Self Management • Social Awareness • Relationship Skills • Responsible Decision Making
Materials / Props	40 foot length of rope

Setup

1. Lay down a rope which is long enough for the number of people in the group to stand opposite one another.

2. Separate participants into two groups with each half standing opposite one another. Group A people are standing on their side of the rope facing people in Group B and Group B people are standing on their side of the rope facing Group A people.

Framing

Included in the procedure

Procedure

1. Ask that each person face someone who is standing opposite them. It is fine if the groups are not even in number.

2. It is important to obtain the group's attention before you proceed further with the directions. Depending on your leadership/facilitator style in calling the group to attention, you may add a whistle or bell into your games bag or simply employ your very best "are we ready yet?" glare.

3. Explain to the group that you will only be stating the goal of the activity one time and, that once you have done so, they should not ask any further questions.

4. Before stating the goal for the activity, you have a great opportunity to re-introduce the value of "Being Safe" in your Full Value Contract. You can remind/ask participants about "Being Safe" – what it means, what it looks like etc., and extract a solemn promise that they will play safe with one another in this activity.

5. In explaining the goal and rules, mixing in humor with a degree of seriousness, speaking in a clear but somewhat dramatic tone tends to work well in peaking the

group's attention and sense of anticipation. It might go something like this...... "OK, are we ready? Here are the rules....Rule # 1 is Attend to Safety. Everyone needs to promise without any fingers, legs or eyes crossed that they absolutely will not hurt anyone else or themselves while trying to reach their goals. No fighting of any kind is allowed...". How well you dramatize the Being Safe value tends to go a long way toward moving people more deeply into their already established cultural mind set that this must be about competition.

6. Explain to the group that the rope boundary which separates the two home lands should be thought of as fixed and hence cannot be moved in any way.

7. Explain to the two groups that they are standing in their own country which is separated from the other country by the boundary rope on the ground. In your explanation, you should play up how their respective countries represent the best of everything. The main idea is to convey the image that the land on their side of the rope is theirs to preserve and protect.

8. State the goal as follows: "The goal for the group on the left side of the rope is to get as many people who are standing opposite them onto their side of the rope. The goal for the group on the right side of the rope is to get as many people who are standing opposite them onto their side of the rope...OK that's the goal..... Ready, Set, Go!" And then start the stop watch.

9. Generally you can let the group work on solving the problem for five to eight minutes, sometimes longer. It is important to allow enough time for group members to act and react to the various behaviors the two groups employ to reach their goals. As they become engaged with each other, it is important to observe the various behaviors that go on as groups/individuals struggle with each other as they try to get folks opposite them over to their side but not allowing themselves to pass over to the other side. More often than not, you will observe a host of futile, non-productive behaviors that more exemplify lose-win and lose-lose behaviors sprinkled with some interactions that are more positive. It is interesting to note that while the goal of the activity is mutual and hence collaborative/ cooperative behaviors work best, most participants have inferred that it is competitive and to win requires that someone has to lose.

Reflection/Closure/Discussion

The simple solution to this problem is for members of each group to quickly change places with one another by stepping across the line which maybe takes one second at best. It is often quite humorous to have people share what they did and didn't do and what was done to them. As importantly, it is interesting to hear why they did what they did.

Some Questions to Consider:
- What was the group's thinking process?
- Based upon what they heard as the goal and rules for the activity, what, if any, were their preconceived notions?
- What assumptions were made based on what they heard?
- What were the behaviors that got played out between you and the person(s) standing opposite you? How about between the two groups?

- Did anyone have a different view about a possibly easier win/win solution to the problem? If yes, what did you try to do to have others accept your view? How did others react to your suggestion?

- How do the trust or lack of trust issues influence your behavior?

- Why do you think you quickly demonstrated more competitive, if not aggressive behaviors, in trying to solve the problem?

- What might be some key learnings you can take away from this activity?

Usually, you will hear some interesting information around the themes such as: winning at all costs; for someone to win, someone has to lose; I'm sticking with my team; I couldn't trust the ideas and suggestions of others in my group or from the other group. What you hardly ever hear, at first, are things that confirm understanding that they were one large group who had a mutual goal in the activity. Because it was a mutual goal, collaborative and cooperative behaviors would have served them much better.

Given the time allotted and the group's energy around the activity and program goals, one can move the debrief further into what it takes for group members and the group to work more effectively as a team. Some sample questions are: What do you believe you now need to think about how to move forward? What about the trust issue? Does the level of trust among members need to be improved upon? What do you want to do differently?

Related to the notion of building effective teamwork and leadership, the relevance of this activity and debrief can easily be connected to:

- Positive interdependence as an essential for improved team performance

- Pre-conditions for Leading and Coaching

- Trust with colleagues and understanding what it takes to build relationships

- Self Awareness: Bringing in and using the information – understanding values and needs

- Self Motivation: Identifying and overcoming external and internal barriers

- Coaching through Barriers – within yourself, your team and associates, organizational and cultural barriers

Crosstown Connections

Overview

An interactive icebreaker of playful greetings. Participants connect with different partners based on a host of novel handshakes. They are then challenged to demonstrate each greeting with the appropriate partner each time a handshake is called. Crosstown Connections is a fantastic way to form partners, connect people, and play!

Group Size	12 or more
Learning Themes	• Fun and Play • Building Trust, Relationships, and Community
Materials / Props	None

Setup

Have the group stand in a circle.

Framing

Say to group:

"Consider meeting someone new for each handshake learned."

Procedure

1. Demonstrate a handshake with a willing volunteer. Invite everyone to find ONE partner to practice the handshake with and return to the circle.

2. It is good to have the facilitator help to match partners during this process, perhaps by calling out, "Partner lost and found!" when working with larger groups.

3. Continue playfully introducing new handshakes. Instruct participants to find a new partner for each handshake. It is fair to introduce three to five handshakes.

4. It may be helpful to have handshake partner reviews between each round.

5. Speed Round: Once handshakes have been introduced and partnerships established, call out the names of the different handshakes that have been taught. Partners are expected to find one another, complete the handshake and be ready for the next handshake to be called.

Reflection/Closure/Discussion

None needed

Tips and Comments

- **Handshakes**

    - **High Five or Low Five**

    - **Rodeo** – Link elbows and circle shouting, "Yee haw!"

    - **Happy Salmon** – Go in for the handshake, pass hands and slap your partner's forearm.

    - **Turkey** – One person makes the feathers (open hand), one person makes the body and the head (closed hand with thumb extended). Upon connection of the body with the feathers, partners gobble like turkeys.

    - **Lumber Jack** – Participants grab their partners' right hands with their right hands and give the thumbs up. They continue stacking and then pretend that they are sawing wood together.

    - **Celebration** – With their hands, have participants slap thigh thigh, clap clap, snap snap, high ten their partners and shout, "YEAH!"

    - **Secret Handshake** – Participants create their own secret handshake known only to them.

- If Secret Handshakes are used in this activity, it is really fun, according to NJ Teacher of the Year, and Middle School PE Teacher, Chip Candy, to call out this handshake in a public space (i.e., school cafeteria). In doing so, people who have a secret handshake partner find their partner, demonstrate their handshake, and then, of course, act as if everything is normal and return to where or what they were doing.

- Use the partnerships associated with different handshakes to form pairs, quads, or teams later in the program. This is effective and efficient when activities call for either a particular grouping or create groups for debriefing.

Variations

- Crosstown Connections works well when the handshakes are introduced with a playful story. Many facilitators like to associate handshakes with particular places or roles around the world. For example, the Happy Salmon may be introduced as a celebration fishermen used after returning to the harbor safely with a good catch. Or, the Lumber Jack is a greeting that loggers from New Hampshire use when they haven't seen each other in a while.

- For a fun challenge and link to the subject of Social Studies, try to connect as many handshakes as possible to either states, provinces, countries, or subcultures, etc. Better yet, introduce a bunch of handshakes and invite your participants to make the connections to these locations or groups. An interesting debrief could be focused on why each handshake was chosen in association with a particular area.

Dinosaur Game

Overview

A silly de-inhibitizer and energizer straight from the Jurassic era. Participants send waves of movement and playful dinosaur sounds around a circle with one simple goal – to keep their teeth covered!!! A ridiculously FUN game for no apparent reason other than a roaring good time!

Group Size	8 or more
Learning Themes	• Fun and Play • Building Trust, Relationships, and Community
Materials / Props	None

Setup

None

Framing

Say to the group:

"This is simply FUN!"

Or:

"Here's a game the dinosaurs used to play!"

Procedure

Warm-up

1. Round 1: Participants stand in a circle holding hands. One person begins by passing a wave, undulating from his or her shoulder, down the arm, and into his or her neighbor's arm around the circle either to the right or to the left.
2. Round 2: Once the wave has passed all the way around, pass it in the opposite direction.
3. Round 3: Now the wave can be passed to either the right or left. For example, when you receive a wave, you may choose to continue the wave or pass it back to the person who gave it to you.

Play

4. Round 4: Add the sound and the covering of teeth. To become the dinosaur, you must use your lips to cover your teeth, add a dinosaur sound (or any silly sound) and a giant, awkward stare at the person you are sending the wave to. The goal is to try to make that person laugh and show their teeth without you doing the same. If anyone reveals their teeth during a laughing fit, they graduate to the outside of the circle and become a distracter. Distracters can make silly sounds as long as there is no breaking the plane of the circle, no touching of participants still in the circle, and no shouting in ears.

Reflection/Closure/Discussion

None needed

Safety

Be sure to assess your group's readiness to safely and respectfully play this game. It may feel like a risk to stand or sit in the center of a group without sight while trying to guess something that everyone else knows the answer to.

Disguised Voice (aka Ducky Wucky Woo)

Overview

A benevolently deceptive energizer that is sure to get a few good laughs. Participants attempt to identify the playfully disguised voices of their group mates. It works both as a venue in which to play, laugh and move on or to more deeply explore topics such as self and social awareness and self management.

Group Size	10 – 15
Learning Themes	• Fun and Play • Building Trust, Relationships, and Community • Self Awareness and Self Management • Social Awareness
Materials / Props	None

Setup

Begin with the group in a circle.

Framing

"Have you ever tried to disguise your voice, attempted to sound like someone else, or tried an accent different from your own? (Invite participants to share their experiences.) We are going to play a guessing game that might give you this opportunity."

Procedure

1. Explain the game.

   a. One person will volunteer to stand or sit in the center of the group with eyes closed or blindfolded.

   b. Once this person has shut his or her eyes or the blindfold is on, a second person will be selected by the facilitator or the group members.

   c. The person selected will then say, in a disguised voice, "Ducky Wucky Woo." Now, it may be helpful to encourage the selected person to try out accents, high or lower tones, impersonations, a muffled tone, etc. Anything that eludes obvious voice recognition.

   d. The person in the center, with eyes shut or blindfolded, will then have three opportunities to guess who owns the disguised voice.

   e. If they answer correctly or use all three guesses, a new person is invited into the center of the circle and the game begins again.

2. Play!

Reflection/Closure/Discussion

1. Do not feel obligated to process the experience. Let it speak for itself with laughter and comments, then move on.

2. If you choose to process this, consider the themes of both self and social awareness as well as self management. Ask participants:

    a. How did you feel while playing this game?

    b. What was different about being the person in the center of the circle?

    c. If it was stressful for you, how did you manage your emotions?

    d. Did anyone consider what other people were feeling or what it might have been like for others as they played this game?

    e. What did you learn by listening to how others felt during the game?

    f. How might playing this game help us to better manage emotions during our time together? How might it help us to better understand or have empathy for one another?

Tips and Comments

- Please note that this activity titled Disguised Voice is different than the activity often referred to as Ducky Wucky. In some circles, Ducky Wucky invites people to sit on the laps of others, Disguised Voice does not.

Variations

- **Team Guess** – Invite more than one person into the center of the circle to guess as a team. These participants may briefly discuss who they believe disguised their voice.

- **Spin It** – Invite the participant in the center to spin around three times to further disorient themselves before listening to the disguised voice and guessing. Monitor for safety.

- **Mix It Up** – Invite participants standing or sitting in the circle to move to a new spot in the circle before or after identifying the person to disguise their voice.

- **New Phrase** – Use a phrase other than "Ducky Wucky Woo." Consider short words of wisdom, familiar song lyrics, or commonly known phrases.

- **Disguised Voice Debrief** – Consider using Disguised Voice as a debrief tool or way to process an experience. If the time and group is right, Disguised Voice could be an effective, albeit humorous, way to engage participants in sharing their perspectives.

Safety

Be aware that this activity generally inspires an exuberant and playful atmosphere. Without extinguishing that spirit, monitor the level of play in relation to the setting. Check in as necessary and adapt as needed.

Don't Break the Ice

Overview

A fun variation of tag that seems to bring out the best in people. Partners attempt to move about while connected through four suspended blocks, simultaneously trying to break the connection of other players. Don't Break the Ice seems to bring about a variety of behaviors from everyone playing which leads to an ideal environment for discussing group norms and establishing a Full Value Contract.

Group Size	12 or more
Learning Themes	• Physical Activity and Movement • Building Trust, Relationships, and Community • Relationship Skills
Materials / Props	• Plastic or wooden blocks – At least 2 blocks per person 1-2 inch blocks work best

Setup

1. Clear an open space. The space does not need to be too large, but does need to be clear.

2. Creatively divide your group into pairs. Consider fun ideas from the list of Snappy Partners in *No Props* or *Count Me In* by Mark Collard.

Framing

Say to the group:

"Relationships are the foundation of a community. We form friendships/relationships that we feel comfortable with and want to maintain."

Or:

"Sometimes we become distracted or exhausted and are challenged to maintain these relationships. Let's explore ways to maintain these connections."

Procedure

1. Tell participants to suspend four blocks in a straight horizontal line between them using only the tips of their index fingers. In other words, participants position two blocks on the tips of their index fingers and connect their two blocks directly to their partners' in a straight horizontal line – to start anyway!

2. State the objective: Participants attempt to move and maintain their connections through the four suspended blocks while trying to break the connections of other partner pairs using their free index fingers only.

3. Explain and demonstrate the rules:

   a. Connection breaking attempts can only happen by participants who are properly connected to their partners.

b. Physical contact should be kept to a minimum. This is a game of finesse and positioning, not asserting oneself physically. Participants should refrain from pushing, blocking, swatting, etc.

c. Participants may box out (as in basketball), move, and position themselves to make their blocks more challenging to knock.

d. Participants may only use the tips of their index fingers to connect through their four blocks. In other words, participants may not link hands, fingers, or thumbs in an attempt to better secure their blocks.

Reflection/Closure/Discussion

- **Full Value Check-in** – Don't Break the Ice seems to bring out the best in people (especially if you omit communication of the particular rules bulleted in the procedure)! Often times, behaviors such as cheating, dishonesty, revenge, competition, and miscommunication are demonstrated. This seems to provide an opportunity to either develop a Full Value Contract or check in with a pre-existing one.

- **Pair Share or Quadraphonic** – In a "Pair Share," two people share responses to a question(s). During a "Quadraphonic," four people share responses to a question(s). Using a "Quadraphonic" debrief provides the option of new pairings after debriefing.

  - Would you say that you and your partner were successful at maintaining your connections and communication?
  - What was allowed for your success or failure?
  - What are some of the best strategies for maintaining connections and communication that you demonstrated or saw another group demonstrate?
  - What are three healthy ways to stay connected to people in your life? What are three unhealthy ways of attempting to stay connected to people in your life?

Tips and Comments

Connecting Variations

- **Switch** – Encourage participants to switch hands or play using their sub-dominant sides.

- **Which Digit?**

  - **Thumbs Up!** – Use thumbs as a connecting point rather than index fingers and, likewise, participants may attempt to break the connection of others with their thumbs.
  - **Pinkies Too!** – Similar to Thumbs Up, participants use pinky fingers for both connecting and disconnecting.

- **Hey, Where Are You Going?** – Players challenge themselves by facing opposite directions.

Game Variations

- Try omitting rule "d." If you do, prepare for an opportunity to process particular behaviors that present themselves without it!

Tips and Comments *(continued)*

- **Ice Breakers** – Similar rules as Don't Break the Ice with one partnering rule change. Once blocks are broken, participants pick up their blocks and re-connect with different partners. See Don't Break the Ice write-up for Framing and Debriefing ideas.

- **Building Blocks** – Same rules as Don't Break the Ice, with one competitive rule addition. Once blocks are broken, participants, whether connected or not and with or without blocks, attempt to pick up as many blocks as possible, re-connect either with their partners or anyone else, and continue playing. Participants may re-connect to another person with as many blocks as they are able and as few as one.

- **Three's a Crowd** – Three participants attempt to remain connected based on the original rules of Don't Break the Ice. Provide time for participants to strategize the best way to connect and play.

- **Connect 4** – Four participants attempt to remain connected based on the original rules of Don't Break the Ice. Provide time for participants to strategize their best way to connect and play.

Falls Ball

Estimated Time

30 minutes

Safety

As described in the overview, Falls Ball is a fast-paced game. Monitor or check in to ensure that everyone feels safe and is demonstrating safe movements while playing this game.

Overview

A fast-paced field game created by blending recognizable influences from soccer, ultimate frisbee, and team handball. Players advance a ball up the field using their feet as in soccer or their hands as in ultimate Frisbee or team handball attempting to score goals on a defending team. While having a traditional sports influence, Falls Ball offers plenty of learning opportunities and is a game you'll want to play game after game, day after day, year after year.

Group Size	20 – 30
Learning Themes	• Fun and Play • Physical Activity and Movement • Relationship Skills
Materials / Props	• 2 Goals/Nets • 1 Dino Skin™ Ball or rubber kickball/playground ball • 4 cones • Colored Pinnies (light weight vests designating teams) for each participant or one team

Setup

- Place the goal/nets 100-150 feet apart

74

- Place 4 cones to mark 4 corners, and ultimately the boundaries, of the playing field. The boundaries should allow for playable space behind the goals.

Framing

Say to the group:

"We know that vigorous physical activity is beneficial to our heart and respiratory systems, and have discovered that it is also healthy for the development of our brains. Let's use our brains as we engage our bodies in a game requiring many aspects of teamwork – communication, inclusivity, and resilient attitudes."

Procedure

1. Creatively divide your group into two teams.

2. Provide colored pinnies to each player to differentiate between teams.

3. Explain and demonstrate the rules:

    a. Each team is trying to score as many goals as they can against the opposing team.

    b. Play begins as soccer does with a coin toss to determine possession and a kick off. The team who earns possession must initially kick the ball forward for the game to begin.

    c. Players may move the ball up and down the field in two distinct ways. When the ball is on the ground, it may only be kicked or contacted with the feet as in soccer. Players may, however, flick the ball with their feet into their own hands or the hands of other players.

    d. When a player is holding the ball in his or her hands, he or she may take up to three steps and may use one pivot foot while trying to pass the ball to other teammates.

    e. Players may intercept the ball or knock it to the ground when it's in the air. Knocking the ball to the ground does not necessarily mean a change in possession and the ball is played live. On the other hand, intercepting the ball does change possession.

f. A goal is scored by throwing or kicking the ball into the net. Teams earn one point by throwing the ball in the net and two points by kicking it in.

g. Goals may be scored by players in front of or behind the net. All goals must be scored through the open side of the net.

h. Possession changes and play continues immediately after a goal is scored.

4. Provide opportunities for strategizing after each goal, game, or a predetermined amount of time. Teams could benefit from a brief reflection on their strategy, analyzing what's working or not, and how people are feeling about being on their team or their team's outcomes.

Reflection/Closure/Discussion

Say to players:

1. Describe your attitude during this game. What was your attitude like when you or your team scored a goal? What about when a goal was scored on your team?

2. Was it helpful to your team and even for your enjoyment while playing?

3. In small groups, reflect on the following questions related to teamwork:

    a. How well did you communicate as a team? What are some effective examples?

    b. Was everyone included by his or her team? What are the effects of being inclusive?

    c. Did anyone demonstrate resilient attitudes? What do resilient attitudes look like?

Invite participants back to a large group and discuss how the qualities of teamwork you just discussed might be helpful for future group work?

Tips and Comments

Variations

- After a goal is scored, consider having the scoring team return to their half of the field before defending their goal.

- Play with two or more balls to increase the action.

- If using a ball that bounces and a surface that enables a bounce, introduce the ability to dribble the ball, as in basketball.

Game Story

Falls Ball is not a new activity per se, however it may not have traveled from the town it was created in. Falls Ball was developed by an inspired and active group of summer program counselors and participants at Mason Field in North Attleboro, Massachusetts. The concept of blending games or activities to create new ones had traveled to this small town. The enthusiastic and empowered counselors of the North Attleboro Park and Recreation Department's Summer Playground Program ran with the idea during the summers of 1994-2001 and created many games legendary to the program. Falls Ball is one of them. It was an active game that was played game after game, day after day, and summer after summer by the 4th-6th grade program and later migrated to the 7th-10th grade program as participants, returning each summer, progressed through the program.

Foot Tag

Overview

A humorous tag game that sends everyone hopping on one foot to tag the feet of others, using an unusual technique. A great opportunity to reflect on safety, Full Value Contract, and goal setting, Foot Tag is sure to get the heart rate going and the laughter flowing.

Group Size	6 or more
Learning Themes	• Fun and Play • Physical Activity and Movement • Building Trust, Relationships, and Community
Materials / Props	None

Estimated Time ◕

10 – 15 minutes

Safety

Participants should be reminded to have a general awareness of body and space given that they will be moving and avoiding tags in unique and unfamiliar ways. Quick movements may result in two or more people bumping into one another.

Setup

Provide a clear and open space.

Framing

Say to group:

"This is a game of balance, quick thinking, and fast feet. It also requires significant attention to safety. Let's play and then check in."

Or

"Balance seems to be one of the continuous challenges of life; for example, balancing speaking and listening, playing and resting, or work and life. Caring for ourselves and others is another area in which we need to consider balance. In this game, you have opportunities to practice balance and caring for self and others."

In the variation, Hand to Foot Tag, the movement needed to make a successful tag lowers the head and may limit visual awareness. Additionally, players may avoid tags by swinging their leg backwards without looking. When playing this variation, participants should be made aware of particular movements, such as bending, lowering the head, and turning quickly, in order to prevent contact to the head – their own and others.

Procedure

1. This is an Everybody's It tag game.

2. To start, each person lifts one foot, while balancing on the other.

3. On a signal to start, participants move around the space by hopping on their grounded foot, while attempting to tag the feet, top only, of other players with their own feet.

4. Once the foot of a player is tagged, he or she is eliminated from the game.

5. To avoid being tagged, players must continue to move by hopping on their grounded foot. If they tire, they may, at any time, switch feet and continue playing.

6. After playing an elimination round or two and actively practicing the rules, provide an opportunity for participants to ask clarifying questions.

7. Continue play with a couple of added rules:

   a. When players are tagged, they must stand where they are. They may stand on both feet to rest; however, if they would like to get back into the action, they must stand on one foot and attempt to tag the feet, tops only, of other players who move by them. If they are successful, they may re-enter the game.

   b. A participant may also re-enter the game by asking for help. To ask for help, a participant must stand on one foot and raise one hand. Anyone who is still moving around may execute an Ankle Shake greeting with the people requesting help, to get them moving again. Players may not be tagged when engaged in the aiding gesture of an Ankle Shake.

Reflection/Closure/Discussion

Fist to Five

Say to group:

1. "Let's check in on safety. Using a Fist to Five, fist being the least and five being the most, how safe did you feel playing this game? Show zero to 5 fingers."

2. "What might we need to do to increase or maintain the safety in this game?"

3. "How does that relate to what we might need to do to increase our safety in school, at home, or anywhere else?"

Full Value Check-in

1. Conduct a Full Value Check-in to explore all Full Value components.

2. In this activity, what does it mean to be a contributing member of a Full Value community?

3. What from this information can we transfer to other settings (i.e., class, school, trip, program, etc)?

Survey

1. How many people got tagged? How many tagged others?

2. How many people "helped themselves" by tagging the foot of another person after being tagged themselves?

3. How many people "helped others" by executing an Ankle Shake?

4. How did it feel to help your self or others?

5. How does helping your self and others improve or maintain a healthy life style?

Tips and Comments

- Initially introducing this game, and other tag games, as a game of elimination provides the opportunity for participants to practice and understand the basic rules of the game. Incorporating the additional rules communicated above increases participation, activity, and learning of all players.

- **Variations**

  - **Goal Setting** – Play Foot Tag as described above within a set time frame – two minutes, for example. Before each two-minute round, provide an opportunity for participants to set a goal. Goals could be set regarding how many tags they can execute within the time frame or participants can set a goal regarding how many people they could help by Ankle Shaking.

  - **Hand to Foot Tag** – Instead of tagging foot to foot, have participants, in pairs, attempt to make a tag hand to foot. All other rules still apply.

Frogger (Re-visited) (aka Amphibian Crossing)

Overview

A tag game with a variety of characters, crossings, and challenges. Players attempt to cross a road, side walk, and river, as in the classic video game, without being tagged. Frogger reminds us that running around, playing tag, and pretending to be frogs, cars, and alligators is a lot of fun! There is much to learn from the intersection of modern systems and nature.

Group Size	20 – 60
Learning Themes	• Fun and Play • Physical Activity and Movement • Self Awareness and Self Management • Relationship Skills • Responsible Decision Making
Materials / Props	• Hula hoops • 4 long lengths of play rope • 5 cones • Carpet squares or floor mats (optional)

Estimated Time

30 – 45 minutes

Safety

- After being tagged, participants should exit on the sides of the playing area when returning to the start.

- For younger participants, the facilitator may need to determine when the next frogs may begin their crossing attempts.

Setup

- Place four play ropes on the ground or floor to mark the start and end lines as well as the sidewalk. The sidewalk will create two spaces – the road and the river – between the start and end lines. The total distance should be about 100 feet.

- Place four or five hula hoops in a row just past the finish line.

- Scatter hula hoops among the "river" section.
- Set four or five cones just before the start line.
- An optional setup would be to set out carpet squares or floor mats among the hula hoops in the river.
- See diagram below.

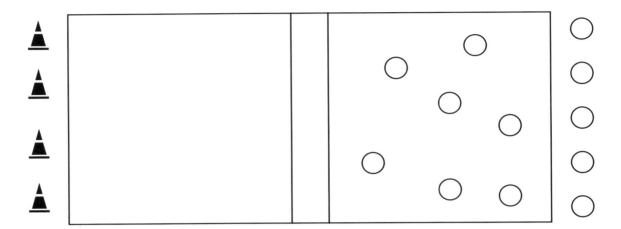

Framing Possibilities

Frogger
Say to group:

"Does anyone remember the arcade or video game called Frogger? What was Frogger's general objective? Yes, the objective was to safely cross the road, the sidewalk, and the river, ultimately ending up on a lily pad. (Or, the objective was to cross the road, the sidewalk, and the river, without getting hit by an automobile, eaten by a snake or alligator, or falling into the river.) Ultimately, Frogger was trying to safely make it to a lily pad. We are going to re-create that classic video game and challenge."

Goals and Obstacles
Say to group:

"Many obstacles or distractions can present themselves while en route to achieving a goal. Recognizing positive assets and finding positive support systems are essential to moving within and beyond these obstacles and distractions."

Amphibian Crossing
Say to group:

"Each spring, in New England, a natural phenomenon happens. On rainy nights in early spring, many amphibians – salamanders, frogs, and newts – attempt to cross road ways to mate. Making the crossing without being squashed by a car or stifled by other hazards is challenging. Subsequently, a social phenomenon occurs. Community volunteers organize to escort or assist these amphibians to the other side of the road and ultimately to their mating areas."

Procedure

1. The goal is for the majority of participants (a.k.a. amphibians/frogs) to attempt to cross the road and then the river, landing safely at their home lily pads (hula hoops), without being tagged by participants assuming the role of automobiles and alligators (select participants).

2. Determine who would like to be automobiles and alligators. The rest will be amphibians/frogs.

3. All participants begin in teams at cones set just before the start line; automobiles begin in the street; alligators begin in the river.

4. On a start signal, the first participant from each team may attempt to safely cross the road and then the river, without being tagged by an automobile or alligator.

5. Once participants enter the road, they may move in all directions, forward, back, side to side, but may not return to the starting location. If they do, another participant on their team may begin his or her crossing attempt and the participant who returned may only attempt another crossing after all other participants on their team have made their attempts.

6. Automobiles and alligators move in any direction needed to make a tag.

7. If a participant is tagged by an automobile or alligator, he or she may also return to their team and another frog may enter the road.

8. Once a participant crosses the road successfully, reaching the sidewalk without being tagged, a participant from the same team may enter the road. For each participant who successfully crosses the road, another participant on their team may begin.

9. There are many ways to determine how the game ends – a competitive race, a cooperative effort, or a version that blends the two. There are even ways to keep the players moving. Play with some of specific ideas in the variations section below and determine which meet your goals and needs of your group.

Reflection/Closure/Discussion

Frogger

1. In order to be successful in this activity, it seems that you need to find a safe route and make healthy choices about when it is safe to move. How did you determine what a safe route was and when it was safe to move?

2. How did it feel when you crossed a section, the road or river, safely?

3. How might focusing on safe routes and making healthy choices lead to a healthy lifestyle?

4. What would you consider safe routes and healthy choices in your life?

Goals & Obstacles

1. How was your experience of trying to reach your hula hoop or goal?

2. Who or what was helpful in your success?

3. How might this be helpful in achieving your goals outside of this activity?

4. What positive assets and support systems exist in your life?

Amphibian Crossing

1. What did you do to help each other cross the road and river safely?
2. What did you learn from these actions and attempts?
3. How might that relate to assisting amphibians cross the road in the spring of New England?
4. What impact does this have on the environment? On people?
5. What should we do with this information?

Tips and Comments

Types of Play

- **Competitive** – Teams of frogs race against each other, attempting to be the first team to get everyone safely to their lily pad home.

- **Cooperative** – Working toward a collective best, frogs play cooperatively, as one team, attempting to get the greatest number of frogs safely to any lily pad home in the shortest time possible.

- **Co-opetitive** – Working toward a collective best, teams of frogs play cooperatively, attempting to get the highest number of frogs safely to their specific lily pad home. In other words, teams of frogs try to get as many players on their team to their team's lily pad. They do so, however, in a cooperative spirit, trying to get the most frogs, each to their own lily pad, by the time one team successfully lands all of its players on their lily pad.

- **Keep 'em Moving** – All of the types of play above limit the participation and movement of players. Once a player makes it all the way across, they are required to sit at their home lily pad and wait for a new game to begin. While this may be an appropriate way to manage some groups in some settings, keeping them moving may better meet the goals of settings such as a Physical Education class. Another variation that could be used with any of the types of play described above, keeps people moving. Try playing in a way that when frogs on any team successfully make it all the way across the road and river, they return (outside the boundaries) to their teams and attempt again when it is their turn.

Vary the Challenge

Over time, whether it is in the same session or over the course of a few sessions or even years, adding more or fewer characters can increase the challenge and provide variety to the game. Doing so will provide a novel setting to learn and grow in while maintaining the fun and adventure!

- **Automobiles and Alligators** – To vary the challenge, either increase or decrease the number of participants playing the role of automobiles and alligators.

- **The Snake** – As participants become more familiar with the game and to increase the challenge, consider adding a snake in the sidewalk area. The snake must run the entire width of the playing area, from one side to the other, before being able to change directions. If tagged, a participant joins hands with and becomes part of the snake. Each player tagged by the snake joins hands with and becomes part of the snake.

Tips and Comments (continued)

- **Logs** – Another way to increase the challenge is to place sections of the mats or carpet squares throughout the river. Just as hula hoops (lily pads) do, these mats or carpet squares, representing logs, could also provide safe zones to frogs while crossing the river.

- **Birds of Prey** – Birds of prey could also be introduced, creating more varied challenges. Birds of prey circle – walk, jog, or run – around the river perimeter and may make one attempt at tagging a frog. To do so, the frog must not be occupying a safe zone – hula hoop or mats or carpet squares – and the bird of prey may only move forward. Whether the attempt was successful or not, the bird of prey must circle the perimeter one full time before making another attempt.

- **Frog Hunters (Characters from "Frogger," original PA write-up)** – Frogger, as it was originally written up by Project Adventure in both *Adventure Curriculum for Physical Education* and *Achieving Fitness*, incorporates frog hunters on the sides of the playing area. Frog hunters attempt to tag frogs jumping from lily pads (spot markers) to lily pads by throwing fleece balls at them. If a fleece ball tags a frog while the frog is in the air, the frog must attempt a river crossing again. In Frogger Re-visited, frog hunters again attempt to tag frogs with fleece balls from the sides of the playing area.

- **Frogger / Dead Ant (Frog) Tag Combination** – As in Dead Ant Tag, when frogs are tagged in either the road, the side walk, or the river, rather than returning to the starting line, they stay where they are, lie on their backs waving their legs and arms saying, "flat frog, flat frog, flat frog…" Other frogs may attempt to assist dead frogs by carrying them to the nearest safe zone – either the side walk or hula hoop. In order to move a dead frog, four additional frogs are required, one on each limb of the dead frog. Any participant connected to the dead frog is safe from being tagged. Dead frogs may not be moved to the home lily pads.

- **Ultimate Frogger** – Combine all of the above, incorporating each additional character and rules from Dead Ant Tag, to play a game of Ultimate Frogger!

From My Perspective

Overview

A problem-solving activity involving the suspenseful collection of different perspectives. A deep box containing clues related to an imaginary crime is surrounded by investigators (participants) who must list all the contents. They may not, however, move from their individual positions and given the side walls obstructing vision, no one person has sufficient view to identify all the contents. From My Perspective is an activity about sharing one's perspective while inquiring about the perspectives of others.

Group Size	4 or more
Learning Themes	• Relationship Skills • Responsible Decision Making
Materials / Props	• Box with a lid • Collection of random items of varying size and function to go into box • Paper and writing utensils

Setup

Place items in a box in such a way that different items are visible depending on the direction from which the viewer is looking. A large box with a partial lid works best, so that, for example, participants who are viewing from behind the box would see the outside of the box and the open lid partially obscuring contents on that side. Cover the box with fabric initially, so that no one can see it until you are ready to begin the activity. This also generates a sense of mystery. Gather participants into a seated or standing circle around the box.

Framing

Say to the group:

"I want you to imagine that you are an investigative reporter who has just stumbled upon a piece of evidence that will potentially break open a very important case. Because the evidence is fragile, you may not touch it. Also, because the person who perpetrated this crime doesn't want you to even go near it, they have rigged sensors all around us. The only movement you may make is to take notes about what you see from the place you are right now. Stay where you are!"

Procedure

1. Instruct participants to write a description of what they see. Allow five minutes.

2. During this time, participants are not allowed to change their positions or touch any of the objects.

3. After five minutes have passed, place the blanket back over the box.

4. Have participants gather into groups of four – groups should be composed of participants from four different perspectives on the box. Have them try to come up with one complete description of the box's contents, based on what each participant wrote.

5. Gather everyone and have a representative from each group share his or her complete description with the class.

6. Unveil the box and let participants walk around and take a look at the complete box and its contents.

Reflection/Closure/Discussion

Ask participants:

1. How did your original location affect what you saw?

2. How accurate was your small group description of what was under the blanket? What helped it to be accurate? What caused it to be inaccurate?

3. How does your perspective in life change what you see?

4. How is it helpful to consider things from multiple perspectives? (This would be a good time to discuss real life examples of the power of talking about one's perspective and how really listening to someone else's point of view can help resolve conflicts.)

Tips and Comments

- As you set up the box, make sure that some things can only be seen from specific perspectives or sides of the box.

- For an interesting twist, use objects that have writing on them.

Full Value Stock Market

Overview

Full Value Stock Market is a game of exuberant card trading resulting in the display of behaviors associated with an exciting and potentially stressful situation. Players attempt to be first to collect a set of matching cards representing helpful behaviors.

Group Size	10 or more
Learning Themes	• Building Trust, Relationships, and Community
	• Self Awareness and Self Management
	• Social Awareness
Materials / Props	• 9 index cards per person
	• Markers

Setup

Prepare stacks of 9 blank index cards for each person.

Framing

Say to the group:

"As we share more time together, it is important that we identify healthy norms, or behaviors that will be helpful to the growth of our group. If you had to select one value, quality, or behavior that has been most helpful to our group and summarize it in one word, phrase, or symbol, what would it be?"

Procedure

1. Distribute nine index cards to each participant. Ask them to think about one value, quality, or behavior that is most helpful to supporting an individual or whole group. Give some examples, e.g., trust, listening to each other, or not judging. Have them record the value, quality, or behavior on each of the nine index cards in the form of a word(s) or as a drawing or symbol. For example:

2. Collect and shuffle all of the cards.

3. Deal out nine cards, without showing what they are, to each participant. Ask players not to look at their cards until the rules have been explained.

4. State the objective: Be the first to collect nine of the same Full Value cards.

5. Explain the rules:

   a. The game has no turns and everyone plays at once.

   b. Players trade with one another by exchanging one to three cards without showing what they are.

   c. To trade, players call out the number of cards they wish to trade until another player holds out an equal number of cards. The two parties then exchange the agreed-upon number of cards face down.

   d. Once a player has all of the same Full Value cards, he or she must call out the Full Value Concept represented, ending the round.

Reflection/Closure/Discussion

1. What were some of the values, qualities, or behaviors represented on the cards? Were any of these demonstrated by anyone during the game?

2. What were other ways that you treated each other as you engaged in this game of exuberant trading?

3. What behaviors would you like to continue? Are there any that your group could do without?

4. Let's put together a set of Full Value cards. These cards should be a set of behaviors that we all agree would be helpful to our individual and group performance as we move forward. We can use them to check in or celebrate at any time.

Tips and Comments

- If using Full Value Stock Market as a way to create a group-generated Full Value Contract, consider recording each behavior, value, or quality as cards return to you and before shuffling the deck. Another way to achieve this is to separate one card from each person before shuffling all of the cards into the deck.

Variations

- **Active Full Value Stock Market** – To make Full Value Stock Market more active, spread hula hoops around the perimeter of a large field, gym, or playing space. Place a 30 foot rope in a circle directly in the center of the playing space. Add the following rules:

  - Agreements to trade must be made in the central circle created by the rope.

  - Trading may only occur in a hula hoop on the perimeter of the space.

  - Each time a trade occurs, a player must return to the center space and make another agreement to trade.

Tips and Comments *(continued)*

- **X Marks the Spot** – Add one to three cards, marked with an X (or skull and crossbones) to represent unhealthy norms or behaviors that would not be helpful to the group. Players trade this card just like any other card. However, a player cannot win if they hold the X (skull and crossbones) card. Adding this rule playfully invites the players to hinder their teammates' progress. On a rare occasion, a player may decide to "break the rules" by removing the unhealthy norm cards from trading all together. Using this variation provides an opportunity to process and identify behaviors that might be unhealthy for the group. And,...allowing players to remove the unhealthy behaviors card creates the space to explore what it takes to stop unhealthy behaviors.

- **Full Value Stock Market Co-op** – Try a more cooperative version by playing until everyone collects a set of the same nine Full Value cards in the shortest time possible. The group can then work toward their best time throughout three to five attempts. Players must still trade without showing their cards. The cooperative version invites reflection associated with traditional teamwork and problem-solving activities, such as trust, commitment, communication, etc. It also integrates goal setting and behavioral norms and their association to performance objectives.

- **Full Value Stock Market Co-opetition** – Lastly, a co-opetition version can be played by blending the competitive energy of the original version and the common goal of the cooperative challenge introduced above. The objective of this variation is for everyone to collect a set of nine matching Full Value cards in the shortest time possible over the course of three to five rounds; however, each player can earn individual points by collecting his or her set of matching Full Value cards before anyone else. Points could be awarded to each player as they complete their individual task. Players can track their individual points or times over the course of three to five rounds. While processing this variation, the exploration between self gain and group gain can be profound.

FVC Origami

Overview

Inspired by an origami exhibit at the Peabody Essex Museum, participants communicate their Full Value Contract through origami. (See explanation of origami at conclusion of write-up.)

Group Size	6 or more
Learning Themes	• Building Trust, Relationships, and Community • Self Awareness and Self Management • Social Awareness
Materials / Props	Origami paper, standard 8 ½ x 11, or flip chart paper

Setup

Open space or cleared tables

Framing

Say to group:

> "How many of you are familiar with origami? What is origami? We are going to use origami, or the art of paper folding, to express how we want to be treated and how we could treat others in this group. In other words, we are going to use it to create and represent our Full Value Contract."

Procedure

1. Provide each participant with a piece of flip chart paper.
2. Have participants think about a behavior/Full Value concept that they feel should be part of the group's norms.
3. Have them fold/manipulate the flip chart paper into a shape, as in origami, that best represents their chosen behavior/Full Value concept.
4. Have participants share with the group once everyone is done.

Reflection/Closure/Discussion

1. What do you notice about the behaviors that are being represented?
2. Do you notice any similarities? Were there many differences?
3. Are there any works of FVC origami that seem to hold significance for you?

Tips and Comments

Relative Information/Variations/Uses

- **What is Origami?** According to Wikipedia, "Origami is the traditional Japanese art of paper folding. The goal of this art is to create a representation of an object using geometric folds and crease patterns preferably without gluing or cutting the paper, and using only one piece of paper."

- **Uses:** Once the FVC Origami has been created, consider using it for the following:

  - FVC Origami – The group could choose the most significant three to five FVC origami and use as a more accessibly condensed Full Value Contract. Another option would be to create like categories of FVC origami.

  - FVC Origami Check-in/Debrief: Use as a symbol during future FVC check-ins or debriefs.

  - Gift Giving/Affirmations: The FVC could be an effective way to affirm the behavior of other group members. It may even spark creativity, as a need may arise for another FVC origami or general origami symbol to convey a specific thought or feeling.

Tips and Comments *(continued)*

- **The Crane:** For thousands of years, the Japanese culture has treasured the crane as a symbol of honor and loyalty. The crane is a majestic bird that mates for life and is extremely loyal to its partner. The bird is strong, graceful and beautiful. Because of the great importance of the crane, the Japanese people feel that a person who folds a thousand cranes will be granted his or her greatest wish. Consider teaching the crane exclusively and using it as a debrief to identify a group member who has demonstrated honor and loyalty. (For instructions, go to: http://dev.origami.com/diagram.cfm)

- **Colors:** Colors are significant and can represent particular meanings. Consider introducing the following colors and meanings associated with origami to the group before they create their FVC Origami.

  - **Red** is the traditional color for roses and Valentine's Day. Red represents strong love, passion and desire. Studies show that a woman in a red dress becomes a focal point in a room! This is a very powerful color.

  - **Dark Crimson** stands for inner beauty and inner strength. It represents soul mates – a connection without words.

  - **Pink** represents happiness, tenderness, best friends and sweethearts. Pink is the fresh blush on a maiden's cheeks.

  - **Orange** is the color of enthusiasm and energy. Orange is the lush autumn foliage and the warmth of a fire.

  - **Yellow** stands for freedom and joy. Yellow is the perfect color to spur creativity, to celebrate the beginning of a new project or the completion of a successful one. Yellow is the bright welcome of sunshine.

  - **Green** is the traditional color of healing – it represents living things growing healthily and with strength. It is the color of harmony and finding balance. Green is the color of luck and wealth. It is, of course, the modern color for St. Patrick's Day! It is the color of grassy meadows and lush forests.

  - **Blue** represents honor and faith. A trustworthy friend or lover is "true blue." Blue is also the color of meaningful spirituality. It represents a bond of the spirit. It is the color of the sea and of the open sky.

  - **Purple** is the traditional color of nobility and courtly love. This is the color of knights and maidens, of princes and princesses. It represents elegance and wine. Amethyst is the stone for birthdays and anniversaries in February.

  - **White** represents the hope for the future, a fresh start, innocence and purity. White has been the traditional color for brides since the Victorian era. In many cultures, white represents a joyous eternity.

  - **White and Red.** A combination of red and white represent unity, of two people who care for each other standing together. It combines the red of love with the white of eternity.

  - **Silver** stands for elegance. Silver has been treasured by people for thousands of years. Silver is the traditional color for the 25th anniversary.

  - **Gold** represents a love and loyalty which is eternal. Wedding bands are made from gold, and a high compliment is to say someone has "a heart of gold." Gold is the traditional color for the 50th anniversary.

> **Tips and Comments** (*continued*)
>
> – **Ivory** stands for luxury and tradition. It represents a quiet, steady, warm caring.
> – **Brown and Beige** colors represent grounding, being down to earth and dependable. This is the trust and loyalty of a true friend.
> – **Tea** is a light brown color representing remembrance and fond memories.
> – **Black** is a classic formal color, the color of black tie dinners and tuxedos. It is the color of strength and stability.
>
> * Some of the origami information (cranes and colors) comes directly from http://www.lisashea.com/japan/origami/sales/

GPS-E

Estimated Time

10 – 20 minutes

Overview

A metaphorical navigation device for setting goals. Individuals use GPS-E as a structure to set goals, guide behavior, and check-in.

Group Size	1 or more!
Learning Themes	• Self Awareness and Self Management • Responsible Decision Making
Materials / Props	GPS-E Goal Setting Sheet

Setup

Consider an appropriate space or time for goal setting.

Framing

Say to the group:
"Has anyone heard of a GPS? What are they used for?

GPS (Global Positioning System) devices are used to help us get where we want to go whether it is in the wilderness, on the water, or in a car. They serve as a guide for when we get lost (and sometimes may even cause us to get lost). In other words, they help us to get to our destination and can be referenced if we start to get off track. We will be using the newest goal setting navigation device, the GPS-E, to guide us as we work to achieve our goals."

Procedure

1. GPS-E is an acronym/mnemonic device for goal setting.

    • **G**oal – What is your goal?

- **P**lan – How do you plan to achieve your goal? How can you accomplish it? What action are you willing to take?
- **S**upport – What support do you need from others in the group to achieve your goal? What support can you give? What resources are available to you?
- **E**valuate – How will you know whether or not you have achieved your goal? What will you use for measuring and tracking your goal?

2. Assign partners or ask participants to find partners who will be their goal buddies.

3. Participants complete their own GPS-E Goal Setting Sheets or simply set their own GPS-Es mentally.

4. Participants share and discuss their GPS-Es with their goal buddies, especially discussing what they need for support and ways that they can support each other.

5. Once participants have met with their goal buddies, they can share just their goals (the "G" of GPS-E) with the rest of the group.

Reflection/Closure/Discussion

Goal Partner Check-in – Throughout the term of the group, have Goal Partners check their GPS-Es with each other to see if they are on track, need to adjust, or completely re-set their goals. Consider recording these check-ins to track over time.

Tips and Comments

- When finding partners consider using Sole Mate, pairing technique found on page 299, or reference Snappy Partners from *No Props* and *Count Me In*.
- Consider blending SMART or STAR Goals with GPS-E, creating the SMART or STAR GPS-E, the most advanced goal setting device.

Estimated Time

20 minutes

Hu Ha Pako *(pronounced 'who ha paco')*

Overview

A quick energizer that progressively grows more intense. Players send a sound and motion around a circle, gradually adding clapping, and then jumping to the movements. Hu Ha Pako provides opportunities to play, laugh, explore accountability, and charge or recharge the group.

Group Size	6 or more
Learning Themes	• Fun and Play • Physical Activity and Movement • Building Trust, Relationships, and Community • Self Awareness and Self Management
Materials / Props	None

Setup

Gather your group into a circle.

Framing

Say to participants:

"Let's play a game sure to build the energy in the group."

Or:

"We are going to play a funn, F-U-N-N, game called Hu Ha Pako. Has anyone heard of the acronym FUNN before? FUNN stands for Functional Understanding Not Necessary. Don't think, just play!"

Or:

"We are going to play a game designed specifically to allow you to make mistakes, also known as allowing you to fail. Hopefully you will learn to let go and have fun. Ready?"

Procedure

1. Explain to the group that they will be passing a sound and a motion around the group. If your group has previous experience with similar activities such as Ah So Ko, Hi Lo Yo, or Yeehaw, it may be helpful to reference these activities, and then continue explaining the rules to this game.

2. Introduce the first two sounds and motions, "Hu" and "Ha".

   a. Saying "Hu" with a swing of the right arm gesturing to the left sends the sound and motion to the left only. Practice this sound and motion.

   b. Saying "Ha" with a swing of the left arm gesturing to the right sends the sound and motion to the right only. Practice this sound and motion.

   c. "Hu" and "Ha" can be used at any time to either keep the sound and motion going in the same direction or reverse the direction. Practice with both.

3. Introduce the third sound and motion, "Pako"

   a. Saying "Pako" while raising both hands over your head and connecting the hands skips the next person in whichever direction the sound and motion is being passed. Provide an example of this.

4. Play with all three sounds and motions – "Hu", "Ha", and "Pako!"

   a. Participants are guaranteed to make mistakes, aka fail. No worries! This is part of the game. Allow opportunities for mistakes and failure, laughter, personal and group accountability. It's all available and all part of the game and inspires the learning. Play on!

5. Once the group has sufficiently played with and demonstrated a good understanding of the base level of this game, sending "Hu", "Ha", and "Pako!" around the circle, introduce the next level, incorporating a clap.

   a. Now, participants must clap when sending any of the three sounds and motions – "Hu", "Ha", and "Pako!" The clap must go in the direction of the original sound and motion. For example:

      i. When sending a "Hu", participants must now send a clapping gesture to the left. Practice.

      ii. When sending a "Ha", participants must now send a clapping gesture to the right. Practice.

Safety

Sound and motion games, such as Hu Ha Pako, can be great fun and a great choice to energize your group. However, there certainly are times when this type of game is not an appropriate choice. For example, this activity may not be a good choice if you are already aware of a participant with a cognitive delay. Otherwise, you'll learn that it may not be a good choice if a participant consistently makes mistakes, struggles greatly to respond, or seems exceptionally uneasy about playing this game. These may be good indicators of what needs to be processed. Take note for future reference, and move on.

      iii. When sending a "Pako", participants must now send a clapping gesture directly above their head.

6. Play with all three sounds and motions – "Hu", "Ha", and "Pako!" – now accompanied by a "Clap!" As the play continues, celebrate those mistakes and failures, leave room for deep belly laughs, and let players call themselves or each other out.

7. Just as the group is feeling grounded and confident with the clap-inspired level, drop the news of yet another level change. For this round, all rules apply with the addition of one more.

   a. Now the three sounds, motions, and the clap will need to be accompanied by a jump, both feet leaving the ground. For example:

      i. When sending a "Hu", participants must now send a clapping gesture to the left while jumping straight up into the air. Practice.

      ii. When sending a "Ha", participants must now send a clapping gesture to the right while jumping straight up into the air. Practice.

      iii. When sending a "Pako", participants must now send a clapping gesture directly above their heads while jumping straight up into the air.

8. Play on! Check out many ways to play in the Variations section.

Reflection/Closure/Discussion

Reflection is not usually needed as this activity is most often used as an energizer. It is possible, however, that there will be a lot of conversation during and after the game. If you choose to process this activity, the themes of engagement, risk taking, letting go of mistakes and accountability can be explored.

A debrief focused on letting go of mistakes and failure might look like:

1. What was your reaction to mistakes or failure in this game?

2. Was your reaction different when you or someone else made a mistake?

3. What might this tell us?

4. Why might mistakes and failure be important to our time together?

5. Do you find that you often accept mistakes or failure in your life or not? How does that compare to how you accepted, or not, the mistakes and failures in this game? Which do you prefer? What do you need to do to live your preference and how might you benefit? What concerns might you have?

Tips and Comments

Variations

Modes of Play

- **Elimination** – When a player clearly makes a mistake or fails to perform the correct sound and motion in a timely manner, including a clap and jump when incorporated, they are eliminated. Eliminated players are asked to simply observe in amusement until the game ends and a new one begins. The games are typically quick and usually entertaining enough to keep players interested and present for the next game to begin. Once the game has been played enough, it can make for a great instant activity for any physical education class or a way for participants to prepare themselves for a meeting, practice, lecture, etc.

Tips and Comments *(continued)*

- **The Distractor** – What better way to engage participants then to provide an opportunity to distract and be the demise of other players? Play games in the elimination mode as described above. However, when participants are eliminated, they may take on a role that perhaps better suits them at the moment – being a distractor. Distractors may do their best to distract other players by making sounds and motions while remaining outside of the circle. They may not visually or physically impede, nor can they interfere with others' abilities to hear what's going on. This mode of play adds another dimension to the game, an opportunity to practice calm and focus amidst the confusion and chaos sure to ensue.

- **Cooperation** – The challenge or goal with this variation is for the group to keep the sounds and motions going for as long as possible, including a clap and jump when incorporated. Now, the group may develop particular strategies while working toward their personal best. This moves the activity from an individually competitive game to a group cooperating toward a common goal.

- **Multiple Games** – If you are working with a group of 15 or more, it may be beneficial to create multiple games after explaining and demonstrating the rules. Doing so will create a space where two, three, four or more games are happening simultaneously. Each game may be played in the cooperative mode as described above. However, if the hope is to get participants playing and interacting with as many people as possible, play multiple games in the elimination mode. When players are eliminated, they leave their original circle and join another game already in progress. An alternative to this variation is to start one game with lots of people and invite eliminated participants to start a new game with other players who have also been eliminated. This creates opportunities for engagement, initiative, and empowerment.

Combinations

- **Hu Ha Pako/Dead Ant Tag Combination** – If the game Dead Ant Tag is known, the caller could call "Dead Ant" and attempt to tag any other players according to Dead Ant Tag. The caller could call "Hu Ha Pako" at any time to resume the game of Hu Ha Pako. The twist: players who are "dead ants" would be required to play Hu Ha Pako in the "dead ant" position. Can dead ants jump? Give it a try, but be safe!

- **Hu Ha Pako/Evolution Combination** – If the game Evolution is known, the caller could call "Evolution", name four characters – Eggs, Chicken, Dinosaurs, and Apes for example – and yell, "Go!" Participants would immediately morph into eggs and begin playing a game of Evolution. The caller could then call "Hu Ha Pako" at any time to resume the game of Hu Ha Pako. The twist: players would be required to play Hu Ha Pako as their current Evolution character. Imagine the ridiculous joy of playing Hu Ha Pako in character. Seriously, can't you just see a person bunched up as an "egg", waddling from side to side, trying to jump, clap, and yell, "Pako!" all at the same time. Hilarious!

Safety

An effective assessment of your group is essential for building trust and rapport with them. This activity should be used with a group who is playful and is willing to follow your lead into the unknown, or else they may feel tricked into doing something they are embarrassed about and begin disengaging.

I'm a Starfish

Overview

A quick energizer of animal-inspired movements. Participants follow the lead of the facilitator by jumping into spontaneous animal driven movements and are invited to add to the mix. I'm a Starfish is a ridiculously fun connection with our friends on Earth.

Group Size	10 or more
Learning Themes	• Fun and Play • Physical Activity and Movement
Materials / Props	None

Setup

Start with the group standing in a circle.

Framing

Say to the group:

"Here's a quick energizer of animal-inspired movements to build our energy. All you have to do is say what I say and do what I do...got it? Oh, and if you are so inspired, feel free to add on!"

Procedure

1. Once the group has confirmed that they 'got it,' crouch down and non-verbally instruct the group to do what you do.

2. Explode into a series of star jumps exclaiming, "I'm a Starfish, I'm a Starfish, I'm a Starfish..." Trust that if you have an accurate assessment of the group and their willingness to play, they will follow your lead and be captivated by the playful energy.

3. Shift spontaneously into the demonstration of another animal movement, typically a crab. The crab shuffles laterally left and right, opening and closing fingers to thumb with claw-like movements while exclaiming, "I'm a Crab, I'm a Crab, I'm a Crab..."

4. Continue shifting through a series of additional animal movements, sounds, and energy.

5. Encourage participants to play along offering additional animal movements.

6. Play for as long as the group seems interested.

Reflection/Closure/Discussion

None needed.

Tips and Comments

- A favorite animal sequence is: starfish, crab, rhino, giraffe, puma, monkey, hawk, frog, etc. because these animals inspire movements that bring the group through a variety of energy levels. It is good to end with something like a slug or sloth to indicate that the players have exhausted themselves and their ideas.

- Use animal figurines or animal cards to help participants think of different animals and how they move.

Ice Breakers

Overview

A fun variation of tag that just got more social. Partners attempt to move and maintain a connection through four suspended blocks, while trying to break the connection of other players. When the connection is broken, it's time to find a new partner. Ice Breakers mixes the personalities and behaviors in the group and often lends itself to a rich reflection on varying strategies, working with different people, and how people were treated and treated others

Group Size	12 or more
Learning Themes	• Physical Activity and Movement • Building Trust, Relationships, and Community • Relationship Skills
Materials / Props	• Plastic or wooden blocks – 2 blocks per person 1 to 2 inch blocks work best

Estimated Time ◔

10 – 15 minutes

Safety

Be aware that this activity generally inspires an exuberantly playful spirit. Without extinguishing that spirit, monitor the level of play in relation to the setting. Check in as necessary and adapt as needed.

Setup

1. Clear an open space. The space does not need to be too large, but playing in a clear, open space is necessary.

2. Creatively separate your group into pairs. Consider a fun idea from the list on page 299 or Snappy Partners in *No Props* and *Count Me In* by Mark Collard.

Framing

Say to participants:

"Relationships are significant to a community. Often times we form friendships and relationships that we feel comfortable with and want to maintain. At times, when other people attempt to disrupt those connections, we do anything we can to keep the relationships safe."

Or:

"Often times it seems that we are challenged to maintain connections and communication in our daily lives. Let's explore ways to maintain those connections."

Procedure

1. Tell participants to suspend four blocks in a straight horizontal line between them using only the tips of their index fingers. In other words, participants position two blocks on the tips of their index fingers and connect their two blocks directly to their partners' in a straight horizontal line – to start anyway!

2. State the objective: Participants attempt to move and maintain their connection through the four suspended blocks, while trying to break the connection of other partner pairs by using their free index fingers only.

3. Explain and demonstrate the rules:.

   a. Connection breaking attempts can only happen by participants who are properly connected to their partners.

   b. Physical contact should be kept to a minimum. This is a game of finesse and positioning, not asserting oneself physically. Participants should refrain from pushing, blocking, swatting, etc.

   c. Participants may box out (as in basketball), move, and position themselves to make their blocks more challenging to knock.

   d. Participants may only use the tips of their index fingers to connect through their four blocks. In other words, participants may not link hands, fingers, or thumbs in an attempt to better secure their blocks.

   e. Once a connection is broken, each individual participant picks up two blocks and finds a new partner.

Reflection/Closure/Discussion

Pair Share or Quadraphonic – In a "Pair Share," partners share responses to a question(s). During a "Quadraphonic," four participants share responses to a question(s). Using a "Quadraphonic" debrief provides the option of new pairings after debriefing.

- Would you consider that you and your partner were successful at maintaining your connections and communication?

- What was it that allowed for your success or failure?

- What are some of the best strategies for maintaining connections and communication that you demonstrated or saw another group demonstrate?

- What are three healthy ways to stay connected to people in your life?

- What are three unhealthy ways of attempting to stay connected to people in your life?

Tips and Comments

Connecting Variations

- **Switch** – Encourage participants to switch hands or play using their sub-dominant sides.

- **Which Digit?**
  - **Thumbs Up!** – Use thumbs as the connecting point rather than index fingers and, likewise, have participants attempt to break the connection of others with their thumbs.
  - **Pinkies Too!** – Similar to Thumbs Up, participants use pinky fingers for both connecting and disconnecting.

- **Hey, Where Are You Going?** – Players challenge themselves by facing in opposite directions.

Game Variations

- Try omitting rule "d." If you do, prepare for an opportunity to process particular behaviors that present themselves without it!

- **Don't Break the Ice** – Similar rules as Ice Breakers, with one partner-restrictive rule change. Once blocks are broken, participants pick up their blocks and re-connect with the same partner. See Don't Break the Ice for Framing and Debriefing ideas.

- **Building Blocks** – Same rules as Don't Break the Ice, with one competitive rule addition. Once blocks are broken, participants, whether connected or not and with or without blocks, attempt to pick up as many blocks as possible, re-connect with either their partner or anyone else, and continue playing. Participants may re-connect to another person with as many blocks as they are able and as few as one.

- **Three's a Crowd** – Three participants attempt to remain connected based on the original rules of "Don't Break the Ice." Provide time for participants to strategize their best way to connect and play.

- **Connect 4** – Four participants attempt to remain connected based on the original rules of Don't Break the Ice. Provide time for participants to strategize their best way to connect and play.

Safety

Select criteria that is safe and appropriate for participants to share publicly.

Identification Numbers

Overview

Identification Numbers provides a unique way for participants to experience and get to know the people in their community. Everyone develops their own ID number based on particular criteria, then shares that information with others.

Group Size	4 or more
Learning Themes	• Building Trust, Relationships, and Community • Self Awareness and Self Management • Social Awareness
Materials / Props	None

Setup

None

Framing

Say to participants:

"While many of you may know the names of other members of the group, this is an opportunity for you to learn something new about each other by generating a special identification number."

Or:

"Jane Goodall continues to make a positive impact on the world through her experience and life work with gorillas and other significant endeavors. During a presentation in Boston, she acknowledged the impact of naming the gorillas in her research and studies, in a non-scientific way. She gave them actual names such as Jamison rather than coding each gorilla with a series of numbers and letters. Can you imagine what it would have been like if she gave the gorillas identification numbers, or names simply consisting of letters and numbers, like the rest of the scientific community? Or…can you imagine what it would be like if we as people were given identification numbers rather than names? We are going to create our own code names to see what that would be like."

Procedure

1. Provide each participant with an index card.

2. Explain to the participants that they will use an example of an identification number, with the criteria for information highlighted, to generate their own code name. For example, an identification number could consist of the initials of a person's address (number, road name, city, and state), the number of countries they have traveled to, the number of books they have read in the previous year, and the number of siblings in a person's family. If Cindy lived on 40 Rubber Chicken Avenue, Adventuretown, PA, has traveled to 11 countries, read 7 books in the previous year, and has 3 siblings, Cindy's's code name would be 40RCAAPA1173.

3. Given the example, have participants generate their own identification numbers and write them on index cards.

4. Once everyone has written their identification numbers on index cards, consider the following options for sharing this information and building community:

   a. Have participants share their identification numbers with partners and encourage them to discuss the information provided by the associated numbers and letters. Participants may then introduce their partners and what they learned about them, according to the identification numbers, to the rest of the group.

   b. Have participants write their code names on flip chart paper or dry erase boards for public viewing. Participants may then guess what identification number belongs to which person.

Reflection/Closure/Discussion

Due to the nature of the activity, identification numbers provide quantified information about players and patterns in the group. These patterns help to highlight commonalities and differences among the group members. Use this information to process these perspectives. It's best to make these comparisons when the code names are listed in one organized location and chart.

1. What similarities or differences do you notice in the identification numbers?

2. What can we learn from the commonalities, differences, and uniquenesses? OR What does this information – commonality, difference, and uniqueness – tell us?

3. How can we use this information as we continue to share time with each other?

Tips and Comments

- Visually posting a sample identification number and clearly labeling the information criteria in a chart is helpful, if not necessary, for participant understanding and keeps the information organized.

- Consider surveying the group for information that they would like to learn about each other.

Safety

Make sure that the ball is sturdy enough to withstand a lot of contact, but light enough not to hurt someone who is tagged with it.

Indiana Jones

Overview

A large group activity designed to generate energy and laughter. Players race around a circular corridor of people avoiding contact with a giant boulder (a large ball)!

Group Size	20 or more
Learning Themes	• Fun and Play • Physical Activity and Movement • Building Trust, Relationships, and Community
Materials / Props	Large inflatable or plastic ball – at least 2 ft in diameter or larger

Setup

Have the group stand in a circle and count off by three. Once everyone has a number, ask the threes to step into the middle of the circle, form a smaller circle and face outward. You will now have two circles facing each other, about six to eight feet apart.

Framing

Say to the group:

"Who remembers the original movie 'Indiana Jones'? Remember the scene in which Indy is running from a huge boulder, that was behind him in a big stone corridor? We are going to recreate that scene here and now."

Procedure

1. Have one volunteer step into the corridor formed between the two circles to be "Indiana Jones." His or her goal is not to be tagged by the boulder (the large ball).

2. Indiana Jones can run in either direction as long as he or she stays within the two circles.

3. The boulder also travels inside the two circles, and is propelled by people on either the inner or outer circle hitting it with their hands. The boulder can also move in either direction.

4. Once Indiana Jones is tagged (meaning the ball hits him or her from either the front or behind), he or she joins the circle and a new Indy is selected.

5. The ball should stay on the ground. It should not be picked up and thrown, kicked or hit with anything except a flat palm.

6. Indiana Jones and/or the boulder may change directions at any time.

Reflection / Closure / Discussion

What strategy did Indiana Jones or the folks in the circle employ during this game? Was everyone included? Why or why not?

Juggle Moves

Overview

A moving variation of the stationary classic Group Juggle. Players move any way and anywhere they want while experimenting with different ways of throwing. The only thing that seems routine is the throwing pattern established prior to moving.

Group Size	10 or more
Learning Themes	• Fun and Play • Physical Activity and Movement • Building Trust, Relationships, and Community • Responsible Decision Making
Materials / Props	One tossable object per person and maybe a few more

Setup

None

Framing

Say to group:

"Being part of a community is significant. It can provide a sense of connectedness, especially as we pursue our many interests, jobs, and activities. Let's practice being connected as a community."

Or:

"Establishing structure in community is necessary for members to feel grounded and safe. Let's establish a structure that provides us with a place where we can play, explore, and grow."

Procedure

1. Begin with participants standing in a circle.

2. Establish a tossing pattern that begins and ends with one person, by tossing one object from one person to the next. Direct all participants to start with their hands up in front of them and once they receive the object to put their hands down to indicate that they have received the object and are already part of the pattern.

3. Once the pattern is complete, have participants indicate who they threw to and who they received from.

Estimated Time

15 – 20 minutes

Safety

Due to the random and irregular movement patterns established by this activity, participants should be reminded to move with responsive alertness.

4. Check the pattern by tossing one object through the pattern again.

5. Once the pattern is set and confirmed, send multiple objects through the pattern one after another. Allow for a few attempts at juggling as many objects as possible.

6. After participants have a good sense of the pattern, explain that they will now have the opportunity to move anywhere they want and throw any way they want. For example, they may run around continuously or run, stop, walk, stop, run while throwing through their legs, around their backs, with their sub-dominant hand, etc. Encourage movement and creative throwing.

Reflection/Closure/Discussion

Connectedness

1. What did you notice as we began to move around and toss creatively?

2. How did it feel to be connected to others in the group?

3. What might that tell us about our connections in general?

4. In what ways can we use this information to create and sustain a healthy lifestyle?

The Value of a Structure/Full Value Contract

1. What was it like for you to establish a structure or pattern?

2. How did it feel to move within that structure?

3. What parallels can you draw between establishing and interacting within a structure and establishing a Full Value Contract?

4. Were your decisions to move or throw in a particular way influenced by the structure we established or the presence or lack of presence of group members?

5. In what ways do other people and norms influence how we choose to act and interact?

Tips and Comments

- This activity is a moving variation of Group Juggle developed by Circus Yoga. Circus Yoga is an engaging experiential blend of circus and yoga, developed by Erin Maile O'Keefe and Kevin O'Keefe. According to their website http://www.circusyoga.com, "CircusYoga is an invitation. Artfully designed to engage all ages, CircusYoga blends the consciousness of yoga with the communal celebration of circus."

Variations

- **Reverse and Forward:** Explain to participants that they can call "Reverse" to direct the group to toss their objects in the reverse or opposite direction. A "Forward" call directs the group to throw in the initial direction. You can also just call out "Reverse" or "Reverse direction" and see how the participants respond.

- **Varying Speeds: Super Slow Motion to Super Fast:** Varying the speed can offer a creative twist, inspiring different movements and perhaps some comedians in the group to emerge and shine. To do this, call out different speeds such as "slow motion," "super fast," "super slow motion," etc. and allow participants to respond in whatever way that they interpret the call.

Jump In, Jump Out (aka Front Back)

Overview

An engaging and playful icebreaker, de-inhibitizer, opener, or warm-up depending on how and when it's used. Beginning in a standing circle, participants attempt to respond to a series of commands communicated by the facilitator. The activity progresses from participants following directions to doing the opposite followed by even more challenging-to-follow commands. The result is often lots of mistakes, lots of laughter and lots of learning! Jump In, Jump Out playfully inspires significant feelings and reactions which may be briefly appreciated or processed more deeply.

Group Size	8 or more
Learning Themes	• Building Trust, Relationships, and Community • Self Awareness and Self Management • Social Awareness
Materials / Props	None

Safety

Be aware that participants are likely to jump in wrong directions and may bump into one another. Monitor the behaviors and responses of the group and check in as necessary.

Setup

Gather participants into a circle with enough space to move back 10 feet or so.

Framing

Say to the group:

"As a community, it can be challenging to live up to our individual and group ideals. This activity will require us to make quick responses as individuals who have influence on the larger group."

Or:

"This activity was intentionally designed for you to make mistakes, maybe even fail. Each round will become more and more challenging. So hold on and be ready to support one another fully."

Procedure

1. Provide the following instructions:
   - "Begin by reaching out to the person next to you and holding hands – yes, holding hands. It is awkward but I know you can do it."
   - "Each round of this game will get more challenging. It is important for us to be gentle with ourselves and each other as we move as one large entity."
   - "Now, as a group, say what I say and do what I say, by repeating after me. For example, if I say, 'Jump in!' you say, 'Jump in!' and everyone takes a jump forward. If I say, 'Jump out!' everyone says 'Jump out!' and we all take a jump backwards together. Let's try this a few times…"

2. Lead several calls pertaining to **say what I say, do what I say**. Add the commands: "Jump right!" and "Jump left!" in addition to "Jump in!" and "Jump out!"

3. Next round. Say to the group, "Now you are going to say the opposite, and do the opposite of each command. For example, if I say, 'Jump right!' you say, 'Jump left' and you jump left."

4. Lead several calls pertaining to **say the opposite, do the opposite**.

5. Final round. Say to the group, "This final round is the most confusing of all, because now you will say what I say, but do the opposite! For example, if I say, 'Jump left!' you say, 'Jump left! but you all jump right!'"

6. Lead several calls pertaining to **say what I say, but do the opposite**.

7. Laughter is encouraged! Mistakes are okay!

8. Bring the activity to a close by having everyone in the circle take a bow together.

Reflection/Closure/Discussion

Acceptance

Creatively separate your group into small groups of three or four participants and ask them to answer the following questions:

1. How did you or others respond when people made mistakes?

2. Was there blaming, shaming, or acceptance? Why?

3. Which round of this activity was most confusing? Why?

4. What would you like to do with this information?

Empathy

Say to the group:

1. As members of a community or society, you play an important role in helping others make good decisions. What can you do to help others navigate through life's academic, work, and social pressures and sometimes confusing 'commands' they are given?

2. How do you respond when other people make missteps?

3. Think back to experiences in your life. What memories stand out in your mind? Did anyone lend a hand to you when you were confused or intimidated?

4. What does this have to do with empathy?

Tips and Comments

- Allow individual participants to step, rather than jump, if it seems more appropriate for them. For some groups, it may be appropriate for the entire group to step rather than jump. Use your judgment to decide what is right.
- Review the calls for each round:
    - First Round: "Say what I say. Do what I say."
    - Second Round: "Say the opposite of what I say. Do the opposite of what I say."
    - Third Round: "Say what I say. Do the opposite of what I say."
    - Fourth Round: "Say the opposite of what I say. Do what I say."
    - Fifth Round: "Say what I say. Jump in any direction you want. Take care of yourself, the people around you, and the space around all of us."

Tips and Comments *(continued)*

- Adapted from an anti-bullying curriculum written by Michelle Wilson and Larry Childs for the North Andover Public Schools called *RAISE -'ing: Active Group Lessons for Bully Prevention and Social Skills Development* (Project Adventure, 2012)

Variations

- Playfully engage the group in a bit of active listening by asking them to repeat what they heard you say. For example, as the facilitator, if leading the first round, you would say, "Say what I say. Do what I say. *What are you going to do?*" To emphasize listening even more, add the phrase, "Hear what I say," to the beginning of every call. For example, "Say what I say, do what I say" would now be "*Hear what I say*, say what I say, do what I say."

- Consider additional rounds with the following calls:

  - **"Say the opposite of what I say. Do what I say."** Now, if "Jump In" is called, the group should say the opposite, "Jump Out," and jump forward. This variation could be facilitated as a fourth round or as a substitute for the final round described above. It typically depends on how overwhelmed or engaged the group seems after the second round. For some people, this call is more challenging than any of the rounds described above.

  - **"Say what I say. Jump in any direction you like while observing this additional rule: take care of yourself, the people around, and space around all of us."** Now the group repeats anything they hear and jumps in any direction they want while monitoring for safety of self and others. Check in around safety as needed. This variation subtly introduces or reinforces both Challenge by Choice and the Full Value Contract and provides the facilitator with an opportunity to speak to either concept or both after the activity is complete.

    Additionally, this variation provides an opportunity to playfully reflect on how well a group is listening to instructions, especially if you ask them to repeat what you said or what they are going to do. Most groups hear the directions for this variation as, "Say what I say, *do what we want.*" It is amazing how many groups convince themselves and believe that they heard, "...do what we want" *and* completely miss the additional rule – take care of yourself, the other people, and space around you."

    Furthermore, this variation, more than any other, invites the opportunity to playfully call other random directions, i.e., "Jump up," "Jump down," "Jump high," "Jump low," etc. And to entertain even more absurdity and silliness, if the moment is right, one could playfully flow into the chorus of the early 90s hit song, Jump Around, by House of Pain:

    > *I came to get down [2x]*
    >
    > *So get out of your seats and jump around*
    >
    > *Jump around [3x]*
    >
    > *Jump up Jump up and get down.*
    >
    > *Jump [18x]*

Tips and Comments *(continued)*

- Jump In Jump Out can be led without holding hands. In this variation, individual actions impact others to a lesser extent but the fun and key learning points still come through.

- For some groups, i.e., groups that have expressed discomfort with holding hands, it may be a better choice to have participants hold a circle of rope or buddy ropes (short lengths of rope held between two people). This enables the group to be connected without having to touch physically. In addition, this variation flows nicely into a Yurt Circle (*Adventure Curriculum for Physical Education High School*, Jane Panicucci et al., Project Adventure, 2003), Knot Race (in this publication), and Pass the Knot Debrief.

- Use cue cards, large pieces of paper or poster boards with words on them, to communicate each call. Produce cue cards with the following phrases:

  – Jump In

  – Jump Out

  – Jump Right

  – Jump Left

  Provide the following instructions for each round.

  – First Round: "Say what you see. Jump in the direction you see."

  – Second Round: "Say the opposite of what you see. Jump in the opposite direction of what you see."

  – Third Round: "Say what you see. Jump in the opposite direction of what you see."

  – Fourth Round: "Say the opposite of what you see. Jump in the direction you see."

  – Fifth Round: "Say what you see. Jump in any direction you want. Take care of yourself, the people around you, and the space around all of us."

- This activity is also known as Front Back. When playing Front Back, most facilitators indicate that jumping is implied and that they will simply call one of four directions – Front, Back, Left, or Right. The group should jump in the appropriate direction based on the call and the directions for each round. For example, if playing the first round, the facilitator would say, "Say what I say, jump in the direction I say" then simply call, "Front." The group would then say, "Front" and jump forward. If the facilitator called, "Back" the group would say, Back" and jump backwards. Calls and responses should be adjusted for each subsequent round.

Jump Tag (aka Jumping Monkeys)

Overview

A simple tag game with surprising moments. Players sequentially share the role of being It. Players are assigned numbers and try to tag others when it's their turn. Players must jump in order to tag and avoid being tagged.

Group Size	10 – 15
Learning Themes	• Fun and Play • Physical Activity and Movement • Self Awareness and Self Management • Social Awareness
Materials / Props *For the Debrief*	• Markers • Index cards

Safety

Movements in Jump Tag can be abrupt, powerful, and explosive at times. Anyone playing should be aware of this as a potentially effective way to play, yet also be aware of other people to avoid collisions.

Setup

Gather your group into a circle and assign numbers from one to however many people plan to play. A group of twelve would be numbered one to twelve. Ask everyone to remember their numbers.

Framing

Say to the group:

Monkeys: "It was once thought that monkeys, such as the Gibbon and Spider Monkeys, played a game of tag that helped them to develop the skills necessary to jump from tree to tree. I'm not sure if it's true, but imagine if it is. Imagine if you could jump like one of these monkeys."

Or:

Awareness: "Awareness is an important life skill. It is essential for personal and group growth as well as for understanding relationships. We are going to play a tag game sure to heighten your awareness. It may surprise you at times."

Procedure

1. Play begins with the group in a standard circle. The group counts to three and all players yell, "Jump" as they jump back as far as they can. Once they've landed, they remain in place until play begins.

2. The person whose number is one begins the game by calling out the number, "One," and then "Jump!" and immediately jumps once in any direction attempting to tag another person. When "Jump!" is called, everyone in the group must jump once. They may jump in any direction to avoid the tag of the current tagger, strategically set themselves up for a future tag, or simply enjoy a carefree and fun jump if they believe they are not close to a potential tagger. *Note: Jumping is the only way to move in this game and tags may occur in the air or on the ground upon landing.*

3. After everyone has landed, player number two immediately calls his or her number, "Two," then "Jump!" and jumps attempting to tag another player. Again, everyone jumps to avoid being tagged when "Jump" is called.

4. Continue playing through the consecutive order and role of being It.

5. If a player is tagged, he or she steps out of the action, yet continues to call his or her assigned numbers followed by "Jump!" When a tagged player calls "Jump," since no tag attempts can be made, it essentially provides an opportunity for strategic placement toward an anticipated tag, avoiding a tag, or just fun!

6. Play until one person remains.

Reflection/Closure/Discussion

Jump Tag is often used as a warm-up and typically does not require much reflection or debriefing. If you choose to debrief the activity, the following questions may be used, based on the initial framing.

Monkeys

1. Based on your experience, do you or anyone else in the group possess the skills of a monkey with the ability to jump from tree to tree?

2. While we may not have the skills for tree jumping, we might have been playing to develop other skills helpful for being (living, surviving) in our human environment. What skills were we developing as we pretended to be monkeys?

3. When and where might these skills be helpful?

4. What skill might you like to practice? Additional skills?

Awareness

1. What reactions, comments, or observations do you have?

2. Did anything surprise you?

3. On a spectrum line-up from self aware to aware of others, re-arrange yourselves to show which was more helpful or important in this game, being self-aware or aware of others. Any questions or comments?

4. Fold the line in half to form partnerships and discuss this question – how does our awareness of self and others affect our relationships?

5. On an index card, write one thing you could do to strengthen relationships in this group.

6. Share responses with the group.

Tips and Comments

Variations

- **Am I Out?** So what happens after someone has been tagged? This would be an excellent question to ask your groups or classes if there is interest in co-creating additional rules and ultimately expanding the experience. Co-creating an experience with your group can effectively increase participant engagement and investment in learning.

Tips and Comments *(continued)*

In addition to your own ideas, consider the following variations to keep all players engaged, even after they've been tagged.

- Tagged players remain standing where they were tagged, adding texture to the playing area.
- Tagged players remain where they were tagged and may attempt to tag the current tagger from their stationary positions.
- Tagged players must remain stationary until their numbers come up. At that point, they may re-enter the game as they call out their numbers.
- Tagged players remain where they were tagged and perform a specified number of fitness-related activities e.g., jumping jacks, squat thrusts, push-ups, sit-ups, etc. and re-enter when their tasks are complete.
- Tagged players remain where they were tagged. If they would like to jump and tag again, they may indicate by extending both hands above their heads. Anyone who has not been tagged may "high-ten" stationary players to bring them back into the game.
- Tagged players add on to the player(s) who tagged them, by holding hands, linking arms, or placing both hands on the shoulder of the player who tagged them or the last person in line. This growing line jumps and tags on the number associated with the player who has not yet been tagged. The player who has not yet been tagged is the only player of the group who can continue to tag other players; however, anyone in this line-up can be tagged by another tagger. Players or groups of players may not jump through these forming teams. Monitor for safety. Some players may think that jumping into and trying to break the line-up of these forming teams is a good strategy. It's not!
- With a larger group, say thirty+, consider playing multiple games of Jump Tag simultaneously in groups of ten to twelve. When players get tagged in any game, they simply leave the game and the group they were playing with moves clockwise, and join another game already in progress. They may join immediately and keep the number they started with, which means that two or more people could be playing in the same game with the same number. No problem. More taggers equals more action!

- **Everybody's It Jump Tag** – While the original or base version of Jump Tag circulates the role of It throughout the group and throughout the game, playing a variation where everybody's It at the same time is a completely viable option. There simply needs to be a cue or signal for when to jump. For simplicity, one person could simply call "Jump" over and over again. Other ideas include jumping to the beat of a drum, jumping only while music is playing, or jumping to the tempo of the music. Incorporating music opens the door to subject, culture, and energy integration.

- **Team Jump Tag** – OK, one more variation…for now! Why not play Jump Tag in small teams of three or four? Team Jump Tag works well with larger groups. This variation invites everyone to play according to the original rules and/or with the addition of any of the above variations. However, each number is assigned to a team of people, instead of an individual. Now when you play, teams of three or four people jump on the same turn and try to tag as many people as they can, during their collective turn. They are welcome to play as independent individuals, jumping in any direction or as a single unit, with well-orchestrated jumps. Provide opportunities for reflection and strategizing between games.

Safety

Given the unique movement of this game, participants should be made aware of the potential of colliding with each other and be especially careful to avoid bumping heads.

Knee Tag

Overview

A tag game full of quirky movements and surprising moments. Players try to tag each other's knees while discovering ways to help themselves, help others, and keep the game moving. Knee Tag also enables the exploration of risk taking and the concept of control to empowerment.

Group Size	10 or more
Learning Themes	• Physical Activity and Movement • Building Trust, Relationships, and Community • Self Awareness and Self Management • Responsible Decision Making
Materials / Props	None

Setup

- Provide a level and open space.
- Gather your group in a circle.

Framing

Say to participants:

"Challenge by Choice (see Introduction) offers an opportunity to stretch from our comfort zones. As we play, consider the choices we make and how they impact our experience. Acknowledge your comfort zone while discovering what your stretch zone is and how it feels."

Or:

"We make lots of choices every day. Similarly, you will have lots of choices as we play a game of tag. In the end, what influences your choices? In the game and in life? We'll play and then check in."

Or:

"Stepping out of your comfort zone means taking a risk. Often times the more risks you take, the more you fail. And the more you fail, the more you learn. Our time together is about risk taking, failing, learning, and oh...having fun! Let's play!"

Procedure

1. Explain to the group that they will be playing a tag game in which everyone is It.
2. Explain and demonstrate the rules:
   a. Everyone is It and attempt to tag the knees of other participants with their hands.
   b. Hands may be used to cover knees and prevent a tag.

c. When hands are on knees, participants may not move their feet. Consider them stuck to the ground like roots of a tree.

d. In order to move, participants must place both hands on their stomachs. With hands on their stomachs, participants may run, walk, skip, hop around, whatever is appropriate for the space and fun of the game.

e. If a participant's knee is tagged, he or she simply takes a knee, or kneels, and remains stationary.

3. Check for understanding of the rules; then play.

4. At this point, the game of Knee Tag is being played as an elimination game – the taggee is no longer involved or able to tag anyone until a new game begins. While this is not the overall intent of the activity, there is value to starting with this variation. This initial elimination round or game provides an opportunity to introduce a manageable number of rules and further check for understanding before adding additional rules. At this point, you are probably ready for those additional rules. Let's go!

5. It is helpful to introduce and demonstrate one of the following rules at a time, inclusively progressing to a game bursting with choices and enthusiastic engagement. Additional rules:

a. If someone is tagged, he or she takes a knee and may tag the knee of someone passing by. The tagged person takes a knee and the person who made the tag remains on a knee. Classically, this is known as "ankle biters".

b. Often the previous rule is combined with an opportunity to re-enter the game. When players are tagged, they take a knee and may re-enter the game by tagging the knee of someone passing by. If successful, the person who was tagged takes a knee and the successful tagger pops up and returns to playing the game. In many tag-playing circles, this is called "pop-up tag" and can be viewed as participants helping themselves.

c. Next, if someone is tagged, he or she again takes a knee and may re-enter the game after receiving a high five from another participant.

6. Between rounds is a great time to briefly check in regarding fun, safety, and risk taking. For example, after playing a few rounds, use a "fist to five" technique, displaying one to five fingers in response to a question, to check in on both fun and safety. Ask the participants to display one to five fingers to show how much fun they are having. Then ask them to display one to five fingers showing how safe they are feeling. Determine if anything needs to change in order to increase the fun and/or keep it safe, then play some more. This type of check-in could be similar for exploring risk taking.

Reflection/Closure/Discussion

Risk Taking

1. Ask participants to display one to five fingers showing how much fun they had playing this game. Invite anyone to share if they would like. If not, move on.

2. Again, ask participants to display one to five fingers showing the level of risk they took while playing the game.

3. Ask the following questions:

a. What influenced how much or little risk you took while playing?

b. Is the level of risk you are taking right for you? What are some ways that might help you to determine this? How much fun are you having? How engaged are you? How content do you feel?

c. Consider taking more risk in the next round or game. Taking more risk could mean less time covering your knees, spending more time in the center of the group or on the perimeter, or asking someone for help. Determine what action you might take to demonstrate this, whether it is one of the examples, or one that you generate, and share with a partner.

4. Play another round or game and check in to see if taking more risks changed participants' experience of the game and one another.

Responsible Decision Making

1. Invite participants to line up on a continuum:

   a. Least fun to most fun

   b. Took less risks to took more risks

   c. Too many choices in the game to not enough choices

2. Fold the line in half to form partners or section off small groups of four participants. Invite them to discuss the following questions:

   a. What made the game more or less fun for you?

   b. What motivated you to take more or fewer risks?

   c. What choices did you make while playing this game?

   d. How did these choices influence you or others who played the game? Did it make it more or less fun or allow for more or less risk taking?

   e. What does that tell us about choices and how they impact our life and the lives of others?

   f. What new choice might you try tomorrow?

3. Return to a whole group to share highlights or summaries of the partner or small group debrief.

Tips and Comments

- Frequently asked questions typically emerge while playing Knee Tag. Here are a few:

  - Can I tag from a stationary position, when my hands are covering my knees? Yes, but you must remove one or both of your hands to do so, which exposes your knees, which means you could get tagged.

  - Can I pivot when my hands are on my knees? No, unless everyone agrees that utilizing one pivot foot is acceptable.

  - Can I walk with my hands on my knees? Nope, see rules c and d above.

  - Can I pull someone's hands off their knees and then try to tag them? No, this is not very Full Value! Model and encourage participants to respect the choices of others.

Tips and Comments *(continued)*

– If someone has been tagged and has his or her hand raised requesting a High Five to get back in, can they tag someone who is trying to help them? Yes, absolutely! This is part of the fun. It also seems to inspire excellent conversations regarding trust, revenge, reacting to surprises, and perspectives of what is fun or not. Another option of course is to provide a space for the group to determine collectively if this is fair and fun or not allowed. Let the group decide. It adds to the depth of learning associated with learning themes such as self-expression, decision making, and establishing group norms.

Variations

• **Creative Movement and Sounds.** Offering a different way to move and make sounds offers more variety and fun. As participants play, explain that in order to move, they may no longer put their hands on their stomachs and proceed quietly. They must now indicate that they are moving by waving their hands above their heads making ridiculous sounds. Participants can also be invited to explore and create their own movements and sounds while trying to tag other participants.

• **Hands Up.** Hands Up is a directive call from the facilitator which adds spontaneous excitement and movement to the game. Once the group is familiar and comfortable playing Knee Tag, the following rule may be added to keep it fresh. When "Hands up" is called, everyone must put their hands in the air and continue to play Knee Tag as they know it, with one exception. Participants may not cover their knees to prevent a tag, but try instead to rely on agility and awareness. They may not cover their knees until they hear the facilitator call "Hands down." "Hands down" indicates that participants return to playing knee tag in a more traditional way.

• **Hands Up, Hands Down, Handed Over (or Hand Over the Controls).** Whether you are looking for even more fun with this game, bordering on the ridiculous, or to experientially introduce the concept of Control to Empowerment, this variation brings it to life! (*Exploring Islands of Healing* p.241) The "Hands Up" variation offers spontaneous moments; however, they are directed by the facilitator. So what happens if you give up the controls and hand them over to the entire group? One has to wonder what the group will do with so much power and control. After flowing through the progression of rules and variations outlined above, or after your group has become familiar with the rules and variations, empower them to call "hands up" and "hands down." With this variation, anyone at any time can call either of these directions and everyone must follow.

Now why would you ever want to give up control? For starters, it's fun! It playfully inspires more learning opportunities. Finally, it especially offers the impetus for a quality discussion about responsible decision making and effective use of power and control. Progressing through all of the rules and variations of Knee Tag is a most concise and engaging way to introduce the concept of control to empowerment. It also helps to develop foundational skills associated with calling group regardless of whether you are in a therapeutic or alternative education setting.

Safety

Advise participants to be self and socially aware while twisting and untwisting the rope, as participants will be stepping over and under the rope while moving in and among other people.

Knot Again (aka Knot Exchange*)

Overview

Knot Again is yet another variation of the popular activity Human Knot. Small groups of participants twist short segments of rope to create a knot for another small group of participants to un-twist.

Group Size	6 or more
Learning Themes	• Relationship Skills • Responsible Decision Making
Materials / Props	One 10-foot length of accessory cord, rope, or webbing per 2 participants

Setup

- Criss-cross cord/webbing/rope at a central point on the floor or ground as depicted in the diagram below.

- Set up three to five ropes to accommodate six to ten people. Provide enough setups to accommodate your class or group size. Smaller groups of six to ten people seem to be most effective.

- Quick Puzzle: Are the lines in the diagram the same length – yes or no?

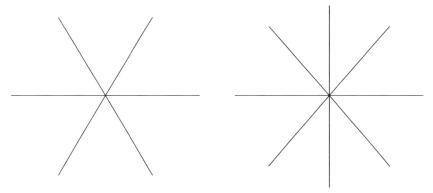

Framing

Say to participants:

Perspective

"'If you change the way you look at things, the things you look at change.' (a quote by Wayne Dyer) What does this mean to you? We all create situations for ourselves. How we view these situations determines whether they are positive or negative experiences. Here's a chance to practice this."

Leadership

"Is it always leaders who create or do we all play a role in creation? In this activity, be aware of the role you and others play while creating a piece of art together. Likewise, notice what role you and others play during the second part of the activity."

Procedure

Say to the participants:

1. "Stand at one end of a piece of webbing/rope.

2. Pick up the end of the rope/webbing.

3. While holding on to your end, twist the rope by moving under, over, and around the ropes of other people. Do this for a few minutes or until the rope or ropes seem sufficiently twisted. Be amazed by what you create!

4. Your task is to enjoy and experience what you created by twisting the rope!"

Facilitation Tip: You may want to briefly process what the participants, individually and as a group, did and how they did it, to create this knot or beautiful piece of art.

Reflection/Closure/Discussion

Perspective

1. How was your experience?

2. How would you describe your attitude and perspective while creating the knot?

3. How was that different or similar to un-twisting the knot?

4. How did this affect your experience?

5. Share a time in your life when you chose to view a situation from a positive perspective and therefore the experience was positive.

Leadership (Rope Sculpt)

1. Notice that you are connected through the rope with one other person. Stay connected.

2. Discuss what leadership you noticed during the activity.

3. Use the rope to sculpt what leadership means to you based on your experience.

Tips and Comments

- While Human Knot and Knot My Problem are widely used variations of Knot Again, there are reasons why a facilitator may choose one in particular. Human Knot literally provides human to human contact, creating a more intimate and personal interaction. Knot My Problem allows connection through a rope allowing focus to be on something other than the people themselves. It also sets up well to debrief with Pass the Knot or segue into a Yurt Circle. Knot Again provides similar yet different opportunities to Knot My Problem.

  Knot Again, like Knot My Problem, allows the focus to be on something other than people, which can be essential for learning social and emotional skills, such as conflict resolution. When resolving conflict, it can be beneficial to take the people out of the problem and focus on the issue itself. In this case, the issue to be resolved is the knot that has been created by the group – not the group itself.

- *Knot Again is also called Knot Exchange which is found in the book *Raptor and Other Teambuilding Activities* (Sikes, 2003).

Safety

- Make sure that participants move safely in and around the rope.

- Do not allow participants to pull excessively on the rope.

- Allow participants to shift their wrist positions if they are uncomfortable

Knot My Problem

Overview

An exceptional problem-solving activity. Each person grabs a section of coiled rope with one hand. This hand can never let go of the rope. Participants may loosen their grip and slide their hands, but may never let go, as the group attempts to untangle the knot. Knot My Problem highlights communication, accountability, and roles within a group.

Group Size	8 or more
Learning Themes	• Social Awareness • Relationship Skills • Responsible Decision Making
Materials / Props	One 30 ft. length of rope per 10 – 15 people

Setup

Pick up a length of rope and tie the two ends together. Do the same for any additional lengths of rope, as needed. Coil each length of rope so that when you lay it on the ground, it looks like several circles of rope piled on top of one another. Finally, separate your participants into groups of 8-15. Clear a large space in the center of the room.

Framing

Say to the group:

"Have you ever worked with a group when one or two group members stood off in the background not participating? Have you ever finished doing your part in an activity and then watched while other participants struggled to finish theirs? In this activity, you will be challenged to stay 'Here' and help the group finish even if you are in the 'free and clear.'"

Or:

"A circle has often been used as a symbol to represent community. We all have a connection to this community and a connected community is able to leverage its connections to solve problems. Working as a community and effective communication will be necessary for what you are about to encounter."

Procedure

1. Have each group circle up around a coil of rope.

2. Participants should reach down and clasp their hands around a piece of rope. Ideally, they will grab a bit of rope that is on the opposite side of the coil from where they are standing.

3. Once everyone in the small group has grabbed a piece of rope, they should stand up, creating a mess of rope in the center of the circle.

4. At this point, no one may let go of the rope. The hand with which they picked up the rope may never completely release the rope. Each participant may slide his or

her hand up and down the rope, but never totally let go. They may use their other hands to assist in moving sections of rope as needed.

5. The goal is to untangle the rope without letting go. Participants must move their bodies through holes formed by the rope. In other words, wherever their hands or sections of rope they are holding go, they go too. The group is done when the rope is one circle, with everyone facing the inside.

6. In their efforts to untangle the rope, a group may not untie the knot that connects the two ends of rope.

Debrief

Pass the Knot Debrief – Ask participants to remain standing, in their circle, with both hands on the rope. Point to the knot that ties the two ends together. Let participants know that when that knot is in front of them, they may choose to respond to the question or pass. If the knot is not in front of them, they need to wait until it is. Ask participants to practice moving the rope around the circle, by passing it to the right. Now ask one of the following questions:

1. What helped the group to be successful in this activity?

2. What from your Full Value Contract was alive and well? Which concepts do you need to work on? Give examples and reasons.

Tips and Comments

- To make this activity less challenging, allow participants to grab a piece of rope that is close to them, instead of reaching across the coil.

- Remind participants that they can slide the hand that cannot let go of the rope. Letting go of the rope entirely makes the problem much easier to solve.

- Invite participants to try this activity without the ability to speak or make any sounds.

- Knot My Problem not only sets up well for a Pass the Knot Debrief as indicated in the debrief section above, but also flows nicely into a Yurt (Rope) Circle (*High School Adventure Curriculum for Physical Education*. Panicucci, Jane et al. Project Adventure. 2003)

Adapted from "Knot My Problem" in *Creating Healthy Habits*, Katie Kilty (Project Adventure, 2006)

Safety

• Discourage participants from tugging the rope or other creative yet mischievous behaviors.

• Warn participants of the potentials of rope burn so they can monitor as needed.

Knot Race (aka NASCAR)

Overview

A timed challenge likely to rev up your group. Participants grab hold of a circle of rope connected by a knot. The group then attempts to move the knot around the circle as fast as they can. Knot Race provides a problem-solving option when space is limited and is ideal for processing behaviors that are helpful and harmful to the success of a group.

Group Size	8 or more
Learning Themes	• Relationship Skills • Responsible Decision Making
Materials / Props	One 30 ft. rope per 8 – 15 people

Setup

Tie the two ends of each rope together. Lay out two rope circles on the floor. Separate the participants into two groups. Have each group gather around one of the ropes. Post the reflection questions in a visual location such as a wall, dry erase board, flip chart, etc..

Framing

Say to the group:

"What is the purpose of rope? How is rope used? In this activity, you will get to use a rope in a whole new way. It will be both an instrument for measuring progress and a way to communicate with one another."

Or:

"Does anyone here watch NASCAR? Does anyone race, or hope to race, cars, go-carts, dirt bikes, or anything similar? While this isn't exactly the same, we have the opportunity to participate in a race. Imagine that the knot is a race car and the rest of the rope is the track. Our goal is to get the race car (knot) around the track (rope circle) as fast as we can. Rev your engines and get ready to roll!"

Procedure

1. Ask participants to pick up the rope without tugging it. Demonstrate what this looks like.

2. Tell participants that they are going to be presented with a series of challenges that involve passing the rope around the circle.

3. Ask each group to locate the knot that ties the two ends together. Explain that this is their marker. Tell them that the knot is similar to establishing a baseline when doing goal setting. It's hard to know where you want to get to if you don't already know where you are. This, in turn, helps you to measure progress.

4. For their first challenge, have participants simply pass the rope 360 degrees around the circle, so that the knot ends up where it began.

5. Have participants see how quickly they can pass the rope around the circle. How long do they think it will take? Have someone in the group be the time keeper.

6. After a few rounds, ask each group to stop and brainstorm ways they can improve their time. Then, give them a few chances to apply their ideas while trying to decrease their time.

7. Other challenges to try:

   a. Pass the knot one round to the right and then one round to the left.

   b. Pass the knot with arms raised over their heads.

   c. Pass the knot with everyone standing on the inside of the circle of rope.

   d. Pass the knot around a Figure-8 shaped track. To create this, cross the rope circle over itself to create the shape of a Figure-8 and race!

   e. Pass the knot with eyes closed. See if participants can guess when the knot has traveled all the way around the circle – ask them not to open their eyes until they think the knot has finished the journey.

   f. After completing the series of challenges, tell participants that they are going to listen and respond to a series of reflection questions about the activity.

8. **(Pass the Knot Debrief)** Ask the first question and tell participants to begin passing the rope around the circle. Tell them that if the knot comes to them and they want to answer the question, they should stop the rope, hold the knot, and respond to the question. If students do not want to answer the question, they are to let the knot pass by them.

9. Allow the knot to travel all the way around the circle for each question, giving each participant an opportunity to answer each question.

10. Continue until several questions have been asked and answered.

11. Sample questions:

12. What is one thing your group did to be successful in this activity?

    • What Full Value Concepts did your group demonstrate during this activity? Give an example of where they came to life.

    • What concepts could use improvement?

Reflection/Closure/Discussion

Processing is integrated into the procedures of this lesson.

Tips and Comments

• If it will help participants to focus or be more productive, consider having more than two circles. Or, if they will not be able to self manage, have everyone gather around one rope.

• If a question does not draw a response, go on to another.

• If the knot is framed as a race car, invite the explosion of revving engines and screeching tires as the activity begins.

Safety

- Given that a certain level of trust is required to effectively support each other, practitioners should consider a GRABBSS assessment and appropriately sequence activities leading up to Lean and Walk.

- Certain types of clothing material, such as nylon, may make this activity more challenging and less safe. Participants should be made aware of the effects of slippery clothing material.

Lean and Walk

Overview

A quick and fun activity that highlights support and spotting. Two people lean into each other's shoulder and walk, trusting one another, yet most likely laughing, as they do.

Group Size	8 or more
Learning Themes	• Physical Activity and Movement • Building Trust, Relationships, and Community • Self Awareness and Self Management • Social Awareness
Materials / Props	None

Setup

None

Framing

Say to the group:

"What does it mean to support someone? Can we agree that in order to support another person, we need to find the right amount of support to give? Can we also agree that supporting someone requires a certain level of give and take? Let's give it a try."

Procedure

1. Establish partners.

2. Describe and demonstrate a lean and walk with a willing participant.

3. To lean and walk, two people stand side by side.

4. Have the participants lean toward each other and connect at the shoulder. Make adjustments as needed to feel safe, secure, and supported.

5. Once the two people are comfortably supporting each other's weight, they attempt to walk while maintaining connection, support, and weight sharing.

Reflection/Closure/Discussion

1. How did it work out?

2. Did the discussion before the activity – supporting someone else requires us to be comfortable and support requires give and take – prove to be true? Explain.

3. How might these ideas be helpful as we move forward with our time together?

4. What role does social support have in creating and sustaining a healthy life style?

5. What are three ways that we can care for ourselves and others?

Tips and Comments

- Lean and Walk makes for an excellent traveling activity. For example, if you happen to be guiding a group on a challenge course and intend to use a low element that may require spotting and physical contact, this activity may be an appropriate choice to offer prior to the low element. If you are approaching the low element from a nearby field or building, using Lean and Walk to get you there productively takes care of two needs – getting to the destination and preparing the group for the low element.

Variations

- **Different Perspectives, Same Direction** – Is it possible to support someone while holding different perspectives? In this variation, participants still connect at the shoulder as described previously; however, they do so while facing in opposite directions. They will still attempt to lean and walk in the same direction – one person will walk forward, while the other walks backward or participants may choose to walk sideways.

- **Back to Back** – A twist on the Different Perspectives, Same Direction. Have two people safely lean and connect back to back. While connected, they again attempt to lean and walk while supporting each other and each other's weight.

- **Mobile Bridges (a.k.a. Hand to Hand)** – Some of you (practitioners) may be familiar with a warm-up called Human Bridges and Human Springs, which prepare participants for an experience on the low element known as the Wild Woosey. This variation is similar to the warm-ups and techniques used on the Wild Woosey. In this variation, two people face one another and connect at their hands, palm to palm only, and without interlacing fingers. Again, while leaning into the support of one another, each partner team attempts to lean and walk.

Left and Right Pairs Tag

Overview

A disorienting and funny tag game requiring more strategy than speed. Participants play tag with one other person in the midst of other players. One player may only turn left while moving and the other player may only turn right. Players move in circles, or squares if we are being technical, attempt to orient and re-orient themselves to tag their partners.

Group Size	10 or more
Learning Themes	• Fun and Play • Physical Activity and Movement • Building Trust, Relationships, and Community
Materials / Props	4 cones to mark boundaries

Estimated Time

10 – 15 minutes

Safety

Bumpers (hands up) should be used, since the pace can be fast and the play space is rather small.

Setup

Have participants partner up and mark the boundaries using four cones.

Framing

Say to participants:

"Catching your partner will be harder than it looks, especially if he or she is a creative problem solver."

Procedure

1. Partners are given 30 seconds to determine who will be the tagger and agree on what three actions the tagger will perform before chasing his or her partner.

2. Players must stay within the boundary area. If the tag-ee runs outside the boundary area, he or she automatically becomes the tagger. If a successful tag is made, players switch roles.

3. The catch of this game is the movement. One person in the pair may ONLY move forward and make 90 degree left turns. The other person may ONLY move forward and make 90 degree right turns.

Reflection / Closure / Discussion

1. What were some of your successes and challenges during the game?

2. What were some ways that you practiced creative problem solving in this game?

3. Why is it important to be a creative problem solver?

Estimated Time

10 minutes

Safety

Sometimes participants can become anxious about being one of the last remaining in the circle especially in the third round. You may want to give little hints if time gets long.

Little Green Straw

Overview

A quick activity that challenges participants to become more aware of their surroundings. Everyone is invited to find a straw multiple times within a particular boundary. The experience and potential learning is surprising!

Group Size	10 or more
Learning Themes	• Fun and Play • Building Trust, Relationships, and Community • Responsible Decision Making
Materials / Props	• A 50 ft. length of rope • One small green straw (or similar object like a pencil or pen)

Setup

Using the length of rope, create a circle on the ground just big enough for the entire group to gather in. Participants should be corralled close together, not touching but with little space between them.

Framing

Say to the group,

"How in tune are we to the world around us? Are we aware of the people around us? Are we aware of the slight changes happening every moment? Reading our environment is an important skill and today we are going to test our ability to read our environment and explore our awareness of what is happening around us."

Procedure

Round One

1. Invite all participants to enter the circle and find a place to stand. The group should not stand in a circle but rather as a mixed crowd facing in different directions.

2. Explain to the group that, in a moment, you are going to ask them to close their eyes (or put on blindfolds) and once everyone's eyes are closed that you are going to hide the little green straw somewhere in the circle. Show the group the straw.

3. Hide the straw on the ground in a somewhat obvious spot and step out of the circle. Stepping out of the circle is important.

4. Once the straw is hidden, invite participants to open their eyes and attempt to visually locate the straw.

5. It's important that participants remain quiet, no talking throughout the entire round. Once participants have located the straw, they should quietly step out of the circle and allow others to find it.

6. Wait for everyone to find the straw to end round one.

Round Two

1. Same rules as the first round except try hiding the straw in a trickier spot like just behind someone's foot.

2. Be sure to hide the straw on the ground again.

3. As in the first round, step outside of the circle once you've hidden the straw.

4. Wait for everyone to find the straw to end the round.

Round Three

1. The rules will be the same as the first two rounds except, this time, hide the straw behind your ear.

2. It's important in this round that you stand in the circle rather than stepping out as in the two previous rounds.

3. It will take much longer for participants to locate the straw in this round so be patient. You may need to remind participants to remain quiet.

4. Wait for everyone to find the straw to end the third and final round.

Reflection / Closure / Discussion

1. What happened in each round? What was different about the third round?

2. What clues or information did you use to help you locate the straw in the third round? Were there any behaviors from other participants that gave you a clue?

3. Did we make any assumptions?

4. What does this teach us about working in a group? How can this be useful as we move forward?

Log Pile

Overview

A fun introductory, problem-solving activity that encourages participants to look past assumptions and think creatively.

Group Size	10 or more
Learning Themes	• Building Trust, Relationships, and Community • Relationship Skills • Responsible Decision Making
Materials / Props	None

Setup

None

Framing

Bring the group together and begin with, "Today we are going to explore different ways of doing things that we may do everyday. For example, shaking hands. How many people have shaken someone's hand? Great, now how many people have tried shaking hands like the Woodcutters of the Northeast?"

Procedure

1. Introduce the Woodcutter's Handshake by asking for a volunteer to be your partner. As your partner approaches, reach out to them with your hand. Your fingers should be tucked back making a fist with your thumb up, as though you were giving your partner the thumbs up. Your partner grabs your thumb as if it were the handle of a saw and puts up his or her thumb for you to grab with your other hand. Finally, your partner, with his or her other hand, completes the stack. Now, both you and your partner will move your arms back and forth together as though you were cutting down a giant tree.

2. Allow participants an opportunity to try this new method for shaking hands with as many people as they can in one minute.

3. Bring the group back together.

4. Explain to the group that, unlike more traditional handshaking techniques, the Woodcutter's Handshake is not simply limited to two people. Ask the group to explore how many people they can involve in a single Woodcutter's Handshake.

5. Ask participants if they can think of a way to involve the entire group in one Woodcutter's Handshake.

Reflection / Closure / Discussion

What can we take from this experience that may be helpful as we face increasingly difficult challenges?

Tips and Comments

Smaller groups of 12-15 participants will be less challenged to involve everyone. Larger groups of 15-100+ may be more challenged to re-think the challenge but may discover more success in shaking hands horizontally rather than vertically.

This activity is a great tone setter for creative problem solving and looking at a situation from every angle.

Longest Shadow

Estimated Time

10 – 20 minutes

Overview

A quick problem-solving activity. The group works together, positioning and re-positioning themselves, to cast the longest shadow possible.

Group Size	6 or more
Learning Themes	• Relationship Skills • Responsible Decision Making
Materials / Props	A bright sunny day or high-powered spotlight!

Setup

Provide a large open space on a bright sunny day or use a high-powered spotlight.

Framing

Say to group:

"Like casting a shadow on a bright sunny day, we leave behind a legacy, a story about ourselves, our family, our communities, and our organizations everywhere we go and as a result of anything we do. Can you recall a legacy about someone you admire?

Who are some of the people you highly regard and what aspects of their legacies do you admire? A legacy is essentially a story that exists after a person or group moves on. Let's explore the legacy that our team is creating as we make our mark in the form of a shadow."

Procedure

1. State the objective: Create the longest shadow cast by your bodies.

2. Explain the rules:

   a. The shadow must be one continuous line.

   b. Each individual shadow must connect to other shadows; however actual people are not required to be connected.

   c. Participants may use their bodies only, which means that they may not use their clothes, bags, accessories, or objects that they find around them.

   d. The group must identify a unique unit of measurement to determine the length of each attempt. For example, if they choose to use the shoe of a participant named Norrie, the group would measure their shadow using Norrie's shoe and record the length as 200 Norrie's Shoes.

   e. The group may make as many attempts as they would like or within a given amount of time and record their efforts.

3. Record and use personal bests, a record of an individual's or group's best performance, to challenge themselves or future groups.

Reflection/Closure/Discussion

1. How do you feel about your shadow?

2. What were some positive qualities of teamwork demonstrated while creating your shadow?

3. Using a fist to five, showing zero to five fingers, rate the quality of:

   a. Sharing of ideas

   b. Listening to each other

   c. Providing feedback in a way that was helpful and heard

   d. Assertive communication

4. What legacy or story about your team might be left behind? Are there any aspects that you might consider to be positive? Any aspects that you might consider negative?

5. What is one thing you can do to reduce a negative aspect of this legacy? What is one thing you can do to maintain the positive aspects of this legacy?

Macro Wave Popcorn

Estimated Time

5 – 10 minutes

Overview

A brief problem-solving activity for any size circle. Participants are challenged to set and achieve goals by sending a popper wave around the circle as quickly as possible. It requires that participants already have an understanding of how to use poppers. Macro Wave Popcorn is an ideal introduction to problem solving and goal setting while having fun!

Group Size	8 or more
Learning Themes	• Fun and Play • Relationship Skills • Responsible Decision Making
Materials / Props	1 or 2 poppers per participant

Setup

Provide an adequate space for the entire group to stand or sit in a comfortable circle.

Framing

Say to the group:

"How many people have been to a sporting event and been part of the 'wave'? Well, we're going to do a similar wave except we're going to use poppers! Let's give it a go!"

Once students have practiced, introduce the next level of the activity by saying,

"How fast do you think we can do this? Let's set a goal and do our best to meet it."

Procedure

1. Participants must use proper popper technique (See Playing with Poppers)
2. Only one popper may be popped at a time.
3. The time starts on the first pop and stops on the last.
4. The group will have three official rounds to do their best.
5. Between each round, the group will be given a chance to discuss and evaluate their progress.

Reflection / Closure / Discussion

1. How were we able to achieve our goal?
2. Did everyone contribute and were ideas shared and heard?
3. Did we learn anything in each round that helped the next?

Tips and Comments

Variation:

This activity is also great as a simple celebration by removing the time factor. Simply ask students to pop through the wave as quickly as possible and finish off with a big "Hurray!" The faster they go, the cooler the sound.

Magic Spells

Overview

In this riddle-type activity, something magical has happened to the way words are depicted. Participants attempt to decode their names or words, which are spelled by literally spelling each letter. Discoveries happen at different moments for each person. Most often, participants help one another to understand. Magic Spells is a great activity to introduce "aha" moments, learning at different paces, and creating a caring learning community.

Group Size	10 or more
Learning Themes	• Building Trust, Relationships, and Community • Self Awareness and Self Management • Social Awareness
Materials / Props	• Index cards • Markers

Safety

Be aware of cognitive strain or strong emotional reaction due to "not getting it." This activity is not for everyone and may make some people feel that they are being tricked or left out. Please be considerate when facilitating this activity.

Setup

Generate 'Magic Spells' cards for names or words related to your framing and desired outcomes using the alphabet code below. For example, if playing the Magic Spells: Name variation, a card for Lisa, Andrew, or Greg's names would look like the following. Do you see it?

eleyeesaye	*ayeendeeareeeeyouyou*	*jeeareeeejee*

Or you could frame the activity differently to introduce words that might be helpful for a forthcoming experience using the Magic Spells: Words variation. Given what you know can you figure out the three words on the next page?

teeareyouestee	seeohememeyetee-emeeeentee	eeeempeeajetee-aitchwye

The following are two Magic Spells variations represented in the Framing, Procedure, and Reflection/Closure/Discussion sections. In each section, two tracks emerge titled as either Magic Spells: Names or Magic Spells: Words. Each track has a slightly different purpose, yet is based in the same 'Magic Spells' concept. Choose one track and follow it specifically to avoid confusion.

Framing

Magic Spells: Names

"I have cards for each of you, but something most extraordinary has happened to them. Someone or something has put a magic spell on them. Help me to get them to the right person."

Magic Spells: Words

"I have cards with words on them that will most likely be helpful for our time together. However, something extraordinary has happened to them. Someone or something has put a magic spell on them. Help me to discover the magic that exists around here."

Procedure

Magic Spells: Names
Say to the group:

1. I am going to pass one card to each of you.
2. Remember – someone or something has put a magic spell on them.
3. Your task is to correctly match each card to the right person in your group.
4. Once you know whose card you have, get it to its rightful owner.
5. Go!

Magic Spells: Words
Say to the group:

1. I am going to place some cards in front of you.
2. Remember – someone or something has put a magic spell on them.
3. Your task is to tap into the magic around here and identify what each card says.
4. Once you think you know a card, put it aside and work on the rest.
5. After deciphering all of the cards, we'll discuss whether they will help to create a magical experience for *all* of us and what our role is in that.

Reflection/Closure/Discussion

Magic Spells: Names

1. Use the concept of Magic Spells as a debrief and to generate a Full Value Contract.

2. Have participants use the Magic Spell Alphabet below to "cast a spell" on a word or phrase that they believe would be helpful for creating a caring learning environment.

3. Have other group members use their newly gained wisdom to unlock the magic.

4. Take the cards with you as you work with this group and use them as debrief cards.

Magic Spells: Words

1. What allowed you to decipher the words or phrases on the cards?

2. Were the behaviors you demonstrated represented on the cards?

3. What might our behaviors during the activity or the words on the cards tell us about our time together?

4. Do you believe that they would be helpful in creating a magical experience for *all* of us?

5. What role do we have in creating that experience?

Tips and Comments

Tip

- Allow for, and notice the timing of, aha moments as participants discover the names or words on the cards. It may provide the opportunity to discuss aha moments, learning at different paces, and creating a caring learning community.

- If you prefer, generate cards on a computer and print rather than using index cards and markers.

Variation

- Use Magic Spells: Words to introduce an established Full Value Contract such as Be Here, Be Safe, Be Honest, Set Goals, Let Go & Move On, and Care for Self & Others. Or use it to reinforce words of concepts that the group has recently been learning.

Magic Spells Alphabet:

- Would you believe that there are people online who have not only considered the concept of how letters are spelled, but are also debating what the best representation of each spelled letter might be? It's true. We've come up with the following. Feel free to search for others or make up your own. The key is to be consistent in representing each name or word.

A – aye	H – aitch	O – oh	V – vee
B – bee	I – eye	P – pee	W – you-you
C – cee	J – jay	Q – cue	X – ecks
D – dee	K – kay	R – are	Y – wye
E – eee	L – el	S – ess	Z – zee
F – eff	M – em	T – tee	
G – jee	N – en	U – you	

Map Making

Overview

A creative process for a positive world. Participants create a map of the world using ropes and other random props and establish behavioral norms. Map Making is a great way to consider how behaviors not only impact an immediate group, but the world at large.

Group Size	4 or more
Learning Themes	• Building Trust, Relationships, and Community • Relationship Skills • Responsible Decision Making

Materials / Props	• 7 lengths of rope
	  – One, 20 foot
	  – Four, 40 foot
	  – One, 60 foot
	  – One, 80 foot
	• Random props (e.g., bean bags, fleece balls, processing cards, etc.)
	• Additional sections of rope

Setup

Place ropes and random props in the center of an open space.

Framing

Say to group:

"A mapmaker's dilemma is that it is impossible to show both shape and size accurately. In order to show true shape for the land masses, as in the Mercator projection, the relative sizes will be distorted. Likewise, if you attempt to display accurate sizes, as in the Gall-Peters Projection, true shapes get distorted. You can probably imagine how challenging this could be. Well, we are going to create a map together."

Or:

"What if you could create your world? What would you create? How would you create it? How would people treat each other?"

Procedure

1. Explain to the group that they will embark in a creative process to create a map of the world that is oriented correctly, yet not perfectly proportioned.

2. Check in at the end of ten minutes to see if the group needs more time to finalize their creation. Remind the group that the map does not need to represent perfect shapes or scale.

3. Encourage the use of additional props to make borders, islands, or places of personal significance.

Reflection/Closure/Discussion

1. What do you have to say about your world?
2. What do you have to say about how you created your world?
3. Did anyone want to keep working on it? Was anyone ready to give up? Why?
4. Did anyone change something you created without asking? How did that feel?
5. What have we learned from this experience?

Continue with these steps to create a group generated Full Value Contract:

6. Identify behaviors demonstrated during the activity that would be helpful in positively creating our world. Write them down on an index card and place them within one of the seven continents.
7. Identify behaviors demonstrated during the activity that would not be helpful in positively creating our world. Write them down on an index card and place them outside one of the seven continents.
8. Let's take a look at what turned up.
   a. Do the behaviors within the continents seem like they would be helpful in creating experiences for our group? How about the world beyond our group?
   b. What impact would the behaviors outside of the continents have on our group? Might that be true for the world beyond our group?

Tips and Comments

- Instead of a world map, consider mapping a specific country, city, or town.
- After the group generates and reflects on what could be their Full Value Contract, consider setting personal behavioral goals related to either the group itself, the greater world, or both. Instruct participants to draw or sketch a map of their group or life goals.

Safety

One challenging aspect of this activity is for the group to determine how to navigate the narrow pathway (through the hoop) set between the starting line and the retrieval zone. Due to the design, participants may come in close contact with each other. Participants should be made aware of this and should avoid physical contact with each other.

Merge

Overview

A fast- paced, problem-solving activity. Inspired by the daily challenge of merging traffic or ants marching, the group navigates a narrow entrance way while trying to retrieve all objects and return them to the starting area in the shortest time possible.

Group Size	12 – 15
Learning Themes	• Physical Activity and Movement • Relationship Skills • Responsible Decision Making
Materials / Props	• Play rope or webbing • Cones • Hula hoops • A variety of tossables (2 – 3 per participant) • Stop watch

Setup

1. Place a play rope or webbing on the floor or ground to indicate the starting line.

2. Scatter objects about 50 feet away in a retrieval zone marked by cones or a roped boundary.

3. Between the start area and the scattered objects, set a narrow pathway marked by cones or rope, and then the hula hoop(s).

Framing

Say to group:

"Have you ever been in a vehicle trying to merge onto an off ramp to exit a highway? Would you agree that it's not an easy task and that there are many different strategies used by many different drivers? What are some of the strategies a driver may use? Would you say that these strategies are good for the individual driver or good for all of the cars attempting to merge? While attempting the next activity, you are asked to find the most efficient solution to merging."

Or:

"Imagine yourself as a team of adventurous archeologists. You have been enlisted to recover lost artifacts of an ancient culture destined to be crushed and lost forever by a precarious tunnel notorious for stopping the most clever treasure hunters. Determine the most efficient way to get the objects out before it's too late."

Or:

"Have you ever watched ants building an ant hill or tunnel? They work systematically, moving one little pebble at a time out of the hole and away from the entrance. They flow in and out of the entrance of the hole hardly ever contacting each other and certainly without jamming the system. (The scattered objects represent tiny pebbles, the hula hoop is the entrance to the hole, and the ropes the pathway to the hole). Your goal is to retrieve the pebbles (objects) and return them beyond the start/finish line in the most efficient manner, just as ants would."

Procedure

1. State the objective. The group attempts to retrieve all objects and return them to the starting area in the shortest time possible.

2. Explain the parameters:

    a. Everyone must start and finish behind the starting line.

    b. Everyone must stay within the boundary. If anyone steps outside the boundary, the entire group must return to the start line and begin again while time continues to run.

    c. Everyone must step within the hoop when retrieving and returning objects.

    d. Everyone must retrieve at least one object.

    e. Objects may not be thrown or tossed. The objects must be placed on the ground or floor beyond the start/finish line, not tossed.

    f. Each person may only have one object in their possession at a time.

    g. Time starts when the first person crosses the starting line. Time stops when the last person crosses the starting line.

3. Check for understanding of the parameters, and then begin.

4. After the first round or attempt, provide time for planning, preparing, and goal setting. Encourage the group to use what they did and what they learned from the previous round to set a goal and plan for additional rounds.

5. Play two to four additional rounds, for a total of three to five rounds, providing opportunities for the group to achieve or revise their goals.

Reflection/Closure/Discussion:

1. Rate your goal or goals using a thumb-o-meter. Show a thumbs up if you felt your goal was challenging, thumbs down if it wasn't challenging at all, or thumbs to the side if you believed it was somewhere in between.

2. What factors helped you to determine your thumb-o-meter rating? How did you respond to the goal that was set?

3. What does this tell us about goal setting?

4. What might be the benefits of a challenging goal?

5. Define a challenging goal for yourself that could be achievable within the next three months and share it with another person in this group.

Tips and Comments

- Play the Dave Mathews Band song 'Ants Marching' while playing Merge or as a part of the reflection.

Variations

- **Don't Touch Me** – Require that only one person may step within the hoop at a time. Add ten seconds to the overall time for each time more than one foot exists in the hula hoop at the same time.

- **Through the Ringer** –Increase the challenge by requiring each participant to pass their entire body through the hoop, from feet to head or head to feet. More than one participant may pass through the hoop at the same time, as long as the hoop does not break. If the hoop breaks, require participants to repair the hoop and attempt again.

- **Change the Movement** – Have participants try moving on all fours in a crab walking or bear crawl position.

- **Multiple Teams** – Consider dividing groups into multiple teams working for collective or competitive goals. This is an effective option when facilitating groups of twenty or more.

- **Choose Your Own Adventure!** – Invite your group to challenge themselves or another group by reconfiguring the narrow passage into the retrieval area. They could change the shape, set obstacles as "booby-traps," or add additional parameters in an effort to increase the challenge and ultimately, the adventure and fun!

Optional Setup Diagrams

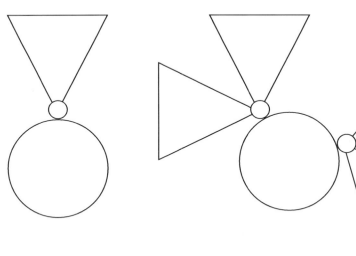

Missile Command (aka Message Command)

Overview

A simple tag game for large groups and big meaning! A select group of taggers are chosen to guard six buckets against the remainder of their group who are attempting to collectively knock over all six buckets. Two framing variations provide opportunities for this activity to be connected to outcomes related to history, a Full Value Contract, and managing all of the message streams we have available to us today thanks to technology. Either way you spin it, Missile Command is sure to be a blast!

Safety

There is a lot of running around in this game as there is with any tag game. Be sure to play on an appropriate and level surface. Additionally, warn participants that quick movements and changes in direction could result in colliding with other players. They should be aware of this and play in a way that demonstrates this awareness.

Group Size	20 or more
Learning Themes	• Fun and Play • Physical Activity and Movement • Responsible Decision Making
Materials / Props	• 6 plastic buckets • 6 spot markers • Two, 30-foot pieces of rope • 4 cones

Setup

- Place six or more spot markers ten-feet apart from one another at one end line to mark where participants line up at the start of the game. These players represent either missiles or messages depending on the framing.

- Place six plastic buckets ten-feet apart from one another and about 60-100 feet away from the spot markers. These buckets represent cities or message centers depending on the framing.

- Place a rope about 20 feet in front of the spot markers marking a tag/no-tag zone.

- Place cones on the two ends of the rope and just behind the line of buckets to mark boundaries.

- See diagram below.

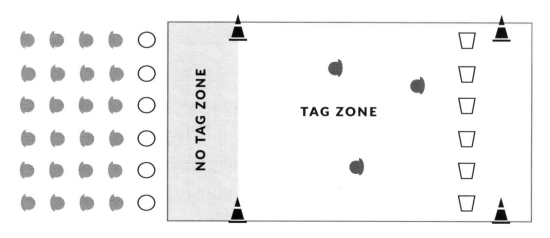

= lines of people
(representing missiles or messages)

◯ = spot markers (starting line)

⊔ = plastic buckets (cites / message centers)

= taggers

Framing

Missile Command

"Six major cities (plastic buckets) in your country are being attacked by a never-ending barrage of ballistic missiles. A select group of missile commanders (taggers) must coordinate their efforts to defend their precious cities, against missiles (the remainder of the group) destined to destroy each city."

Message Command

"Thanks to technology, multi-tasking has become more common place for many people. We now have the ability to call, text, email, message, chat, video chat, tweet, and update our status – to name a few options. Imagine all of this information flying your way through wireless and broadband networks and showing up on various devices. How do you effectively communicate with everyone without getting overwhelmed? In other words, how can you best manage your stress with all that comes your way? Let's play a game that highlights this and explore how we fare!"

Procedure

1. Creatively choose three taggers to protect the six plastic buckets. Invite them to stand within the "tag zone."

2. Separate the remaining people into four to six lines with approximately the same number of particpants in each line. Direct these participants (representing missiles or messages) to line up behind a spot marker and give each line a number.

3. State the goal. The goal for the participants starting behind a spot marker is to knock over the six buckets. The taggers try to prevent this by tagging anyone they can.

4. Explain the rules:

    a. The first person in each line may make their attempt when their line number is called by the facilitator.

    b. Taggers may attempt to tag other people only after they enter the tag zone.

    c. Once a person leaves the no tag zone, he or she may not return to avoid a tag.

    d. If a person gets tagged by a tagger, he or she must leave the tag zone boundary and return to the end of any line and wait for another turn.

    e. The game continues until all six buckets have been knocked over.

5. Once a game has finished, select three new taggers and play again!

Reflection/Closure/Discussion

Missile Command

The Missile Command framing is intended to provide a playful context in which to run around and play tag. You may choose to let it be and not reflect or process the experience. However, it may provide opportunities to check in regarding the Full Value Contract or connect the experience to history, war, and social relations on a global scale. Consider these as themes to reflect on and learn about.

Message Command

1. Would you say that our message receivers were effective or not effective in their task of responding to the multitude of messages that came their way? Support your response with some examples.

2. For those who were message receivers, how did your approach affect your stress level as you played?

3. Are these examples representative of effective and ineffective strategies to manage messages that show up on all of our devices in our everyday life?

4. Are there other examples of effectively or ineffectively managing all of our means of communication that didn't show up during this game? Name a few.

5. What is one practice you would like to continue or one way that you want to try to be more effective in responding to messages from others and reducing your stress? What is one practice you would like to let go of?

Tips and Comments

- The facilitator should randomly call line numbers at a pace that seems to make the game interesting and challenging. Calling line numbers slowly at first and speeding up as the game continues is a great way to meet this goal. Basically, the pace of the calls and consequently, the intensity of the game should increase as the game progresses. If done well, the game will eventually end due to an overwhelming flurry of people, too much for any team of taggers to manage.

- There are two framings offered above, drawing on different metaphors. Did you follow them and make the connections? Here is a brief review:

  - **Missile Command Framing** – Plastic buckets represent cities. The taggers trying to protect the cities are missile commanders. The people trying to destroy the cities are ballistic missiles. If the missiles achieve their goal of destroying all of the cities by knocking over all six buckets, a new game begins. If the missile commanders are successful with their task, which is by design nearly impossible, then the game would continue for a while and everyone would become exhausted!

  - **Message Command Framing** – Plastic buckets represent various message centers, e.g., phones, computers, tablets, mailbox, etc. The taggers trying to prevent messages from "overwhelming" their message centers are considered message receivers. The rest of the players trying to knock over the buckets represent messages in a variety of forms, e.g., email, text, tweets, wall posts, phone calls, etc. If these people are successful in overwhelming the message receivers by knocking over all six buckets, a new game begins. Similar to Missile Command, if the message receivers are keeping up with the frantic pace set by the facilitator, the game is likely to drip with exhaustion.

Variation

- Increase or decrease the number of taggers and lines of people trying to knock off the buckets, based on group size.

Name Stock Market

Overview

Looking for a name game that does not require participants to announce their names to the group at the start? Name Stock Market is a noisy, enthusiastic card trading game resulting in the discovery of who's in the group. Players attempt to be first to collect the letters of their name by trading with others.

Group Size	10 or more
Learning Themes	• Fun and Play • Building Trust, Relationships, and Community • Relationship Skills
Materials / Props	Index Cards

Setup

Distribute index cards to each person. Have them write each letter of their first name on individual index cards. For example, Ethan's cards would look like:

Framing

Say to the group:

"We can learn a lot about each other by playing games. The game we are about to play is a fast-paced, highly interactive game that could be stressful. It is modeled on playing the stock market. We will trade the letters of our names instead of stocks and have an opportunity to discover who's in our group. We might even discover how we treat each other in times of stress."

Procedure

1. To begin, collect and shuffle all of the cards.

2. Deal nine cards, without showing what they are, to each participant. Ask players not to look at their cards until the rules have been explained.

3. State the objective – be the first to collect the letters needed to spell your own name.

4. Explain the rules:

    a. The game has no turns and everyone plays at once.

b. Players trade with one another by exchanging one to three cards without showing what they are.

c. To trade, players call out the number of cards they wish to trade until another player holds out an equal number of cards. The two parties then exchange the agreed-upon number of cards face down.

d. Players may use any appropriate letter card to spell a name. In other words, players are not limited to the letter cards they wrote (produced). For example, if a couple of players were named, Aaron and Matt, either player could use the index card with the letter 'a' on it that they produced. Or, Aaron could use the index card with the letter 'a' that Matt produced. Likewise, Matt could use the index card with the letter 'a' that Aaron produced. Furthermore if there was a player named Brian playing as well, he could use the index card with the letter 'r' on it that he wrote or the one Aaron wrote.

e. When a player has all of the letters needed to spell his or her name, he or she will call out, "I'm done, I'm done!" ending the round.

Reflection/Closure/Discussion:

Name Stock Market is a playful way to energize the group before asking people to introduce themselves, so you may not want to process it beyond sharing names after the trading has subsided. If you choose to process the experience, consider these questions:

1. How would you describe the general feel of the group as they played this game?

2. Did anyone feel the stress of the game? Did that affect how you traded with other people?

3. How does stress affect how we appear to others?

4. How can we care for ourselves and others in stressful situations?

Tips and Comments

- **Level the Playing Field** – Since our names vary in the number of letters, level the playing field by ensuring that everyone starts with the same number of cards. To do so, determine who in the group has the most letters in their first name and give each player this number of cards. For example, if the longest first name in the group is Jonathan, give each person eight cards. Have each person write each letter of their first name on individual index cards, as noted in the setup above. However, ask anyone with first names fewer than eight letters, such as Jim, to also use letters from their last name until they reach eight cards of letters. So if Jim Schoel were playing, Jim's cards would look like:

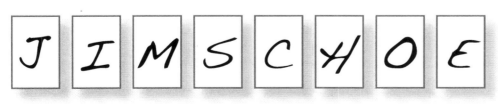

J I M S C H O E

Tips and Comments *(continued)*

If there is a very long first name and a very short combination of first and last name that doesn't match the number of letters used in the longest, get creative! Use middle names or nicknames.

Variations

- **Active Name Stock Market** – To make Name Stock Market more active, spread hula hoops around the perimeter of a large field, gym, or playing space. Place a thirty foot rope in a circle directly in the center of the playing space. Add the following rules:

  - Agreements to trade must be made in the central circle created by the rope.

  - Trading may only occur in a hula hoop on the perimeter of the space.

  - After each trade, a player must return to the center space and make another agreement to trade.

- **I Got Your Name** – If players are familiar with each other's names, play a variation where anyone can collect any name in the group. Once they collect all of the cards needed to spell the name of another person, have them yell out, "Mike, I got your name!"

- **Name Stock Market Co-op** – Try a more cooperative version by playing until *everyone* collects a set of cards that spell their name in the shortest time possible. The group can then work toward their best time in three to five attempts. Players must still trade without showing their cards. The cooperative version invites reflection associated with traditional teamwork and problem-solving activities, such as trust, commitment, communication, etc. It also integrates getting to know each others' names while setting goals.

- **Name Stock Market Co-opetition** – Lastly, a co-opetition version can be played by blending the competitive energy of the original version and the common goal of the cooperative challenge introduced above. The objective of this variation is for *everyone* to collect the cards needed to spell their names in the shortest time possible. This would occur over the course of three to five rounds; however, each player can earn individual points by collecting his or her name before anyone else. Points can be awarded to each player as they complete their individual tasks. Players can track their individual points or times over the course of three to five rounds. While processing this variation, the exploration of self-gain and group gain can be profound.

Name Trains

Overview

A name game and problem-solving blend, Name Trains invites participants to arrange themselves in a circle (or line) by connecting "shared" letters at the beginning and/or end of their names. Name Trains will challenge any individual or group to learn the names of other group members, practice letting go and moving on, and seek unseen solutions while connecting with each other.

Group Size	6 or more
Learning Themes	• Building Trust, Relationships, and Community • Self Awareness and Self Management • Social Awareness • Relationship Skills • Responsible Decision Making
Materials / Props	None

Setup

Prepare an open space. A room with furniture (i.e., desk, chairs, tables, etc.) could work as well. Since this is not an extremely active game, groups can work in and around the furniture.

Framing

Say to the group:

"During our time together, we will build community. To build community, we need to form connections. To form connections, we need to share our names. Sharing our names may help us build community. As we attempt to build community, we may find that connections are sometimes easy to come by and sometimes not. When you are most challenged, you may discover that seeking unseen or unspoken solutions leads to a connected community."

Or:

"Have you noticed that some people seem to connect quickly while others feel completely left out. This seems to be a common norm among groups of people. Would you like this to be your norm? What would you like? Let's practice that."

Or:

"Would you agree that compassionate communities are inclusive? Being inclusive will be helpful in what we are about to experience."

Procedure

Say to the group:

1. Think about your name.
2. Identify the first and last letter of your name. For example, the first and last letters of Bryan's name are 'B' and 'N.'

3. Using these letters, create a circle (or line) in which everyone is connected or connected with as few gaps as possible. (or: Using these letters, attempt to connect the entire group in a circle (or line) with as few gaps as possible.)

4. To connect with someone you must share a letter in common. For example, Bryan and Norrie can connect by "sharing" the 'n,' the last letter in the name Bryan and the first letter in the name Norrie – Bryan_Norrie

5. Names can be used spelled backwards. For example, the name Michelle spelled forward can connect with the name Nate spelled backwards, or etaN, by sharing the 'e.' – Michelle_etaN

6. There may be a point where you get stuck, or feel like you are not able to connect the entire group. Think creatively and share your ideas. There are many names and many solutions. Hint: Participants may use middle names, last names, nick names, names in a different language, etc. Do not disclose this information directly but, rather allow for the group to discover the opportunity created by unseen and unspoken solutions.

Reflection/Closure/Discussion

Reflection 1: Creating Community and Building Trust

1. What do you have to say about your experience?

2. Was it easy to find connections with one another?

3. Were there any challenges that arose? What were some of the challenges?

4. How did the group manage these challenges?

5. What does this tell us about our community?

6. How can it help us to continue to build community as we move forward together?

Reflection 2: Creating Community and Building Trust

1. Before beginning the activity, we agreed to practice a particular norm. Do you recall what it was?

2. Was this demonstrated through our behaviors or did a different norm emerge?

3. Is there a particular behavior that we should continue practicing? Are there any behaviors that we should let go of?

4. How can we check in on this in the future?

Reflection 3: Self-Awareness and Self-Management

1. Line up on a spectrum ranging from – the group was very inclusive to – the group was not inclusive at all. Line up on a spectrum ranging from – as an individual I was very inclusive to – I was not inclusive at all.

2. Was there a difference between where you lined up when reflecting on the group's behavior and when reflecting on your own?

3. Line up on a spectrum ranging from: I feel connected to the group to I do not feel connected to the group. Line up on a spectrum ranging from: I stayed connected to the people I connected with early on to I switched many times so that others could connect? Line up on a spectrum ranging from: I was aware and helped others find a connection to the group to I was unaware and did not help others connect.

4. What did staying connected to someone mean for you? How might it have impacted others? How do you feel about this?

5. Line up on a spectrum ranging from: In the future I hope to be more aware of myself to I hope to be more aware of others. Line up on a spectrum ranging from: I hope to be inclusive and care for others to I hope to care for myself and my friends.

Reflection 4: Relationship Skills and Responsible Decision Making

There are times when it seems that one or two participants are left out entirely and the group seems to struggle to find a way to connect these individuals. If this is the case, consider using these questions:

1. How is it going? What's happening right now?

2. If you are connected, how does it feel? If you are not connected, how does it feel? Is this what we desire?

3. Can you think of any other solutions? Who else could you connect with?

4. How could we re-arrange ourselves with these potential solutions so that we are all connected or do we need to let go and move on?

5. What from this experience will help you make responsible decisions in other areas of your life?

Tips and Comments

- For your reference, below is a sample Name Train using the names of some former and current PA trainers. Do you recognize any of the names or remember any of the people?

  Tara_Alison_Nate_esiobmaD_drofwarC_Childs_Suze_eneR_Ryan McCormick_ kecsnjnalK hciR_reteP_Paul_Lisa_Angel Krimm_MB Buckner

- Participants in a group will often connect quickly according to the guide-lines, stand together, and look at the participants who are still not connected. Likewise, participants who are not connected often stand around looking at those who have already connected or each other, feeling, perhaps, left out. If using this activity to meet a particular objective related to being considerate, inclusive, or finding solutions, consider the reflection questions under heading Reflection 2.

Variations

- **Silent Name Trains** – As with many activities that invite participants to line up in a particular manner, consider conducting this activity as a muted activity. In addition to the rules described above, add the rule that no talking is allowed. Feel free to add that no sounds – stomps, claps, groans or even gestures – are allowed. Ask for the group's commitment to the rules and proceed. In fairness, this variation should only be used if the group has a sense of one another's names and is up for the chal-lenge of recalling, trusting, and potentially failing.

- **Visual Name Trains** – For some participants, it may be appropriate to allow the use of name tags, or cards, or the creation of letter cards representing the first and last letters of their names before engaging in the activity. Doing so would place more focus on connections and a bit less on problem solving, although there is likely to be some.

Tips and Comments (continued)

- **Trains** – Instead of names, use cards with the words or pictures of particular content being explored to create "trains." Use the rules above and replace names with the words associated with particular content. This may allow for the opportunity to discuss connections among the actual concepts being used in addition to the challenge of connecting the words.

- **Trains of 2, 3, or 4** – Use Name Trains to form partners or small groups. So instead of participants trying to connect the entire group, they only need to find connections for partnerships or small groups. Below is a sample write-up.

Framing

Say to the group:

"Connections with another person can be tough to come by. When we find them, we often want to keep them. However, there are times when we need to let go of a connection so that we can connect with others. We are going to make connections with each other using our names in a particular way. Consider each other as you make connections."

Procedure

Say to the group:

1. Think about your name.
2. Identify the first and last letter of your name. For example, the first and last letters of Bryan's name are 'B' and 'N.'
3. Using these letters, find a partner you connect with.
4. To connect with someone you must share a letter in common. For example, Bryan and Lucien can connect by "sharing" the 'n,' the last letter in the name Bryan and the first letter in the name Lucien. Bryan_neicuL

Debrief

Say to the group:

1. What do you notice about our group right now? (Most likely, not everyone will be with a partner)
2. How does it feel to have a partner?
3. How does it feel to be without a partner?
4. Are you happy with this situation?
5. What would you like our group to look like?
6. Does anyone have any solutions?
7. Let's try them!

Tips and Comments:

- Most participants in a group will quickly partner according to the guidelines, stand together, and look at the participants still without partners. Likewise, participants without partners often stand around looking at those who have already partnered or each other, feeling, perhaps, left out.

- If using this as a partnering activity, the facilitator may direct/ask participants without partners to pair up. However, if using this activity to meet a particular objective related to being considerate, inclusive, or finding solutions, consider the reflection questions.

Ninja

Overview

An interactive tag game that has gone viral. If you don't know this one, you should or will soon enough. Participants circle up, jump back and prepare to orchestrate their best ninja-inspired moves. With one ninja-like movement, players take turns trying to tag the hand or avoid the tag of another player. Ninja is a FUNN game that most groups initiate after learning how to play!

 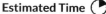
Safety

Monitor for appropriate and safe tags.

Group Size	8 or more, although even 2 people can challenge one another to a Ninja duel
Learning Themes	• Fun and Play • Physical Activity and Movement • Building Trust, Relationships, and Community
Materials / Props	None

Setup

Stand in a circle.

Framing

Say to participants:

"When I shout 'NINJA!', you will assume your most Ninja-inspired position joined by a Ninja state of mind (whatever comes to mind when you hear 'Ninja'!)."

Or:

"Ninjas are best known for their discipline, covert tactics, and stealthy maneuvers. Bring forth a playful Ninja spirit and let's begin Ninja training."

Procedure

1. The goal of the game is to be the last Ninja standing.

2. Tags are sequential, and only one person may attempt a tag at a time.

3. The game starts with everyone in a tight circle. One person shouts, "Ninja!" and everyone shouts their most Ninja-inspired sounds, "Waahh!", while simultaneously jumping backwards, landing in their most Ninja-inspired poses and holding steady.

4. The person who initiated the game may, as the current tagging Ninja, attempt to tag (with his or her hand) the hand of ANYONE in the group. To do so, they must move in one fluid, often Ninja-like, movement. To avoid a tag, a player who has been approached by the tagging Ninja, may defensively move from his or her held position, also in one fluid movement. He or she must then hold whatever new position is assumed.

5. Once the tag attempt has occurred, whether successful or not, the tagger must also hold his or her final position until it is his or her turn to be the tagging Ninja.

6. If a player's hand is tagged by a tagging Ninja, he or she is eliminated from the game.

7. After the tagging Ninja has attempted to make a tag, the person standing to his or her right becomes the new tagging Ninja. Remember, only one person may be the tagging Ninja at a time. This process continues until everyone has been eliminated and there is only one Ninja left.

Reflection/Closure/Discussion

Most groups desire to play Ninja for fun and often initiate their own games once they have learned how to play. While this is often the case, Ninja is a wonderful opportunity to facilitate a Full Value check-in or explore the choices being made during the game.

Tips and Comments

Variations

- Allow both hands to be tagged before being eliminated.
- If a player is eliminated, he or she may start a new game of Ninja with others who have been eliminated.

ONE WORD

Overview

This is a quick and easy brain teaser that challenges participants to think about how they interpret directions. Participants rearrange letters to spell "one word." ONE WORD is a wonderful way to introduce "ah-ha" moments, discovery, and surprise.

Group Size	2 or more
Learning Themes	• Fun and Play • Responsible Decision Making
Materials / Props	Index cards and markers

Setup

The set up is minimal but should be done prior to meeting your group. Write each of the following letters on separate index cards: N W O D E R O (one letter per card). Depending on the size of your group, you may want to create two or more sets.

Framing

The framing is important so be careful and brief. After you've handed out the index cards, simply say, "Using all the letters I've given you, spell ONE WORD."

Procedure:

1. Distribute the index cards with the letters N W O D E R O printed on them.

2. State the directions to the activity, "Using all the letters I've given you, spell ONE WORD."

3. Participants must use each letter. They may only use each letter once and may not add any additional letters.

4. **Solution:** It is impossible to spell one word using these letters, but you can literally spell "ONE WORD"

Reflection / Closure / Discussion

So what have we learned from this? This activity, although fun in itself, addresses an interesting piece of the communication puzzle – how we interpret information. This can be a great jump start to a variety of communication-based discussions from misunderstandings to assumptions and should motivate participants to ask questions, explore multiple view points and ideas, and seek understanding.

Tips and Comments

If a group is struggling to solve this puzzle, it may be helpful to re-state the directions slowly and clearly. You may also ask the group to think about how they are interpreting what you are saying.

Variation

- Include the words "just" or "only" and associated letters to the mix challenging the group to spell either "JUST ONE WORD" or "ONLY ONE WORD."

- Use wooden, plastic, or foam letters instead of index cards.

Partner Get-Up

Overview

A humorous activity leading to profound insights. One person attempts to instruct his or her partner to stand up from a position of laying face down on the ground or floor by communicating effectively. However, this rarely happens easily or well because the person lying down is asked to assume a particular state of having never stood up before in their life and therefore are unable to initiate their own movements and only move according to the specific movements communicated by their partner. If a communicated movement is too general, no movement occurs. Partners exchange feedback and insights and then switch roles. Partner Get-Up provides many significant learning opportunities as indicated in the framing. Take a look!

Group Size	10 or more
Learning Themes	• Self Awareness and Self Management • Social Awareness • Relationship Skills
Materials / Props	None

Setup

Provide an area or clear a space where people are willing and able to lie down on the ground or floor.

Framing

Say to the group:

" We are about to engage in an excellent activity that allows people to focus and explore what they need from one another when they are in either a leader or follower role, how to understand and empathize with other people's needs, how to respond to those needs and what it takes to build a better rapport with one another. Specifically related to one's role as a leader or coach, this activity serves to expand one's awareness of how to increase motivation and productivity for the learner."

Procedure

1. Ask everyone in the group to choose a partner. If the group size is not even in number, a triad can also work well.

2. Ask that one member of the partnership lay on the floor/ground. This person represents the person who is learning or being coached. Ask the other member to start by standing up next to his/her partner. This person represents the leader or coach.

3. The goal of the activity is for the leader (coach) to communicate with the learner (coachee) so that the coachee is able to move from a lying down prone position to a standing position.

4. The learner/coachee is not allowed to initiate any of his/her own behavior during the session, but can do exactly what the coach tells or asks him/her to do.

It is important to emphasize that all people who are being coached should not anticipate and/or exercise movement or action of any kind on their own. Creating an image that the coachee is in an infant state and really does not know how to get up on his or her own helps the coachee not to initiate any of his or her behavior.

5. The coach is asked to give single, clear, uncomplicated instructions about how to get to a standing position. Each individual movement required to get up must be given by the coach on a step-by-step basis – one instruction at a time. Large sweeping instructions like "roll over", "sit up" or "just stand up" are far too broad.

6. Once a coach has been successful in getting the coachee to a standing position, they should change roles and try again.

Reflection/Closure/Discussion

Some key learning points you may want to highlight during the debriefing are:

1. Good coaches/leaders are able to empathize with those whom they are coaching/ leading. An example might be the leader(s) who didn't remain in a standing position once the activity began – the leaders who were willing to also get down on the floor and put themselves in the same body positions throughout the process.

2. What works for the leader doesn't always work for those being led.

3. Pursuance of the issues around when and why to be more directive and using the telling mode versus the when and why of using a more questioning technique. Telling does not allow for following the interest or capability of the learner.

4. Discussion can focus on how empathy is linked to self-awareness, one of the pre-conditions for coaching others.

5. Discussion can link self-awareness with self-responsibility, which in turn leads to motivation and commitment.

Tips and Comments

As the facilitator, you may want/need to walk around the pairs to make any corrections about the rules and observe some of the humor that ensues if not the frustrations that can arise. You may choose to provide some initial help to the partnership(s) but only by asking good coaching questions such as: What are you feeling now? What do you need to do differently? What would help you as a coach or coachee to be able to do this?

Also, as you are walking around, observe the interactions of the various partnerships. Look for examples of effective questioning techniques versus the just telling behaviors. These represent the behaviors you may want to focus on during the debriefing session.

Phonetically Speaking

Overview

A puzzling challenge of discovery that could be ph-rus-tr8-ing and ph-un. Participants discover an emerging message as they attempt to phonetically order specific sounds. Phonetically Speaking is a unique experience involving humorous sounds and interactions, highlighting communication and patience, among other concepts.

Group Size	6 or more
Learning Themes	• Building Trust, Relationships, and Community • Relationship Skills • Responsible Decision Making
Materials / Props	Phonetically Speaking Cards

Setup

Print and prepare Phonetically Speaking Cards. Below is a sample set of cards for the phrase, "Together Everyone Achieves More." We recommend laminating the cards.

too	geth	rrrr	ev	ree	wun

ach	eee	vsss	mmm	or	rrrr

Framing

Say to the group:

> "What we say and how we say it has significant impact on how well we understand each other. We are going to play a game that may demonstrate this for us. The goal is to discover a hidden message by placing yourselves and your respective cards in the correct order."

Procedure

1. Explain that a card will be passed to each person and that they may not look at the card or share it with any group member until the facilitator says so.

2. Randomly distribute one Phonetically Speaking Card to each participant. Remind them not to look at their cards or share them with anyone.

3. State the objective of the game. The goal is for the participants to discover a hidden message by placing themselves and their cards in the correct order. Or "The goal is to discover a hidden message by placing yourselves and your respective cards in the correct order."

4. Communicate the rules:

   a. Participants may **not** share or show their cards to any other group members. Once participants have looked at their cards, recommend that they put them in their pockets or return them to you.

   b. Participants may **only** say the phonetic sound represented on their card and may **not** say anything else.

5. Say, "Go!" and watch the challenge, humor, frustration, and fun unfold!

Reflection/Closure/Discussion

1. Display a face that demonstrates how you felt during this activity.

2. What feelings could you identify in the facial expressions? Did we miss any?

3. How were these feelings expressed and demonstrated during the activity?

4. How did the expression of these feelings affect your interactions as a group? Is this true of daily interactions?

5. How can we best manage our feelings and express them appropriately?

Tips and Comments

Tips

- Passing the cards out in sequential order seems to make the activity a bit less challenging.

- Create your own Phonetically Speaking Cards using short commonly known phrases or sayings. Better yet, have participants create their own Phonetically Speaking Cards to challenge themselves or other groups.

Variations

- Partner or group people if the group size is larger than the number of cards.

- Try the variations below. While the goal remains the same as in the original Phonetically Speaking, the introduction of a slight rule change in each of the following variations shifts the way the participants communicate with each other and ultimately how they achieve the goal.

  - **Phonetically Speaking *and* Seeing** – Participants discover an emerging message as they attempt to phonetically and visually order specific sounds.

    Framing and Objective: "Communication is one key to an effective team and caring community. What we see and hear can greatly impact our interactions and understanding of one another. Let's explore this idea. The goal is to discover a hidden message by placing yourselves and your respective cards in the correct order."

Phonetically Speaking was first published on the High 5 Adventure Learning Center's blog "By the Handful..." on May 20, 2010.

Tips and Comments *(continued)*

Rules:

– Participants may **only** say the phonetic sound represented on their card and may **not** say anything else.

– Participants may look at their own card and share their card with others.

– **Phonetically Speaking *without* Seeing** – Participants discover an emerging message as they attempt to phonetically order specific sounds while blindfolded or with eyes shut.

Framing and Objective: "Communication is one key to an effective team and caring community. What we see and hear can greatly impact our interactions and understanding of one another. Let's explore this idea. The goal is to discover a hidden message by placing yourselves and your respective cards in the correct order."

Rules:

– Participants may **not** share or show their card to any other group members. Once participants have looked at their cards, recommend that they put them in their pockets or return them to you.

– Participants may **only** say the phonetic sound represented on their card and may **not** say anything else.

– Participants must remain blindfolded or with eyes-shut for the duration of the activity.

– **Phonetically *Seeing, But Not Speaking*** – Participants discover an emerging message as they attempt to visually order specific sounds without saying them.

Framing and Objective: "What we see and perceive (think we know) can influence how we interact with each other. We will play a game that may highlight this for us. The goal is to discover a hidden message by placing yourselves and your respective cards in the correct order."

Rules:

– Participants may **not** look at their own card.

– Participants may **not** speak during this activity.

– Just before they begin, participants will place their cards on their foreheads so that other group members can see them.

– **Phonetic Shuffle (aka Foe-net-ick Sh-uh-ph-lll)** – Participants work together to shuffle cards into the correct order while only saying the sounds represented on the cards.

Additional Setup: Randomly scatter the cards face up on the ground, floor, table, or desk.

Framing and Objective: "Look, listen, and discover. That's all you need to know how to be successful in this next activity. The goal is to discover a hidden message by placing the cards in the correct order."

Rules:

– Participants may **only** say the phonetic sound represented on the cards and may **not** say anything else.

Pitball

Overview

A highly interactive blend of dodge ball and speed ball. Players avoid the tag of one or more balls (appropriate for dodge ball) thrown by the person who has possession. The player with possession must adhere to some challenging parameters keeping the game fun, safe, and challenging.

Group Size	10 or more
Learning Themes	• Fun and Play • Physical Activity and Movement • Building Trust, Relationships, and Community
Materials / Props	Dino Skin™ Ball or Beach ball

Setup

Best played in a fenced-in area, pit, or space with walls, but an open space will work as well.

Framing

Say to group:

> "Let's put our Full Value Contract to the test. Better yet, let's play, and then reflect on how we played (or chose to play)."

Procedure

1. Explain that this is a dodge ball kind of game in which anyone can be It when they have possession of the ball or balls.

2. Explain that the object of the game is to be the last person remaining in the game by tagging others with the ball and avoiding the tag of others.

3. State and demonstrate the rules:

   a. Participants may not move (run, walk, crawl, etc.) when they are holding the ball. In order to move, they must put the ball on the ground or floor and may move the ball by hitting it with an open hand only. This includes a gentle tapping he ball back and forth between their hands. Also, they may not pick up the ball from the ground or floor.

   b. Participants may flick the ball in the air with their feet, and then catch it with their hands, before making a throwing tag attempt.

   c. When the ball is in the air, participants may catch it. If it was thrown, the person who threw it is out.

   d. If the ball contacts a person below the shoulders, he or she moves outside of the area of play. Again, participants who catch a ball that is thrown at them eliminate the person who threw it.

   e. The game begins by randomly tossing the ball in the air.

   f. A new game begins after everyone has been eliminated.

Estimated Time

20 minutes, or as long as there is interest!

Safety

- As with any dodge ball activity, ensure that the head is not an acceptable place for a tag.

- Monitor the participants' interactions and conduct safety or Full Value check-ins as needed. Remember that check-ins should include all safety aspects of a person – physical, emotional, social, etc.

Reflection/Closure/Discussion

Say to group:

1. On a spectrum from most to least, line up based on:
2. How fun this game was for you.
3. The action you took to make the game fun for your self and others.
4. How safe you felt playing this game.
5. The action you took to make the game safe for your self and others.
6. What did you learn from these spectra?
7. What is the significance of having a Full Value Contract that we are all committed to?
8. How did our Full Value Contract influence how you played this game?
9. How might our Full Value Contract or your own values influence decisions you make in other settings? Or what influences decisions you make in other settings?

Tips and Comments

Variations

- Add one or more balls, depending on group and space size, to increase action and activity.

- Allow players to move without having to place the ball on the ground, attempting to "dribble" by hitting the ball up and down with their hands. Doing so is a risk as other players may intercept or deflect the ball away to change possession.

- The rules above represent an elimination type of game. To increase participation, risk taking, and supportive behaviors, provide opportunities to return to the game. Check out these ideas:

  1. If a participant is tagged, he or she must move outside the area of play. Participants still engaged in the game may pass a ball to those on the perimeter of play. These players must pass directly back to the person who threw the ball to them. This is simply a way to provide additional options to keep more people involved.

  2. Additionally, if a player on the perimeter of play receives the ball from a player in the play area, he or she may attempt to tag someone still in the area. As in the game, if players in the play area are tagged, they transition to the perimeter of the play area. Also, a person who makes a successful tag from the perimeter of the play area can be allowed to re-enter the game.

  3. A player could also re-enter the game by simply receiving a pass from someone in the play area as described above.

  4. Aside from these ideas, the game can be played in teams of three to five. If a player has been tagged, he or she will still leave the play area, however, if a teammate tosses a ball to them, they may return to the game.

- Consider a framing variation that introduces a twist on competitive play. For example, what if each tag represented a compliment or good deed and the goal was to give as many compliments or good deeds as possible. What would happen to our world?!

Playing with Poppers

Overview

A series of simple and engaging warm-up challenges using poppers. Participants playfully explore poppers creating personal challenges, stunts, and games. Playing with Poppers is a great way to engage a group in whatever is next, most likely another popper-related activity!

Group Size	10 or more
Learning Themes	• Fun and Play • Building Trust, Relationships, and Community • Responsible Decision Making
Materials / Props	1 or 2 Poppers per participant (Poppers are also known as Noodle Bits – soft foam, half-moon shaped pieces)

Setup

Little setup is needed as long as there is adequate space, free of obstacles, in which the group may freely move about.

Framing

Say to group:

"I want to introduce you to something new – the popper. Now in order to use the popper, you're going to need to dedicate some time to skill development and learn proper popper technique."

At this point, demonstrate how the popper works using your index finger and thumb, rounded side facing out. Give the participants some time to practice

Procedure

This activity is relatively loose in structure, allowing participants to learn through exploration. The rules are few and simple. Players must use the proper technique at all times.

Gripping the Popper

- Hold the popper between the thumb, pointer finger and middle finger with the rounded side of the popper facing the space to which you would like it to travel.
- Extend your arm away from your body, keeping it slightly bent.
- Aim the round part toward the space or target.
- Squeeze the popper with both thumb and fingers equally.
- Release the popper toward the space, target or partner.

Once participants have a good sense of basic popping, introduce new challenges such as:

1. Pop with your non-dominant hand.
2. Pop a popper into the air and catch it.
3. Pop two poppers into the air and catch them both.
4. Pop a popper, do a 360, then catch it.

Once participants appear to be ready to move on, introduce some partner or small group challenges such as:

1. A simultaneous popper exchange
2. A long distance pop
3. Popping through the legs or over the head

Try a popper swat. One partner pops a popper at his or her partner who swats it back with an open hand. The original partner tries to catch it.

Ask participants to work with their partners to come up with their best, most challenging popper trick.

In conclusion, ask students to showcase their best partner challenge to the entire group.

Reflection / Closure / Discussion

None necessary

Tips and Comments

- Given the loose structure of the activity, it works well if you, the facilitator, immerse yourself in the play as well. Doing so adds value and models a playful approach. Get the play started, but don't overdo it. Allow your participants to explore, discover, share and shine!

- Direct partners to join another pair to form a group of four. Invite small groups to continue playing with and exploring the use of poppers creating more challenges, stunts, and games suitable for four players or more! If the numbers don't work out, don't worry, a group of five or six can work too.

Pogo Stick Tag

Overview:

An exciting twist on the game of tag that gets everyone hopping around. Participants play tag with a partner while pretending to be on a... pogo stick! Pogo Stick Tag most often leads to humorous exhaustion, like rolling on the ground laughing, as people discover the creativity, comedy, and fun that emerges by engaging in this activity.

Group Size	10 or more
Learning Themes	• Fun and Play • Physical Activity and Movement • Building Trust, Relationships, and Community • Responsible Decision Making
Materials / Props	None

Setup

Creatively separate the group into pairs. See ideas on page 299.

Framing

Say to the group:

"Here's a chance to exhaust not only your body, but also your creative humor."

Or:

"Would you be up for playing a traditional game of tag with a twist? I will explain the basic rules and then add the twist."

Or:

"How long do you think you can hop around on one foot? Let's try it for a minute. Okay, let's play with that movement. The longer you hop, the longer you'll last."

Procedure

1. Explain to the players that they will be playing a tag game with just their partners, yet among everyone else.

2. Ask each pair to choose one player between themselves to be IT.

3. Explain the rules:

   a. The Its chase and tag their own partners.

   b. When a player is tagged he or she becomes It, but before chasing their partner, he or she must spin around once.

4. Convey the twist of playing pairs tag as if everyone were on a pogo stick. For example, you might say, "Now, most tag games are played by running. There is no running in this game. Instead envision yourself playing tag on a pogo stick." Demonstrate by jumping or hopping around as if you are on a pogo stick, then yell, "Go!"

5. As the game goes on, feel free to encourage participants to play as if they were on a mini pogo stick, or giant stick for that matter, and watch the creativity and laughter unfold.

Reflection/Closure/Discussion

1. On a scale of 0-5, use your fingers to show how fun this game was.
2. On a scale of 0-5, use your fingers to show how creative you were while playing this game.
3. How does our creativity or lack of creativity impact our experience?
4. What does it take to be creative or humorously creative?
5. Are their times in your life when you are creative? Are there times when you are not so creative? Which do you prefer?
6. What is one thing you can do to be more creative in your life?

Tips and Comments

Pogo Stick Tag requires confidence and committed acting on the part of the facilitator to portray the concept of playing tag on an imaginary pogo stick as an appealing idea. A good sell will most likely result in humorous engagement, lots of interaction and laughter, and eventually physical exhaustion, both from movement and laughter. If you are ready to present this game with humor and confidence, go for it. If not, play something else until you build up the courage.

Variations

*   **Pogo Stick Tag Squared** – As with the activity Pairs Tag, there is a variation in which two players link arms and play tag with another pair also linked at the arm. This variation is called Pairs Squared. So, now why not play Pairs Squared with the twist of being on a pogo stick together? Help the participants find a partner. Direct them to link arms at the elbow and stand near another pair doing the same. Explain that the two pairs of people standing next to each other will be playing tag exclusively with each other as individuals did in Pogo Stick Tag above. The twist now being that each pair of people must hop around as if they are on a pogo stick together. Now, I'm sure the participants will experience everything from awe-inspiring synchronized movement to uncoordinated collapsing collisions. Be safe and have fun!

Power Ball

Overview

A physically active field game inspired by the American Gladiators event by the same name. Multiple offensive teams play either competitively against or cooperatively with one another, while attempting to score points against one defending team. Power Ball is a demanding activity that engages most groups and is perfect for, although not limited to, very athletic groups. It provides insights into topics of significance such as competition and cooperation, bullying, and personal effort in general.

Group Size	10 or more
Learning Themes	• Fun and Play • Physical Activity and Movement • Building Trust, Relationships, and Community • Responsible Decision Making
Materials / Props	• Mass Pass Deluxe Kit (Plastic Buckets, Foam Balls, Webbing, Stop Watch). • Pinnies

Safety

Participants should be made aware that other participants, on both offensive teams and the defensive team, will be moving in multiple directions and could abruptly change direction to avoid a tag, score a point, or return to the safe/start zone. Participants should be prepared to avoid collisions and care for self and others.

Setup

There are a variety of setups depending on the group size and goals. In general, place four or five buckets within a square boundary or triangular boundary (if three teams). Use rope or webbing to create the square or triangle. Consider the rope or webbing to be the start line. The area within the start line (inside the square or triangle) is called the scoring zone, while the area outside the start line (or outside the square or rectangle) is called the safe zone. See setup variations below.

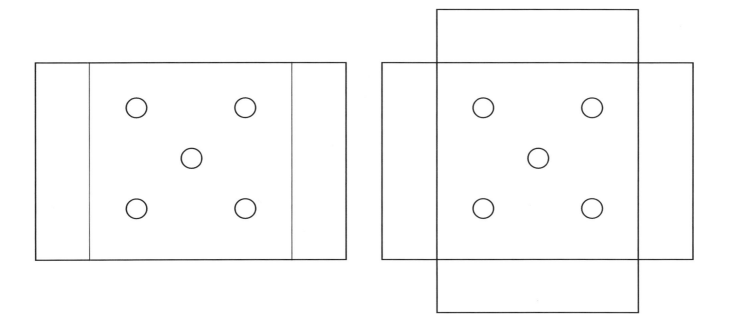

Framing

Co-opetition

Say to the group:

"As offensive teams, consider yourselves one department with multiple sub-teams. Your task is to score as many points as possible and work toward continuous improvement over the course of three rounds. Before each round, each offensive team will have time to develop and revise a strategy for completing the task. The defending team should develop and revise a strategy for limiting the number of points scored."

Bullying

Say to the group:

"Have you ever felt attacked or bullied by others in your community? Have you considered a way that you and others could work together to keep each other safe? Or if having a plan or strategy would be effective when managing bullies? During this activity, some of you will function as teams of bullies, while others will function as teams of people defending the bullies. Consider the offensive teams to be bullies and the foam balls, bully-like actions or statements. (Have the group record bully-like actions and statements on tape and attach to the foam balls.) Consider the defending team to be community members who have organized to prevent the bullies from harming the community (represented by the buckets) with their actions and statements (foam balls). (Have the group record people or places most likely to be affected by bullies.) The bullies (offensive teams) will attempt to affect the community as much as possible (get as many foam balls in the buckets as possible) while the community members (defending team) will attempt to prevent as much harm as possible."

Procedure

1. Separate participants into three teams – two offensive teams and one defensive team. Provide pinnies to the defensive team.

2. The two offensive teams begin in one of two safe/start zones. The participants of the defensive team begin any where in the tag zone.

3. State the goal. On a Go signal, both offensive teams attempt to score as many points as possible by placing a foam ball/object into one of five bins placed within a tag zone.

4. Explain the rules:

    a. Neither bins nor boundaries may be moved.

    b. Defenders may prevent scoring by tagging participants on either offensive team.

    c. If a participant of an offensive team is tagged or steps outside the boundary, he or she must return, and may return with the foam ball/object, to a safe zone before attempting to score.

    d. Any object that ends up on the ground/floor during play must be retrieved and returned to a safe zone by an offensive player before being deposited in a bin.

5. Play three rounds, two to three minutes each. Rotate teams so that each team has two turns in an offensive role and one in the defensive role.

Reflection/Closure/Discussion

Co-opetition

1. What strategies (either offensive or defensive) were developed? Were there strategies that seemed more effective than others? What made these strategies more effective?

2. How were strategies developed? What determined whether a strategy would be used or not?

3. When was it discovered that the offensive teams could work together? Did this discovery influence your strategies or process to develop a strategy?

Bullying

1. What behaviors did you observe from both offensive (bullies) and defensive (community members) teams?

2. How did these behaviors influence the culture of the game?

3. What strategies were developed to defend the buckets (community people and places)? Were any strategies more effective than others? What made these strategies more effective?

4. In small groups of four, reflect on bully behavior and statements written on the foam balls, then discuss and record a strategy for dealing with (managing) these behaviors and statements. Be prepared to share with the rest of the larger group.

Tips and Comments

Additional Framing Ideas

- **Bucket Fillers** – This variation offers a completely different framing and perspective on bullying. Instead of the offensive team representing bullies and the defenders representing allies, consider a new metaphor. In this framing, the offensive team represents people who are practicing being bucket fillers as described in the book *Have You Filled a Bucket Today?* by Carol McCloud, and the defenders represent the obstacles that get in the way of filling our own or other people's buckets. A significantly related debrief could follow along with a reading of, and reflection on, the book. This framing is wonderfully loaded. Thanks to a PA Physical Education Health and Wellness Institute (or PEHWI and affectionately known as "pee-wee") group and their trainer who shared this little nugget of insight!

- Offensive team is a disease; defensive team is immune system/white blood cells. How many people are needed to build our immune system to effectively reduce the likelihood or prevent disease? What can we do to build our actual immune systems?

- Team sports: What qualities make up an effective offense? What qualities make up an effective defense?

Variations

- One's the Limit – While there is no rule stating how many balls each player may possess at a time, you may desire to limit players to one ball at a time. There seem to be benefits and limitations either way. Choose what seems right for your group, setting, and however you like to play.

Press Conference

Overview

A playful icebreaker in which participants enter a frantic press conference looking for information. Participants quickly "interview" their neighbors, then report out. Press Conference is a quick way to learn about group members with the potential for significant subtleties to surface.

Group Size	8 or more
Learning Themes	• Building Trust, Relationships, and Community • Self Awareness and Self Management • Social Awareness
Materials / Props	It is possible to do this activity without props; however, it is much more exciting and easier to retain information if each participant has a writing utensil and a piece of paper.

Setup

Invite participants to gather in a circle and greet their neighbors. Pass paper and pencils to each participant.

Framing

Say to the group:

"In a moment, you are going to have the opportunity to join a press conference during which you will be charged with getting the inside scoop on a particular person attending the conference. This conference, however, is only going to last two minutes. As challenging as it may be, you'll have to get to know this person and be ready to report back later."

Procedure

1. During the two-minute round, participants attempt to gather as much information from one another as possible and write it down (or remember it).

2. Possible questions include:

    - Favorite food, place, or joke
    - Number of siblings
    - Favorite activity or sport
    - Name, middle or last
    - Street name
    - Any pets
    - Nicknames

3. Wait until you start the timer before you announce who each person will be interviewing.

4. When the timer starts, instruct participants to begin interviewing the person directly to their left.

5. Once two minutes is up say, "Stop!"

6. Ask a volunteer to introduce their interviewee and give the group their story too. Continue with other introductions until everyone has had a chance to introduce the person whom they interviewed. Or provide another minute or two to gather more information and then facilitate introductions and reports.

Reflection/Closure/Discussion

This activity is typically used as an icebreaker and usually does not require much reflection or debrief. By its very nature, however, Press Conference, as with any activity, may organically spark significant dialogue. Often times, participants willingly volunteer how they felt during the activity or that they were concerned that they might misrepresent or provide misinformation about the person whom they interviewed. Be prepared to acknowledge and process this information as needed.

Tips and Comments

- **Press Conference Free-for-all** – Instead of playing in the format of a circle, give your group free reign to find out as much as they can about each other in two minutes and let them run wild! After chaos ensues, pause to listen to some reports and send participants on another reporting mission to frantically gather more information.

- **Press Conference Debrief** – Press Conference makes for a great debrief as well. Provide a few simple debrief questions or prompts and jump into the game!

Quick Math

Estimated Time

10 – 20 minutes

Overview

A de-inhibitizer, quick response game that allows group members to take some risks, make some mistakes and appear inept in front of others – all in good humor. Quick Math also serves as an interactive activity geared to learn/review the four basic math operations. Above all else, it is fun. Play on!

Group Size	6 to 20
Learning Themes	• Fun and Play • Building Trust, Relationships, and Community • Self Awareness and Management • Responsible Decision Making
Materials / Props	None

Setup

Begin with the group standing in a circle. Clear sufficient space as needed.

Framing

Say to the group:

> "How do you feel about math? Are you aware of how you feel when you answer a question correctly or incorrectly? Are you aware of how feelings may influence how we act or behave? Have you noticed the impact of your behaviors – positive or negative? Let's play a game requiring basic math skills and see what turns up."

Procedure

1. Begin the activity with you, the facilitator, standing in the center of the circle to model the role of this player.

2. Explain that, as the person in the center of the circle, you will point to someone in the circle and call out two numbers that are to be added together such as 8 and 9. The person you pointed to then ducks or bends downward.

3. The participants who are standing to the immediate left and right of the person you pointed to must shout out the answer (17) as quickly as possible. When shouting out the answer, they point to each other.

4. The person who points most quickly with the correct answer wins. The person who did not win, or lost, now assumes the role of the person in the center of the circle.

5. Tell the group that they will play with addition only and the use of single digit numbers – 0,1,2,3,4,5,6,7,8,9 – to start. Add ideas from the variations section below to enhance the game.

6. Play the first four to five rounds while the facilitator remains in the center of the circle providing an opportunity for participants to get used to the game while also setting the pace.

Reflection/Closure/Discussion

Feelings

1. What feelings were you aware of when you answered correctly? What feelings were you aware of when you answered incorrectly or slower than another person?

2. How did you act, perhaps, because of these feelings?

3. Have you noticed whether these behaviors have impacted your life or those around you in the past?

4. Have you experienced this before?

5. Are these desirable outcomes for you?

6. What will you do now that you have acknowledged this?

Resiliency

If some players find themselves answering incorrectly more often than not, there may be an opportunity to explore what it takes to stay committed and remain as players even when they are more often wrong than right. The questions above regarding feelings may lead you there, especially the questions later in the sequence. Overall, it may provide an opportunity to further explore resiliency and the power that it can offer an individual and a community.

Risk Taking

1. How would you describe this game to a friend?

2. Would you say there was any risk involved? Share some examples.

3. What did you personally do to commit to the perceived risk?

4. What might that mean as we journey together or in your life specifically?

5. Are there areas in your life in which you would like to take more risks? Think of a few and share with a partner.

Tips and Comments

- Consider separating larger groups into two or more smaller groups to increase participation and interaction.

- Celebrate delays, mistakes, failures, and losses. Perhaps, a round of applause or a special cheer. If you are familiar with Benjamin Zander's presentation on the Art of Possibility on Ted.com, you might offer an uplifting, call of "How fascinating!" indicating that you are letting go and moving on.

Variations

- **Change the Operation** – Play multiple rounds with addition as the only operation option. Then change the operation to one of the following: subtraction, multiplication, or division. Now the person in the center points to someone in the circle and shouts either "add," "subtract," "multiply," or "divide."

- **Use Any Operation** – Play as described above in Change the Operation, however, once the group has proven their skill in one operation or the other, or just before the game becomes boring, invite the person in the center to choose from any of the operations – addition, subtraction, multiplication, division.

- **Spinning the Consequence** – Play any of the variations above with a slight change of rules. It seems that with games such as this, it is often the result of being slow, making a mistake, or failing that earns a player entry to the role in the center of the circle. Let's spin it! This time whoever points first and responds correctly, or wins, replaces the person in the center. Not every group will present such motivational behavior, but some will and you can offer this variation to them. Lucky you!

- **Math Sentences** – Instead of saying two numbers followed by a specific operation, invite callers to point at someone standing in the center of the circle and state a math sentence such as $7 + 5$. The participants who are standing to the immediate left and right of the person pointed at must shout out the answer (12) as quickly as possible. Depending on the type of play, the person who either won or lost enters the center of the circle.

- **Multi-step Math** – Ready? 5 plus 6 minus 7 times 4 divided by 4 times 10 equals...40. You got it! Oh, but the person you pointed at didn't. "How fascinating! (Applaud)" They are now in the center! If you didn't see it coming or didn't follow that brief exercise, allow participants to call multiple steps to be solved.

- **Multiple Callers** – As the game and group advances, and to add a bit of controlled chaos and confusion to the mix, invite more than one person into the center of the circle to call. Keep adding people to the center to add intensity until the game folds under the pressure of its own fun!

- **Racing The Wave** – Play a standard version of Quick Math; however, invite participants to race players beyond their initial challenger. To play this variation, the person in the center of the circle points at one person and calls two numbers and an operation or a math sentence to be solved. The person who was pointed at ducks, while the players on his or her immediate right or left race to point first and answer correctly. The player who points first and responds correctly remains standing while the person who was slower to respond or incorrect ducks or sits. The center person then calls another set of numbers and operation or math sentence for the previous winner and the next person in the circle on the losing side race to point and answer. Continue playing until the "wave" makes its way around the circle. Playfully, you could see which side of the circle, Team A or Team 1, has made more progress than the other. Likewise, an individual player could determine how many times he or she answered correctly. Play this variation as a culminating version.

Rock, Paper, Scissors Baseball

Estimated Time 🕐

5 – 10 minutes

Safety

- When running the bases, encourage players to move at a speed appropriate to greeting other players, to avoid collisions and ensure that the fun of the game will continue.

- Some groups have been changing the traditional language of Rock, Paper, Scissors from "Rock, Paper, Scissors, shoot" to "Rock, Paper, Scissors, show" in an effort to use language less associated with guns. Determine what is appropriate and works best for your site.

Overview

A fun take on America's pastime. A player form each team runs bases, one in the typical direction (counter clockwise) and the other in the opposite, atypical direction (clockwise). When players meet, a match of Rock Paper Scissors determines who advances. Rock Paper Scissors Baseball invites players to practice good sportsmanship, alertness, and support of others. Easy to learn and a blast to play!

Group Size	10 or more
Learning Themes	• Fun and Play • Physical Activity and Movement • Building Trust, Relationships, and Community
Materials / Props	4 spot markers or bases

Setup

Set up spot markers or bases in a traditional baseball diamond shape (size may vary). Creatively divide your group into two teams.

Framing

Say to the group:

"We are going to play a unique game of baseball in which Rock Paper Scissors determines who scores a run and who doesn't. You have to pay attention because the game can change at any moment."

Or:

"Baseball can be a stressful game. It requires great focus, precision, and the ability to let go and move on. It is also a game that requires the team to support individual efforts. We will have the chance to practice all of this while we play a game of baseball with a twist."

Procedure

1. Invite both teams to home plate to review the rules of Rock, Paper, Scissors. Start with the hand motions – a fist is "rock," flat palm is "paper" and two fingers out (like a peace sign) is "scissors." Two people face off, count to three then show one of the symbols. Remind players that Rock beats Scissors, Scissors beat Paper, and Paper beats Rock. If both players show the same symbol, they try again until someone wins. Play a few matches to ensure that everyone is familiar with Rock Paper Scissors.

2. The game is played with both teams trying to score runs at the same time. One player from each team begins at home plate and begins to run the bases, one in the typical, counter clockwise direction and the other in the opposite atypical, clockwise direction.

3. When players meet, they greet in some engaging manner such as a high ten and then play a match of Rock Paper Scissors.

4. The winner advances, while the person who did not win runs directly to home plate to high ten the next runner on their team. This runner then begins running the bases in his or her team's direction.

5. Play continues in this manner until a run is scored (which is harder than you think) or when a pre-determined number of runs or time has occurred.

6. Play additional games as time allows.

Reflection/Closure/Discussion

1. What reactions did you notice while playing Rock Scissors Baseball?

2. Did you notice any moments of focus or lack of focus? How did that affect your team?

3. What have you learned about being focused in stressful situations?

4. What is one area in your life where you would like to be more focused? What will you do to make that happen? What support do you need?

Tips and Comments

Players should be encouraged to cheer for everyone and the love of the game.

Variations:

- **Play with the Prime** – Playing with the prime, the ritual used to get players into sync with each other so they can deliver their throws simultaneously, (e.g., "Rock Paper Scissors – Shoot" or "1, 2, 3,") could increase the energy and engagement of the activity and add more fun to the game. For more information on Rock Paper Scissors, go to http://www.worldrps.com. Examples of alternative primes:

- Ta-Da! – Participants hop left and right to the rhythm and sound of "Ta-Da (left), Ta-Da (right), Ta-Da (left) Ta-Da (right) Ta-Da (left), Shoooooooooooow!"

- Bunny Hop – Participants step left and right, finishing with three hops as in the Bunny Hop. An example may be, step right right, step left left, step right, step left, hop hop hop (forward), Whoooooooooooaaaaa! (show)

- Rocky/Eye of the Tiger – Similar to above, participants hop to the beat of the song Eye of the Tiger. Bant (left), bant (back) bant (right) bant (front), bant (left) bant (back) bant (right), bant (front) bant (back) bomb (front).

- Beyond these energizing prime variations, acknowledge and appreciate that the prime through different countries and regions around the world are different. Learning and using the local prime, wherever you may be, typically engages the participants further resulting in their feeling recognized and accepted. Beyond this, when playing with people from different countries, regions, and cultures acknowledging that everyone may have different primes, timing and language, and that before each match players should determine how best to play with each other subtly introduces the topic of diversity and social justice. Subtle yet great potential for profound dialogue!

- **Heel-Toe Running** – While running makes this game exciting, changing the way players run the bases makes the game humorous and fun. Instruct players to connect their heel to their toe when "running" the bases. In addition to the silliness that ensues, this variation is a great alternative for a small or indoor space.

- **Which Team Am I On?** – Play Rock Paper Scissors Baseball as described above, however, when a player loses a match have them join the opposing team. The goal now is to not only to score runs but to acquire as many players from the other team as possible.

- **Rock Paper Scissors Baseball (Alternate Version)** – This version involves more consistent activity from all players and may be a better choice if the goal is physical activity and movement.

  - Separate your group into two teams.

  - Players from each team face off at home plate. Winners of either team run to first base where they face off with a winning player from the opposite team who also advanced to first base. Winning players advance to second base to play other winning players. This pattern continues around the baseball diamond.

  - Players who do not win at any point in the game remain where they are and play others who also did not win at that location. As noted above, winners continue to advance to play other winners, while those who do not win remain where they are until they win a match.

  - Players who win advance to the next bases and eventually score runs for their team. It may be helpful or not to keep track of runs scored.

Rock, Paper, Scissors Championship

Overview

This quick and simple activity is a great way to energize a group, and create an atmosphere of support. The entire group pairs off to play Rock Paper Scissors. The winning player or team of each match continues, while the other becomes the winner's biggest fan. Rock Paper Scissors Championship invites players to practice playfulness, good sportsmanship, resiliency, and support of others. It's a joy to play regardless of the outcome!

Safety

Some groups have been changing the traditional language of Rock, Paper, Scissors from "Rock, Paper, Scissors, *shoot*" to "Rock, Paper, Scissors, *show*" in an effort to use language less associated with guns. Determine what is appropriate and works best for your group.

Group Size	20 or more, ideal for groups of 40 plus!
Learning Themes	• Fun and Play • Building Trust, Relationships, and Community
Materials / Props	None

Setup

Gather the group into a circle while directions are given.

Framing

Say to the group:

"We are going to have a contest to see who among us is the champion of Rock Paper Scissors. When it's all said and done, there will be one clear winner and one clear winning team!"

Or:

"Have you heard of the phenomenon that's buzzing around the world? There are Rock Paper Scissors Championships happening everywhere. Rumor has it that the circuit is looking for some strong teams to join the tourney. They are looking for people with playful spirits, resilient character, and positive energy. Do you have what it takes? Let's play and find out!"

Procedure

1. Review the rules of Rock, Paper, Scissors. Start with the hand motions – a fist is "rock," flat palm is "paper" and two fingers out (like scissors) is "scissors." Two people face off, count to three and show one of the symbols. Here is how you win – Rock beats Scissors, Scissors beat Paper, and Paper beats Rock. If both people show the same symbol, they try again until someone wins.

2. The tournament will start with everyone finding a partner and playing one round of Rock, Paper, Scissors.

3. When someone wins the round, he or she moves on to play someone else. The other person then becomes their biggest fan. This person stands behind the 'winner' and chants their name – the more exuberantly the better.

4. Those who win continue to find other competitors to play, while those who lose join the other person's fan club.

5. Eventually, there should be two people left in the tournament. At this point, the chanting may be chaotic, and it can be fun to stop the action, and make a presentation of the last two people playing and their fan clubs.

6. Once you declare a champion, you can play additional rounds as time allows.

Reflection / Closure / Discussion

1. How did it feel to support others in the group?

2. Were you able to let go of your "loss" and be genuinely supportive of someone else?

3. How did it feel to be supported?

4. Which role did you like best?

Tips and Comments

- Given that this is a "pro" Rock Paper Scissors Championship, there is no trash talking. Participants may only cheer for and positively encourage the team they are on or whom they support!

- If using the first framing where there will be "one clear winner and one clear winning team," the winning team, when you consider the rules of the game, is your entire group. Celebrate accordingly!

- Be aware that in the actual championship match, the final two participants could have high social and emotional stakes. Be prepared to have an energizing finish to bring the entire group back together. For example, you could reinforce that there is one winning team, and that winning team should follow you in a victory lap. Arms stretch out like wings of an airplane running around shouting and eventually re-forming a circle.

Variations

- **Playing with the Prime** (Footnote: The Prime is the ritual used to get players into sync with each other so they can deliver their throws simultaneously. For more information on Rock Paper Scissors go to http://www.worldrps.com/)– "Rock Paper Scissors – Shoot" or "1, 2, 3," – could increase the energy and engagement of the activity. Examples of alternative counts:

  - Ta-Da! – Participants hop left and right to the rhythm and sound of "Ta-Da (left), Ta-Da (right), Ta-Da (left) Ta-Da (right) Ta-Da (left), Shoooooooooooow!"

  - Bunny Hop – Participants step left and right, finishing with three hops as in the Bunny Hop. An example may be, step right right, step left left, step right, step left, hop hop hop (forward), Whoooooooooooaaaaa! (show)

  - Rocky/Eye of the Tiger – Similar to above, participants hop to the beat of the song Eye of the Tiger. Bant (left), bant (back) bant (right) bant (front), bant (left) bant (back) bant (right), bant (front) bant (back) bomb (front).

- Beyond these energizing prime variations, acknowledging and appreciating that primes through different countries and regions around the world are different. Some have more or less pumps to the prime while others use different languages. Learning and using the local prime, wherever you may be, typically engages the participants further, resulting in their feeling recognized and accepted. Beyond this, when playing with people from different countries, regions, and cultures acknowledging that everyone may have different primes, timing and language, and that before each match, players should determine how best to play with each other subtly introduces the topic of diversity and social justice. Subtle yet great potential for profound dialogue!

- **Rock Paper Scissors Team Championship** – While Rock, Paper, Scissors Championship is somewhat oriented toward the individual with support from other individuals, adding a simple rule changes the focus from individuals to team. Play Rock, Paper, Scissors Championship as described above with the winning player continuing to be the main player, the person who throws Rock Paper Scissors in a match with another winning individual. The twist here is to require this player to briefly consult their group and determine as a team which symbol (Rock Paper Scissors) to throw. So, just before the next match, instruct the winning players about to face off to quickly and collectively decide with their respective teams what they, the person who has not lost a match yet, should throw. Doing so slows the game down just a bit, but playfully introduces decision making and more connection to the results of each match. Whether a team wins or loses, everyone contributed to the results.

Shake It Up

Estimated Time

20 minutes

Overview

A quick problem-solving activity, literally! Participants attempt to shake hands with everyone in the group as quickly as they can. Shake It Up is a great activity for introducing problem solving, goal setting, and an overall good time!

Group Size	8 – 30
Learning Themes	• Self Awareness and Self Management • Relationship Skills • Responsible Decision Making
Materials / Props	None

Setup

Provide enough open space for quick movements, or running around, depending on the variation that you choose.

Framing

Say to the group:

> "How quickly can you shake hands with someone in this group? Try it! Go! Now how long do you think it would take for everyone to shake hands with everyone else? You never know unless you try. After trying once, you may have a better idea of what an appropriate goal for the group would be."

Procedure

1. Inform your group that the goal of the activity is to shake hands with everyone in the group as quickly as they can.

2. Explain that the challenge is to do so while observing the following rules:

   a. Each person must shake hands with all group members at least once.

   b. The event is timed. Time begins when you, the facilitator say, "Go!" Time stops when the final handshake has occurred and the entire group or at least one person in the group says, "Stop!"

   c. There are three to five trials to refine possible solutions, set goals (as needed) and achieve the best time.

   d. Planning, preparing, and practicing may occur between trials.

3. Check for understanding of the goal and rules, and then direct the group to begin.

Reflection/Closure/Discussion

1. Did you meet your goal?

2. What allowed for your success? Or not?

3. Have you worked toward personal goals in ways that are similar or different from the ways you worked during this activity? What has been similar and what has been different?

4. What did you learn from your experience with this activity that might be helpful when working toward any goal?

Tips and Comments

Variations

- Add an element of running to the challenge by providing a start/finish line and an area defined as the "shaking space," where players must perform all of their handshaking action before returning to the start line. Players would then begin behind the start/finish line. On a start signal, everyone would be required to run to the shake space, approximately fifty feet away, shake hands, and then run back to the start/finish line. Time begins on the start signal and ends when the last person crosses the start/finish line.

- Likewise, start participants standing in a circle on spot markers. On a start signal, players would move within the circle of spot makers to shake hands before returning to their original spot marker. Time begins on the start signal and ends when the last person returns to their spot.

Sneak Attack (a.k.a. Collaborate or Perish)

Overview

A uniquely engaging, problem-solving activity reminiscent of Red Light Green Light. A group attempts to snatch a rubber chicken, or another enticing object, from behind the back of a watchful guardian. When the guardian turns, everyone must freeze, or all are sent back to the starting line. Once obtained, the bird or object must be strategically carried back to the starting line without the guardian noticing. Sneak Attack involves the retrieval of an enticing object, evokes primal stalking and hunting skills, elicits positive peer pressure, and guarantees highly-engaged giddy fun.

Group Size	12 persons
Learning Themes	• Fun and Play • Self Awareness and Self Management • Relationship Skills • Responsible Decision Making
Materials / Props	• 1 rubber chicken or some other enticing object, e.g., a unique stuffed animal, a bell, or even your car keys all seem to work well. • 1 30-foot length of rope or whatever works to establish a starting line • 1 spot marker

Setup

- Direct participants to stand behind a starting line in a group of 5-15.

- Place the enticing object of choice on a spot marker 20 to 60 feet or more from the starting line, depending on physical space available.

- As the facilitator, assume the role of monitor or 'guardian' and stand with your back to participants on the far side of the chosen object. Eventually this role may be passed on to a few participants in the group.

Framing

Say to the group:

"Have you ever wondered how the human species ascended to the top of the food chain despite our comparatively scrawny physique, lack of retracting claws, propensity to drown after a few minutes under water, and challenge to fly when dropped from high places? Well, this activity will tune you on to our evolutionary secret (whispered): An extraordinary ability to collaborate on the hunt. Yes, by working together we were – and still are – able to run down any of the tasty ruminating mammals grazing our planet. In this activity, you will work on this essential stalking skill – a skill that also has many modern urban applications. For instance, have you ever attempted to sneak up and surprise a friend only to be foiled by others too restless or clumsy to creep with the same stealth? To succeed in the hunt and this activity 'Sneak Attack' you need to be not just 'sneaky', but able to coach, persuade and otherwise infuse your teammates with a commitment to practice this survival skill. Play the game and hone your skills for a congenial sneak-up prank on a buddy, an exotic hunting vacation to a remote indigenous game reserve, or perhaps (hopefully not) a grim post-apocalyptic world in which you'll be competing with other desperate humanoids to propagate in an ever dwindling gene pool."

Or:

"Consider yourself a pack of coyotes. Go ahead – give a loud, howling cry. Now, I am the guardian of this chicken and sadly the coyotes (all of you) have taken all but one chicken of my precious flock. I refuse to let this chicken go easily. In some cultures, the coyote is considered a great trickster and teacher and, as a pack of coyotes, you will have to discover a way to trick me while learning from your experiences regardless of how successful it is. I have learned a lot from many coyotes like you and it will likely take more than one trick to trick me!"

Or:

"Has anyone played Red Light/Green Light before? What are some of your memories? This game is similar to Red Light/Green Light but with a significant twist. Here's how we play."

Procedure

Tell participants that their task is to capture the chicken, poised on a spot marker and guarded by a guardian, and then to carry it back behind the group starting line.
As the group sneaks up to obtain the chicken, the guardian may turn around at any time. Everyone must then freeze (as in Red Light/Green Light). If anyone in the group is caught moving by the guardian, the entire group must begin again. The guardian is the judge of movement and his or her decision cannot be contested. Rules are:

1. Everyone in the group must touch the chicken before it arrives behind the start line.
2. The chicken has no feathers and therefore cannot fly (must be handed not tossed).
3. The group may discuss strategy behind the start line and between their setbacks.
4. Once the chicken is captured, the guardian continues to turn causing participants to freeze. While frozen, the guardian gets one or two guesses as to who they believe has the chicken. When the guardian points or calls out a name, the accused must toss their arms in the air (opportunity for drama) to reveal whether or not they have the chicken. If it is seen by the guardian, it is returned to the guardian's 'chicken spot'.
5. The guardian may not walk around to gain a better vantage point in search of the chicken.
6. The chicken may be shielded by bodies but not concealed under or within clothing.
7. After the chicken has been obtained (meaning touched but not yet retrieved), participants are no longer obliged to return to start line due to movement infractions or lost bird. If participants fail to freeze during this 'retreat' phase, the chicken returns to the spot but participants need not return to the start line. That said, concealing the chicken is more the objective than the freeze.
8. Participants self-monitor to assure that everyone touches the chicken before it lands behind the start line.
9. Once the group succeeds, play another round allowing one or two participants to become guardians while the facilitator joins the group (or helps others get started if group size demands more than one game).

10. See Tips and Comments below regarding advice for guardians as well as comments pertaining to the activity as a whole.

Reflection / Closure / Discussion

Ask participants:

1. What made this so much fun?

2. What strategies emerged as effective or ineffective?

3. How did you respond to setbacks? (Responses might include negative behaviors such as complaining about the guardian and blaming each other for setbacks, etc.)

Ask the participants who assumed the role of monitor/guardian:

4. If you were monitor/guardian, how did you decide on the level of challenge you would give participants?

5. How well did you use the planning opportunity between setbacks or rounds?

6. If you were coached by the group to slow down or otherwise adjust your behavior, how did you receive their feedback?

7. What are a few guidelines for giving and receiving feedback?

8. What important team concepts emerged? (Individual accountability to the team effort is typically a prevalent theme as one person can interfere with success.)

Tips and Comments

- Use your judgment regarding how quickly and frequently to turn when in the role of guardian. Challenging the group and suspense are important so vary your pace and be quick enough to catch someone moving. Sending players back at least a few times forces them to adjust strategy and make behavioral adjustments. That said, avoid making it so difficult that they never attain the bird. Consider using a verbal cue, such as "one fish, two fish, red fish, blue fish" before turning around, especially with younger participants.

- Consider sending individual players, rather than the whole team, back to the start when caught moving by the guardian. This varies the challenge and serves as a great introductory round.

- Have two participants serve side-by-side as guardians after you have modeled the role. This allows more people to experience this role and forces some entertaining coordination. Continue to swap roles with successive rounds.

- When in the role of guardian, knowing names to call out is helpful and better than pointing. Calling out individual infractions in the presence of the group supports development of a safe and trusting team setting in which mistakes are allowed and treated as learning (vs. shaming) opportunities.

- Suggest that players try out different roles round to round.

- This is a very effective activity for handing responsibility to the group for game control usually reserved for the facilitator. The authority associated with guardian feels like being teacher/boss/traffic cop/or principal.

- If group size exceeds 15, two or more games are recommended. Have one group demonstrate initially. This is an engaging activity to watch and observers generally talk strategy, so don't worry about down time.

Tips and Comments *(continued)*

- Important themes are: team problem-solving, impulse control, individual accountability and practicing feedback. The chicken tempts people to move quickly, yet the freeze requirements make fast movement ineffective. Think tortoise and hare. If speedy individuals don't get the hint at first (despite repeated violations and required returns to the start line), peer pressure usually kicks in eventually.

- Take a moment with each freeze to enjoy the frozen gleeful faces and positions.

- This activity builds trust and resiliency as the team becomes habituated to individuals being called out for mistakes.

Estimated Time 🌓

20 minutes

Safety

- Be aware that participants will be running randomly throughout the space.

- Highlight the awareness that reaching or bending down and then quickly moving may result in collisions. Players should be especially mindful of their heads.

Sonic 1

Overview

An exciting twist to Everybody's It tag. Players try to collect as many wiffle balls as they can while avoiding the tag of others. Sonic 1 is a great warm-up, fitness, and movement activity that explores personal efforts and the ability to "let go and move on."

Group Size	12 persons
Learning Themes	• Fun and Play • Physical Activity and Movement • Self Awareness and Self Management
Materials / Props	3 – 5 wiffle balls per person

Setup

Distribute wiffle balls in a large open space.

Framing

Say to participants:

"Has anyone heard of Sonic the Hedgehog™? Sonic was an extremely fast hedgehog who ventured everywhere collecting golden rings while in search of seven chaos emeralds, in an effort to save the world. We are going to play a game inspired by this video game."

Or:

"Have you ever felt like you were running from one place to another trying to hold on to too many things when suddenly something causes you to drop everything? As we play, be aware of your body, your emotions, and behaviors."

Or:

"Have you ever been interrupted from a task or thought and felt like you had to start over because you felt so lost? As we play, be aware of sensations in your body (somatic awareness), as well as your emotions and behaviors."

Procedure

1. State the objective. Everyone tries to collect as many points – wiffle balls – as possible without being tagged by another player.

2. Explain and demonstrate the rules.

   a. Everybody is It.

   b. Wiffle balls are worth one point.

   c., In order to tag, a player must have at least one wiffle ball, in his or her hand.

   d. If tagged, a player must toss their wiffle balls into the air and start again.

   e. If tagged without any objects, players must stop and remain where they are. The stopped player may re-enter the game by asking for help from other players. To help, other players must hand a wiffle ball to a player who would like to re-enter the game.

3. Check for understanding of the rules, then say "Go" and begin.

4. Play until either:

   a. All objects have been collected and are no longer on the ground or floor.

   b. Three minutes have passed.

5. Then play again!

Reflection/Closure/Discussion

1. What emotions did you experience? Did they show up anywhere in your body?

2. What behaviors did you demonstrate or notice?

3. Have you experienced any of these feelings or demonstrated any of these behaviors before? How has that affected your life?

4. What might you do in the future if you experience some of these feelings?

Tips and Comments

Variation

- Sonic Team Tag – A variation can be played in small teams of three or four. Teams of three or four particpants collect objects as described above, but, in doing so, try to bring objects back to a team bucket or hoop. Once an object is in a team's bucket, it may not be removed. Game ends when all objects are in the buckets. Points are then tallied. Wiffle balls are worth one point. Playing additional rounds allows a team to analyze their strategy and develop goals.

Game Inspiration

- This game is inspired by the video game, Sonic the Hedgehog™. For more information about this legendary video game, visit:

  http://en.wikipedia.org/wiki/Sonic_the_Hedgehog_(video_game)

  http://www.sonicthehedgehog.com/

Sonic 2 (aka Sonic and Tails)

Overview

A fast-paced game of maintaining focus amidst distracting chaos. Players try to prevent their buckets of collected wiffle balls from being dumped by other participants. In Sonic 2, as well as in life, a dumped bucket is an opportunity to re-gain focus and practice resiliency.

Estimated Time

20 minutes

Safety

- Instruct players to hold buckets away from their bodies and especially their faces to prevent or limit bucket to face contact, especially as the bucket is hit by a fleece ball.

- Participants should also be made aware that reaching or bending down and then moving quickly may result in collisions. Players should be especially mindful of their heads.

Group Size	10 or more
Learning Themes	• Physical Activity and Movement • Building Trust, Relationships, and Community • Self Awareness and Self Management • Relationship Skills
Materials / Props	• 3-5 wiffle balls per person • 1 fleece ball per person, in a variety of colors (red, yellow, green, and blue) • 1 small plastic bucket or flower pot for each participant • Flip chart paper (for reflection) • Markers (for reflection)

Setup

1. Distribute wiffle balls in a large open space.
2. Give each person a plastic bucket.

Framing

Sonic 2

"In Sonic the Hedgehog 2™, Sonic's sidekick, Tails, was introduced. Tails supported Sonic during his adventures and allowed him to collect more golden rings. The container represents Tails. In the video game, it is important to be aware of and care for Tails, likewise it is important to be aware of and care for the container."

Resiliency

"What does resiliency mean? We have a chance to practice resiliency in this next game. Be aware of what resiliency looks like, sounds like, and feels like."

Focus

"Is there anyone here who is easily distracted? Sometimes it is difficult to stay on task when distractions exist around us. We may lose focus or drift into the distraction, but it subsequently provides an opportunity to discover strategies for staying focused. We are going to play a game that may help us discover some of these strategies. As we play, notice when you are distracted and when you are focused."

182

Procedure

1. Direct participants to balance a container in the palm of one of their open hands. Explain that hands must be kept flat and may not grip the container.

2. Provide an opportunity for participants to practice moving while balancing the container.

3. Tell participants to distribute themselves among the wiffle balls.

4. Explain and demonstrate the rules:

   a. Attempt to collect as many objects into the containers as possible.

   b. The hand holding the container must be kept flat and may not grip the container.

   c. While collecting objects, participants may also pick up fleece balls and throw them at the containers of other participants attempting to empty the contents.

   d. Participants may only throw fleece balls if they are balancing a container on their hands.

5. Check for clarity of the rules, then play!

Reflection/Closure/Discussion

Sonic 2

1. Were you able to protect Tails?

2. What were some of the challenges with protecting Tails?

3. What were some of the strategies to protect Tails?

4. Is there anything or anyone you protect in your life?

Resiliency

1. Pi Chart Resiliency

   a. Pi charting utilizes the symbol "π" to create a graphic organizer with three distinct columns.

   b. Separate into groups of 3-5 participants.

   c. Have participants reflect on their experience and pi chart "resiliency," by brainstorming and recording what resiliency looks like, sounds like, and feels like.

   d. Encourage participants to draw pictures or quote words that they heard while playing.

Resiliency		
Looks Like	Sounds Like	Feels Like

Focus

1. How did you feel playing this game?

2. While playing, were you more distracted than focused or more focused than distracted?

3. How do we balance being distracted and being focused?

4. What are the benefits of balancing focus and distractions?

Full Value Check-in

1. At the end of play, let the fleece balls remain where they are.

2. Ask participants to consider their Full Value Contract and reflect on how they interacted with each other while playing Sonic & Tails.

3. Ask participants to determine if the behavior they are thinking of is something they believe needs to stop, is concerning, or would like to continue.

4. Invite participants to move to:

    a. A red fleece ball if they observed a behavior they believe should stop.

    b. A yellow fleece ball if they observed a behavior they believe is concerning.

    c. A green fleece ball if they observed a behavior they would like to see more of.

5. Invite participants to share their perspectives.

Tips and Comments

Variations

- **Time It** – Play multiple two to three minute rounds.

- **In the Bucket** – Instead of throwing a ball at another player's bucket, have participants place a fleece ball *into* another player's bucket. If successful, a player who has a fleece ball in their bucket must immediately empty the contents of his or her bucket and begin again. Fleece balls must be placed, not thrown or tossed.

- **Alternate Prop Version** – Replace buckets with small plastic containers such as food storage containers or yogurt containers and replace wiffle balls with plastic poker chips. Keep the fleece balls flying though!

- **Bucket Filler's Reflection** – Read *Have You Filled a Bucket Today?* by Carol McCloud after playing Sonic and Tails. Compare and contrast the experience of the game and the experiences described in the book, and then identify ways to fill the buckets of others.

Game Inspiration

This game is inspired by the video game, Sonic the Hedgehog 2™. For more information about this video game, visit:

http://www.sonicthehedgehog.com/

http://en.wikipedia.org/wiki/Sonic_the_Hedgehog_2_(16-bit)

Sonic 3 (aka Sonic and Knuckles)

Overview

A game of shared focus in the midst of a disruptive mess. Partners try to prevent their bucket of collected wiffle balls from being dumped by other players. In Sonic 3, a dumped bucket is an opportunity for partners to re-evaluate their strategy and attempt to communicate more effectively.

Group Size	12 or mroe
Learning Themes	• Physical Activity and Movement • Building Trust, Relationships, and Community • Relationship Skills
Materials / Props	• 3-5 wiffle balls per person • 1 fleece ball per person (mixed colors) • 1 small plastic bucket or flower pot per two participants • Flip chart and markers for debrief

Safety

- Make participants aware that they will be moving randomly among many other participants while connected through the bucket to their partners. Attention should be paid to sharing this space safely.

- Participants should also be made aware that reaching or bending down and then moving quickly may result in collisions. Players should be especially mindful of their heads.

Setup

1. Distribute wiffle balls throughout a large open space.

2. Creatively separate your group into pairs. Consider asking your group to line up on a spectrum ranging from "prefer to work alone" to "prefer to work with others." Ask people to share where they are standing and why. Fold the line in half and direct participants to partner with the person opposite them.

Framing

Sonic 3

"In Sonic the Hedgehog 3™, Sonic and Tails again find themselves connected in pursuit of the chaos emeralds, this time on a floating island. A novel setting provides new experiences and new challenges."

Collaboration

"Working with others can re-define an experience. For some people, working with others can be very easy; for others, it can be extremely difficult. You will have an opportunity to work with another person, develop strategies, and experience moments of leading and following. Additionally, you might note the impact that communication has on your experience."

Procedure

1. Tell participants to suspend their containers between them and their partners using only one index finger each. Two fingers may be permissible.

2. Allow a moment for participants to practice moving while suspending the container between them and their partners.

3. Explain the objective: On a start signal, partners attempt to gather as many wiffle balls into their buckets as they can.

4. Explain and demonstrate the rules:

   a. While collecting objects, participants may also pick up fleece balls and throw them at the buckets of other participants attempting to empty the contents.

   b. Participants may only throw fleece balls at the buckets of other participants if they and their partners are suspending their buckets.

   c. Participants may not attempt to dump the contents of other players' buckets with anything but a fleece ball. In other words, players can not kick, hit, or walk through other players' buckets.

Reflection/Closure/Discussion

Sonic 3

The Sonic 3 framing is intentionally a more playful framing linked to the story of the video game. If you decide to process the experience, consider exploring what new challenges emerged and how they were managed.

Collaboration

1. Non-verbally demonstrate your communication during this activity.

2. Non-verbally demonstrate a moment when you were working well with each other. Non-verbally demonstrate a moment when you were not working well together.

3. Find another team and share what you learned about working in tandem. Identify one key learning that you would be willing to share with the rest of the group and who will share that.

4. Share key learnings.

Tips and Comments

Variation

- Instead of suspending the container with index fingers, buckets can be suspended on fixed strings. Drill holes near the top of two opposing sides of the bucket, then attach a string through each hole. Do not allow participants to wrap the string around their fingers or hands while playing.

- This game can also be played in this way – instead of throwing a ball at another team's container, a player may attempt to place – not throw or toss, but place a fleece ball into the bucket of another team, which then causes them to empty the contents of their container.

Game Inspiration

This game is inspired by the video game, Sonic the Hedgehog 3™. For more information about this video game, visit: http://www.sonicthehedgehog.com/

http://en.wikipedia.org/wiki/Sonic_the_Hedgehog_3

Space Invaders

Overview

A playful spin on a classic video game. Communication centers (composed of both sighted and non-sighted individuals) work together in an effort to proactively contact alien life forms (with fleece balls) before they reach planet Earth. Space Invaders is a fun exchange of communication, the exploration of feelings and, of course, the frantic response to the classic story of aliens attacking Earth. Perhaps, we could attempt to make contact and communicate with aliens before assuming that they are coming to attack us. What do you think?

Group Size	20 or more
Learning Themes	• Fun and Play • Physical Activity and Movement • Building Trust, Relationships, and Community • Relationship Skills
Materials / Props	• 20 – 30 Fleece balls divided among Throwers • 3 – 5 blindfolds or bandanas • 30 Hula hoops • 5 play ropes, masking tape, or chalk (alternative set-up materials) • 10 cones

Setup

1. Place hoop in six staggered rows of five Hoops. The hoops mark obstacles that must be passed in a particular way resulting in a uniform zig-zag pathway that participants must follow (see diagram on the following page). The zig-zag pathway could also be formed by drawing the lines with chalk, tape, or long pieces of rope.

2. Place five cones at both ends of each zig-zag pathway.

Framing

Four Variations

Making Contact:

"There is much debate regarding the existence of aliens. There is also much concern that if aliens do exist, they will invade planet Earth. As earthlings, we tend to fear the unknown and unfamiliar. However, we also know that establishing contact and engaging in effective communication improves our understanding of the unknown."

Making Contact 2:

"Imagine that aliens were about to arrive on Earth. If you had a chance to contact them before they arrived, what would you say? What would you want to know? In this activity, some of you will play the roles of aliens while others will play the roles of

Safety

- Appropriately assess the group's readiness for this activity, given that participants are invited to be non-sighted and throwing fleece balls at one another. Additionally, ensure that participants are informed of the responsibility of caring for self and others (physically, socially, emotionally, spiritually, etc.), especially those who are non-sighted.

- Ensure that weather conditions are appropriate, if using sponges and/or water balloons as described in the prop variation below. Note too, that sponges will pick up dirt from the ground and may soil clothes.

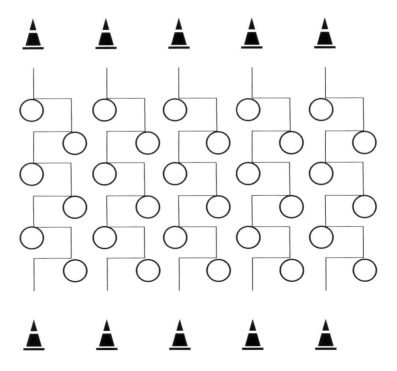

communication center members here on Earth. Communication will play a significant role in working toward a more peaceful existence."

Communication:

"Communication comes in many forms – verbal, non-verbal, visual, written, etc. While it is important to send information out, it is equally important to receive information. Developing good listening skills and reflecting what was heard are essential to understanding others."

Original Video Game Framing:

"Hoards of aliens, portrayed by some of you, are attacking Earth! Others of you will attempt to defeat the aliens and save planet Earth by shooting cannons from individual defense centers. Working effectively in teams will be necessary for the success of each team's objective."

Procedure

1. Invite 6-10 volunteers to form 3-5 paired teams of non-sighted throwers and sighted guides. Have the pairs line up behind the cones on one side.

2. Instruct all other players to create five lines of space invaders behind the other set of cones.

3. State the goal. The goal is for at least one space invader to tag at least one of the non-sighted throwers. The throwers, directed by their guides, try to contact as many space invaders as possible with a thrown fleece ball before this occurs. Throwers try to fend off the space invaders as long as they can or until all space invaders are eliminated.

4. Explain the rules:

    a. When the game begins, space invaders attempt to move closer and closer to the throwers by following the pre-determined zig-zag pathway.

    b. Space invaders may take only one step, either forward or to the side, at a time.

    c. Space invaders may only step forward with a forward lunge, or duck walk.

    d. In order to move sideways, space invaders must use a side-stepping squat.

    e. Also, space invaders may only move forward or to the side when another space invader in front of them has to move on, leaving room for the step. This creates a movement pace that is self-managed.

    f. As space invaders advance, the three teams of non-sighted throwers and sighted guides attempt to contact them with fleece balls. Sighted guides direct non-sighted throwers on where and how to throw fleece balls at the space invaders. Guides can retrieve fleece balls during play.

    g. Space invaders must continue to stay on their pre-determined path, but may avoid contact with an oncoming fleece ball by either finishing a move already in progress or moving only their upper body if pausing before another step.

    h. If a space invader is hit by a fleece ball, they are eliminated.

    i. Play continues until either one of the space invaders tags a thrower, all of the space invaders have been eliminated, or a set period (e.g., three minutes) of time has expired.

5. Start a new game after one ends or try some of the variations below to keep participants involved and moving.

Reflection/Closure/Discussion

Making Contact:

1. Were you successful in making contact with the aliens?

2. What allowed for your success?

3. How did your feelings play into this or affect your outcome?

4. How do feelings affect our communication when interacting with something or someone unknown and unfamiliar to us?

5. Can you identify a moment of effective expression and communication from your life?

Making Contact 2:

1. How effective were the communication center teams?

2. What role did communication play in establishing the effectiveness of your teams?

3. Can you identify a moment during the activity when you engaged as a leader while communicating? Were you engaged as a follower while communicating?

4. What does it mean to be a leader or follower while communicating?

5. Where do you positively serve as a leader or follower while communicating in your life?

Communication:

1. How would you describe the communication between you and your partner?

2. Describe your experience with the specific communication role you played, e.g., able to see but not speak, speak but not see, relay information without seeing it directly, etc.

3. What is one part of communication that you did well?

4. Do you demonstrate this often in your life?

5. What could you do to make it happen more often?

Original Video Game:

1. Were you able to complete your mission of either reaching earth, if you were an alien, or preventing the aliens from reaching earth if you were a defense center?

2. What do you need to do to be effective aliens or protectors?

3. Given two sides with opposing missions, how might both groups work to resolve this issue?

4. Could that information be applied to any situations in your life?

Tips and Comments

- This activity was inspired by a classic video game called Space Invaders. The first two framings, however, are written from a perspective different from the original. Instead of attacking space invaders for their presumed threat, the focus is on seeking first to understand and then be understood. In other words, to understand those who are different from us rather than attacking them first.

- Play with the variations below and try your own variation ideas to keep participants involved and moving.

Variations

- **Play Variation** – There are many ways to keep the game and participants involved and moving, rather than simply eliminating players and having them wait for a new game to start. Below are a few ideas to try. If a space invader is hit with a fleece ball, he or she:

  - Returns to the end of a space invader line and continues to play

  - Become retrievers of fleece balls. Incorporating fleece balls keeps the game moving or at least gives the throwing team a chance!

  - Take the place of either a sighted guide or non-sighted thrower.

  - Join another space invader who has also been hit and form a new team of sighted guide and non-sighted thrower. This variation builds the game's intensity while keeping everyone involved.

Tips and Comments *(continued)*

- **Communication Center Variations** – While the description above establishes a sighted guide and non-sighted thrower in a team of two, there are a couple of additional ways to accommodate more people.

  - Eyes, Body Mouth Inspired – Try a variation incorporating a third person using a technique from the activity "Eyes Body Mouth" (*Creating Healthy Habits*, p. 185). Have two participants from each team stand back to back – one person directly facing the aliens and the other facing away from the aliens. Instruct a third person to stand facing the alien line-up a short distance from the person facing the opposite direction of the aliens. The person closest to and facing the aliens is the thrower and is non-sighted, either eyes closed or wearing a blindfold. While these players cannot see, they may talk and receive information directly from the voice of the operation. The person facing away from the aliens is the voice of the communication center. He or she views the non-verbal communicator in front of them and directs the throwers where to throw. The third person, placed a short distance from the two participants standing back to back, is the eyes and non-verbal communicator of the operation. He or she can see but may not talk and must communicate non-verbally with the voice of the operation, on where to throw. He or she may also retrieve fleece balls from the playing field.

  - Play as described above adding a fourth person in the role of retriever. He or she is able to enter the playing field, retrieve fleece balls, and return them to the throwing team resulting in a nearly endless supply of fleece balls to keep the game moving.

- **Movement Variations:**

  - **Line Dance** – Have the aliens move by following a popular line dance. Incorporating a line dance such as the Cupid Shuffle, Electric Slide, or the Cotton Eye Joe provides a fun and distracting movement alternative for the aliens while incorporating music and dance into the activity.

  - **Other Movements** – Another possibility is to have the aliens move in a crab walk, bear crawl, or their most inspired Break Dancing Robot. These movements not only add variety, but also provide an opportunity for developing muscular strength and endurance in different regions of the body.

  - **A Movement All Their Own** – Once participants get a sense of how the game is played, provide the opportunity for them to create any movement pattern they like.

- **Prop Variation for a Hot Summer Day!** – Replace fleece balls with saturated sponges or water balloons.

Safety

Given the competitive aspect of this game and associated variations, monitor the appropriateness of interactions and provide opportunities for Full Value Check-ins as needed.

Spoon Jousting Tag

Overview

A spin-off of an old tag game involving swatting spoons, precarious ping pong balls, and style! Spoon Jousting Tag, an extension of Spoon Jousting first published by Karl Rohnke, is a game of focus and balance in which people attempt to balance a ping pong ball on a spoon as long as they can while avoiding the swatting spoons of others.

Group Size	8 or more
Learning Themes	• Fun and Play • Physical Activity and Movement • Building Trust, Relationships, and Community
Materials / Props	• 1 ping pong ball per person • 2 spoons per person

Setup

Prepare an open space.

Framing

Say to group:

> "Have you ever noticed how challenging it can be to balance your own tasks when you are focusing more on the tasks of others? Consider this as we play a game requiring balance and focus."

Procedure

Warm-up – Spoon Jousting

1. Have participants find partners. Ideas for pairing follow.
2. Provide each person with two spoons and one ping pong ball.
3. Participants prepare to face off by assuming the official Spoon Jousting position – one spoon with a ping pong ball held a few inches from the belly button and the spoon with no ping pong ball extended toward the opponent.
4. On an agreed-upon start signal, all players attempt to dislodge the ping pong balls from their opponents' spoons using the spoons without ping pong balls.
5. Participants may shuffle and move forward and backward to avoid their opponents' spoons.
6. Once a ping pong ball is dislodged, players re-set and play again.
7. Provide opportunities for participants to switch and play other people, then transition to Spoon Jousting Tag or another activity.

Round 1 - Spoon Jousting Tag

8. Provide each person with two spoons and one ping pong ball.

9. Direct participants to balance and hold the ping pong ball in one of their spoons, leaving the other spoon empty.

10. On a start signal, participants move around a specified space balancing ping pong balls on their spoons.

11. Participants attempt to knock the ping pong balls out of the spoons of other players using only their empty spoons.

12. Players who no longer have ping pong balls in their spoons must stand still where they are. The game can be played until there is one obvious winner.

13. Add two additional rules in subsequent rounds to increase activity and learning:

Round 2 – Look Out!

14. During round two, players who are required to remain still because they no longer have ping pong balls may attempt to knock the ping pong balls out of other players' spoons, still using one of their ping pong ball free spoons.

Round 3 – Help!

15. A third round allows a player who still has a ping pong ball in their spoon to help another by scooping a ping pong ball off the ground and putting it in the spoon of a player who is not able to move.

Reflection/Closure/Discussion

Ask participants:

1. Did you focus more on your task to balance your ping pong balls or dislodging the ping pong balls of others?

2. What did you notice about your ability to balance or focus?

3. How might this information be helpful in the tasks you have to do every day?

Tips and Comments

As described in the procedure, the first round implies a more competitive approach to Spoon Jousting Tag in which players are eliminated with the eventual outcome of one winner, the person who was not eliminated. More participation opportunities emerge in the second round. The third round depicts a more cooperative variation building on the physical skills needed to play the game. Choose the variation that best meets given goals or specific learning objectives.

Tips and Comments *(continued)*

- **Variation:**

  - **Tandem Spoon Jousting Tag** – Tandem Spoon Jousting Tag is a variation of Spoon Jousting Tag using the squared concept of linking two people together described in Pairs Squared (*Middle School ACPE*). Invite two people to link arms. Provide two spoons and one ping pong ball to each linked pair. Every pairing is It and can attempt to knock ping pong balls off of anyone's spoon, as long as they are linked to their partner. Follow the flow of rounds described in Spoon Jousting Tag. Round one is an elimination round leading to one obvious winner. In round two, participation is increased by allowing those who have lost their ping pong balls to still play but without moving from the spots where their ping pong balls were lost. The final round presents a more cooperative approach in which people can help others re-enter the moving around aspect of the game.

Estimated Time

5 – 10 minutes

Safety

- Participants may lose balance and fumble or tumble toward the ground or floor. Ensure that there is enough space between people and objects so that participants can regain their balance or have a clear landing to the floor or ground.

- Shoes may be scuffed during this activity. Participants should be made aware of this. If they are concerned with the appearance and care of their footwear, they may not want to participate or perhaps the activity should not be selected.

Stationary Foot Tag (aka Top It)

Overview

A combination of the classic activities, Snoopy and the Red Baron (*No Props*, p.79) and Toe Tag (*No Props*, p.97), this activity creates an interactive warm-up of balance and flexible, quick, foot-flying fun! Participants face off in pairs and attempt to tag the top of their partner's foot with the bottom of their own. In Stationary Foot Tag, balance and quick feet are key and fun is the result!

Group Size	12 or more
Learning Themes	• Fun and Play • Physical Activity and Movement • Building Trust, Relationships, and Community
Materials / Props	None

Setup

Creatively pair participants (e.g., ask participants to call out their favorite footwear and partner with someone who has an entirely different favorite.). See more ideas on page 299.

Framing

Say to the group:

> "This is a game of fast, flexible foot-flying action requiring balance, flexibility, and quick thinking."

Procedure

1. Two participants face one another and determine who is It and who is Not It.

2. Each person lifts one foot while balancing on the other.

3. The foot that is grounded, or touching the ground, may not move from that spot.

4. The person who is It, attempts to tag his or her partner's foot, top only, with their non-grounded foot while the person who is Not It attempts to avoid being tagged by moving his or her non-grounded foot.

5. After a tag is made, participants switch feet and roles and continue.

6. At this point, you may choose to transition to another activity or continue with the following. Choosing the following additional steps allows for more interaction among group members who may further develop particular skills or the group as a whole.

Switch It Up

7. After play has continued for a bit and the timing for something new seems right, switch it up. Have participants switch partners and play on.

Mix It Up

8. Once everyone has had a chance to develop some skill and has had some fun while playing their partner, perhaps even playing other people, have them try a mixing version.

9. To play:

    a. Everyone begins on one foot as described above.

    b. On a Go signal, participants move toward other people by hopping on one foot.

    c. They then indicate their interest in challenging another person by giving an affirmative, chin to chest, head nod.

    d. The recipient of such an invitation has the option to accept or decline. To accept, he or she responds with an affirmative, chin to chest, head nod. To decline, the participant gives a negative, side to side, head shake and moves on to challenge someone else or accept the challenge of another person. (This is an effective way to expand the understanding of Challenge by Choice within the group.)

Reflection/Closure/Discussion

1. How'd it go? Any reactions or comments?

2. Did you develop any particular strategies for tagging or avoiding the tag?

3. Are there any highlights that you would like to share?

Variations

- **Tag Either Foot** – Allow for either foot, the grounded or non-grounded foot to be tagged. Doing so adds even more dynamic fun to the game.
- **Stationary Foot Tag in a Circle** – Stationary Foot Tag can also be played in a circle or perhaps even concentric circles. For the basic circle variation, have the group stand in a circle. Once in a circle, direct them to hold hands and stand on one foot. Thus the game begins. Participants try to tag the top of other people's feet, while attempting to evade the tags of others. Once tagged, participants are considered out of the game, but are encouraged to start another game with those who have been eliminated from a previous game.
- **Stationary Foot Tag/Snoopy & the Red Baron Combination** – Play Stationary Foot Tag and Snoopy & the Red Baron simultaneously. This combo provides plenty of fun and challenge to fully engage participants' bodies and brains. The combination of arm and hand movements in Snoopy and the Red Baron and leg and foot movement in Flying Feet crosses both the vertical and horizontal mid- lines of the brain and body.
- **In the Family** – Check out 'Foot Tag' a Stationary Foot Tag spin off also offered in this activity guide.

Game Story

Stationary Foot Tag was discovered while facilitating a workshop with Andrew Siems, a new trainer at the time. I had introduced Snoopy & the Red Baron in the usual way, "Does everyone remember Snoopy? Right, Snoopy, the dog from Charlie Brown, the Peanuts comic, not Snoop Dog the rapper!" After we accurately identified the Snoopy, I guided the group to recall the different activities that happened at Snoopy's doghouse. Responses quickly made their way to the usual response, "Flying a fighter plane...the Red Baron!" Affirming the response, yet looking for more, I responded, "Yes, of course... what else happened on Snoopy's dog house?" Other recollections rolled in, "That yellow bird – Woodstock – would hang out. Snoopy slept on the roof. He decorated it for Christmas. Yeah, and wrote stories." "Exactly, he would break out the typewriter – 'it was a dark and stormy night...' – Snoopy's doghouse was a place of imagination. Engaging in Adventure requires imagination. We are going to engage in a game requiring you to imagine yourself as the greatest World War I flying ace of the comic world, Snoopy & the Red Baron." I explained the rules and demonstrated play, including sound effects, and off they went, flying, gunning sounds, and laughter.

As the group was completely absorbed by their own creativity and I prepared to resume play with my partner, Andrew, he asked, "Have you ever played this with your feet?" I replied, "No, have you?" thinking, "Sweet! this new guy is comfortable sharing new ideas." With a laugh, Andrew, said, "No." Synergistically we said, "Let's try it." And off we went playing, laughing, and sharing an impromptu variation of Snoopy & the Red Baron. Overjoyed, we said, "Try this, we just made it up!" Turns out, that when played, the activity seemed to be a successful cross between Snoopy & the Red Baron and the activity Toe Tag.

The significance of this story is twofold. By asking a simple question, "Have you played this with your feet," Andrew, introduced a possibility. Secondly, when you combine two activities you create or discover a new one that deserves a new name, and ultimately an identity of its own. The thing is, this experience actually inspired a whole family of Foot Tag activities. Here's to Stationary Foot Tag. Snoopy & the Red Toe Tag just didn't sound right or safe!

Stationary Handshakes

Overview

A simple greeting sure to stretch your group and build your community. Participants attempt to greet their group mates in a variety of ways – using only one pivot foot, with feet planted on the ground, and by moving about. Stationary Handshakes is an ideal large group opener that highlights Challenge by Choice while giving participants an opportunity to interact with one another.

Group Size	12 or more
Learning Themes	• Physical Activity and Movement • Building Trust, Relationships, and Community • Responsible Decision Making
Materials / Props	None

Safety

Some participants may be moved to help and support one another as they stretch by providing a counter weight or pseudo-spot. Be aware of how this is happening, as some participants may attempt to do this while adhering to particular parameters such as both feet on the ground or only one pivot foot. Leniency is encouraged.

Setup

1. Begin with the group in a circle in an open space.
2. Have participants casually greet the participants to their immediate right and left with a resounding "Hello!", "Good Morning!", "Buenos Dias!", or the like.

Framing

Say to participants:

"We have an opportunity to create our community. How far are you willing to reach out to meet community members?"

Or:

"Challenge by Choice provides an opportunity to challenge or stretch ourselves. How far are you willing to stretch your selves? What do you need as you leave your comfort zone?"

Or:

"We are about to engage in a challenging stretch or stretching challenge. Consider what a good stretch is for you."

Or:

"I've got a challenge for you individually and as a group. Here's how it works."

Procedure

Say to participants:

1. "With both feet planted on the ground (like the roots of a tree), attempt to shake hands with as many people as you can again with a resounding greeting, 'Good Morning!'
2. Next, see how far you can stretch to again greet as many people as possible, this time using only one pivot foot (keep one foot planted, while stepping with the other).

3. This time when I say 'Go', move around and greet as many people as you can and return to the circle when I raise my hand.

4. Finally, take a minute and scan the group, be aware of whom you have greeted and whom you have not. Greet anyone you didn't greet in the previous round. 'Go!'"

Reflection/Closure/Discussion

Possible questions:

1. How did it feel to stretch? Did you feel that you stretched too far? Did you feel that you did not stretch as far as you could?

2. How many returned to their original spot in the circle? Did anyone end up in a different location in the circle? What's up with that?

3. Did you notice the progression of greetings – beginning comfortably and then providing more and more opportunities to stretch yourself?

4. What might that tell you about our experience together?

5. How does this relate to Challenge by Choice?

Tips and Comments

- Just for fun or for a different approach, attempt to introduce this activity non-verbally or with limited talking.

- This activity seems to be a great tone setter for the day, a safe way for participants to begin meeting one another, and emphasizes Challenge by Choice.

- Consider suggesting or requesting ideas for additional handshake challenges such as shaking hands through your legs – right hand to the left, left hand to the right. Or shaking hands by passing the right hand behind the back and left hand in front of the chest.

- Consider shaking feet instead of shaking hands. Why not?

Step Tag

Overview

This activity involves Tag at a slower pace where everyone seems but a step away. Players move one step at a time while avoiding the tag of one or more players who are 'IT'. Step Tag works well in an indoor space, or any space really, and provides an opportunity to playfully explore balance and fairness.

Group Size	10 or more
Learning Themes	• Fun and Play • Physical Activity and Movement • Building Trust, Relationships, and Community
Materials / Props	Fleece Balls (Tagger Identifier)

Setup

Identify one person per every ten participants as a tagger. Create a small space for the activity.

Framing

Say to the group:

"When the tagger is within one step of catching you, it will be awfully tempting to take an extra step to escape. What will you do when confronted with this situation? Will you take the extra step or will you accept the consequence and get tagged?"

Procedure:

1. The goal is for the tagger to successfully touch anyone who is not a tagger on the shoulder with a free hand (no throwing the fleece ball). If successful, the tag identifier is passed off.

2. Tag backs are not allowed. New taggers may not tag the person who just tagged them.

3. Step size is limited to your maximum step length before falling.

4. If you step outside the boundary to avoid a tag, you automatically become the tagger.

5. Each time the tagger takes ONE step, he or she must yell, "STEP!" The rest of the group may then take ONE step in any direction in an effort to avoid getting tagged. The tagger may not take another step until the group has completed their one step.

Reflection / Closure / Discussion

1. What happened during the game? Did people play fairly?

2. What does the game look like when people choose to play unfairly and/or fairly?

3. Why is it challenging to accept that you have been caught?

4. How does this game relate to accepting responsibility for mistakes?

Tips and Comments

Variations:

- Play Step Tag in the style of 'Everybody's It.' Now, anyone can tag anyone else. If tagged players remain where they are and may tag anyone they can reach given the use of one pivot foot. This variation requires a bit more strategy and is typically more fun!

- Step Tag can also be played in pairs, one partner chasing the other within a small boundary. Same rules.

Estimated Time

15 – 25 minutes

Sticky Snakes

Overview

A challenging, think-before-you-act, knotted rope initiative. Participants attempt to untie a rope with knots in it. They must plan well for when their hands touch the rope, they become stuck. Sticky Snakes is sure to challenge a group to think about their actions while providing humorous moments of letting go.

Group Size	10 or more
Learning Themes	• Relationship Skills • Responsible Decision Making
Materials / Props	One 25 – 30 ft. length of play rope per 10 participants

Setup

Tie two or three simple overhand or figure eight knots into each length of rope. Remember, the greater number of knots and the more complicated the knots, the more challenging the initiative will be. Place the knotted rope(s) on a clear, open surface. If you are using more than one rope, be sure to space the ropes a good distance apart.

Framing

Say to the group:

> "Oh no! Do you know what these are? They're called Sticky Snakes and it looks like they've somehow gotten themselves all knotted up. Let's try to help them out by unknotting them. Before we begin, it's important to know that when Sticky Snakes are in distress, like these knotted snakes, they become incredibly sticky. If you touch them, your hand will stick in place until all the knots are out and the snake relaxes."

Procedure

1. Explain to the group that the goal is to untie each knot in the length of rope.
2. Explain the rules:
   a. Once you touch the rope, your hand is stuck to it and must remain in place until all the knots in the rope are untied.

b. You may only use your hands to work out the knots in the rope; however, it is OK for other parts of your body to touch the rope.

c. If the group decides to give up on an attempt and lets go, another knot will be added to the snake. (Optional)

d. Once all the knots are out, participants may let go of the rope.

Reflection/Closure/Discussion

1. Did the group come up with a plan before jumping in? What was the plan?

2. Did it work or did it require a change of plans in the middle of the activity? What was that like?

3. What was most challenging about the activity?

Tips and Comments

Variations

- Use several short three to five foot sections of rope, each with a single knot. This slight variation will create quite a different dynamic.

- See an alternative framing and debrief of Sticky Snakes called Lifeline in *Creating Healthy Habits* by Dr. Katie Kilty (Project Adventure, 2006).

Stomp Clap Groove

Estimated Time

30 minutes

Overview

A game of creative coordination. Participants create movement patterns and attempt to flow through them...together. Stomp Clap Groove is great fun and a true test of a group's creativity and coordination. When groups excel, they get in a groove.

Group Size	10 or more
Learning Themes	• Fun and Play • Physical Activity and Movement • Relationship Skills • Responsible Decision Making
Materials / Props	• Foot, hand and arrow spot markers • Additional paper or card board • Markers

Setup

Establish a pattern of movements by placing feet, hand, and directional markers in a straight line on the ground or floor.

Framing

Say to the group:

"Determining how we want to treat one another can have a significant impact on how we discover solutions to the challenges we face, create a safe space where creative risks can be celebrated, and learn to be more cohesive."

Or:

"A community is a collection of individuals learning to understand one another and flow as one unit. Let's explore this!"

Or:

"Play Hard, Play Safe, Play Fair, and Have Fun is a Full Value Contract that we have established for the group. Within that agreement, it is important for you to establish a more specific Full Value Contract for yourselves. At the end of this activity, you will have an opportunity to establish a FVC of your own."

Procedure

1. Challenge participants to move from Start to Finish, clapping when they pass a hand and stomping when they pass a foot.

2. Invite participants to:

    a. Attempt this first by themselves.

    b. Try it in pairs, with partners attempting to clap and stomp simultaneously. Provide an opportunity to explore this with different partners.

    c. Finally, try the challenge as one coordinated group.

3. Once the group has completed their initial pattern, invite them to add, change, and delete movement markers creating a new pattern to try. Then…play again.

Reflection/Closure/Discussion

1. What did you notice or experience as we moved as individuals, pairs, and a whole group?

2. What would you say were the differences in moving as individuals, in pairs, and as a whole group?

3. Were there any specific challenges or successes that you want to highlight?

4. What did you learn about being part of a community?

Tips and Comments

This game builds from an individual challenge to a paired challenge, and then ultimately leads to a challenge of team coordination.

Variations

- Create additional movement markers to offer more variety, increase challenge, and further explore creativity. Consider movements such as jumping, hopping, sliding, spinning, etc. Invite participants to create their own movement markers.

Tips and Comments *(continued)*

- Create additional markers to add sounds to the flow.

- Establish a power point presentation of movement and sound patterns to project and challenge the group to follow. Better yet, have small groups of students create their own power point presentations for their group to follow. Consider projecting these presentations on the wall, ceiling, floor, or outside at night!

- Have half the group hold a movement and/or sound card and demonstrate as the others attempt the challenge as individuals, pairs, or the entire group. Then switch.

Super-Smile

Estimated Time

10 – 20 minutes

Overview

A silly de-inhibitizer, energizer, or warm up, sure to bring out the biggest smiles and maybe even some belly laughs. Participants stand in a circle and send a smile around the circle as quickly as they can. Once a smile has been received, the sender may start jumping up and down. Time stops when the entre group is jumping. Super-Smile is an activity that has innate health benefits and reminds us all of the significance of the simple things in life, like a smile. I bet you just smiled! You did, didn't you! Thank you, now I am jumping up and down!

Group Size	8 or more
Learning Themes	• Building Trust, Relationships, and Community • Self Awareness and Self Management • Social Awareness
Materials / Props	None

Setup

Gather participants into a circle, standing at about an arms-length from the next person.

Framing

Say to the group:

"Smiles are a simple way to put ourselves and each other at ease. We are going to test the theory that, like yawns, smiles are contagious. We will see how quickly a single smile can travel to everyone in our group."

Procedure

1. Explain that you, the facilitator, will start time on a stop watch and then send a single smile across the circle by making eye contact with someone and smiling. Once the receiver makes eye contact and smiles, the sender (facilitator) starts gently jumping up and down in place, to indicate that the first smile has been sent.

2. Now, the receiver of the first smile sends a smile to someone else who is standing in place and so it continues... the sender can only start jumping up and down once the receiver has made eye contact and smiled back.

3. Everyone may send only one smile and receive only one smile.

4. Once everyone has successfully sent a smile and the entire group is jumping up and down, time stops.

5. Play for several rounds. See how quickly you can send the secret smile, and enjoy the laughter! Follow the same sequence or create new ones. Either way, don't take it too seriously!

Debrief

1. How does smiling impact you?

2. How can it impact an entire group?

3. How might you carry this activity beyond this room?

Tips and Comments

- Allow participants to fake a smile if needed. Fake smiles are likely to become real. Besides, there are many benefits to smiling regardless of whether it is genuine or fake. According to About.com, "Smiling is a great way to make yourself stand out while helping your body to function better. Smile to improve your health, your stress level, and your attractiveness." Smiling is just one fun way to live longer, read more at:

  - http://longevity.about.com/od/lifelongbeauty/tp/smiling.htm
  - http://www.livestrong.com/article/18859-health-benefits-smiling/

- Adapted from an anti-bullying curriculum written by Michelle Wilson and Larry Childs for the North Andover Public Schools called *RAISE -'ing: Active Group Lessons for Bully Prevention and Social Skills Development* (Project Adventure, 2012)

Variations

- Establish small groups self-timed by participants.

- Allow variation in the height or energy applied to the jumping.

- Add the rule that if someone stops smiling, he or she must stop jumping until someone sends them a smile again. This will certainly impact the time, but may also increase the likelihood of belly laughs.

Tail Tag: Power Stealing/Power Sharing

Overview

A classic and engaging game of tag with a focus on bullying. Participants attempt to take the tail (bandana) of other players. If a player is without a tail, they must kneel and may take tails from other players passing by. While Tail Tag is commonly known, Tail Tag: Power Stealing/Power Sharing explores social power as it relates to bullying and the ability to prevent, manage, and resolve interpersonal conflicts and social pressure.

Group Size	10 or more
Learning Themes	• Physical Activity and Movement • Building Trust, Relationships, and Community • Relationship Skills • Responsible Decision Making Skills
Materials / Props	• Bandanas or small colored flags/scarves (one for each player) • Cones for marking boundaries

Safety

It is very important to remind players to keep their heads up when playing to avoid collisions. Players need to be aware that if a scarf is on the ground, it can be slippery.

Setup

- Clear a flat open space for playing tag within boundaries.
- Set boundaries for play.
- Give each player a bandana or small colored flag/scarve.

POWER STEALING

Framing

Say to the group:

"This game will help us to better understand social power. We will experience power-stealing and power-sharing as related to bullying."

Procedure

1. Give each player a colorful flag as his or her tail or "power."
2. Demonstrate that a fistful of the tail must be tucked into the back waistband. Tucked tails must be visible and grab-able at all times.
3. Everyone is It.
4. The object of the game is to gather as many tails as possible and collect them in your waistband at the back or side (not in the front, as this in not an appropriate place to grab each other).
5. Once players steal a tail, they have five seconds to tuck it, and must count to five out loud "1, 2, 3, 4, 5." If a player is not able to tuck the tail in five seconds, he or she must drop it and let someone else gather it from the ground.

6. If players are without tails, they must kneel down and can only move again if they are able to steal a tail from a passerby.

7. Instruct players to spread out within the boundaries. The game begins on the facilitator's cue.

8. Play the game for two rounds or five to ten minutes, re-setting tails if need be.

Debrief

Option #1

1. How did the power shift from the beginning to the end of the game?

2. What did it feel like to take a tail? What did it feel like to have your tail taken?

3. How might this game be similar to or different from bullying?

Option #2

1. One way of respecting others is following rules and playing with intent to challenge rather than harm. Engagement in this activity is respectful. Related questions about how respect is experienced in this activity:

2. Did you feel respected? Why or why not?

3. Did you behave in a respectful manner towards others? If so, what were the behaviors that would have communicated respect? If not, what communicated disrespect?

POWER SHARING

Overview

Participants continue playing Tail Tag as described above with the addition of helping another player who is without a tail. Players now may help one another and explore the difference between this variation and the first. Tail Tag – Power Sharing further explores social power as it relates to bullying and the dynamic of helping other people.

Setup and Framing (Continued from variation #1)

Procedure

1. Same rules as the original game of Tail Tag, with the additional twist that you can choose to give tails away to help people who are kneeling down.

2. Note: If you give away your only tail, you must kneel down.

3. Spread out within the boundaries. The game begins on the facilitator's cue.

4. Play the game for two rounds or five to ten minutes, re-setting tails if need be.

Debrief

Option #1:

1. Ask students to line up on a "Yes"... "Maybe/Not Sure" ... "No" continuum in response to each question Give them an opportunity to share information and respond to the follow-up questions which are italicized. Be sure not to judge participants for their honesty:

   a. Was this round more fun for you? *How was this round different from the last one?*

b. Did you choose to give a tail away? *What did it feel like to give a tail away?*

c. Did you receive a tail? *What did it feel like to receive a tail?*

d. Did anyone want to get back at someone or pay someone back during the game? *How does this relate to bullying or bullying prevention? Sometimes we may want to get back at other people who have hurt us... what are some healthier ways to "take our power back?"*

e. Have you ever supported anyone who seemed powerless in everyday life?

f. Have you ever been supported by someone when you felt powerless in everyday life?

g. Did anyone form an alliance at any point in either round of Tail Tag? *How did you feel if you were with an alliance? How did you feel if you were without an alliance?*

h. Did this game make you think about how you treat each other?

Team Tail Tag

Overview

A fast-paced, team-oriented tag game great for increasing the heart rate and exploring team work. Rather than playing independently, participants play Tail Tag in teams, trying to pull scarves (or bandanas) from other players. Team Tail Tag enhances an already fun game by increasing the interactive connection among players.

Group Size	12 or more
Learning Themes	• Fun and Play • Physical Activity and Movement • Relationship Skills
Materials / Props	Juggling scarves (or bandanas) for every participant (Red/Orange/Yellow)

Estimated Time 🕐

5 – 10 minutes

Safety

It is very important to remind players to keep their heads up when playing to avoid collisions. Players need to be aware that if a scarf is on the ground, it can be slippery.

Setup

Pass out the scarves. Participants tuck the scarves into their back waist loop or pocket. Participants will be separated into three teams based on the color of the scarves they are wearing.

Framing

Say to participants:

"Working well together as a team will keep your team in the game."

Procedure

Say to participants:

1. "The goal of the game is to pull scarves from other teams, which will leave them frozen.

2. If your scarf is pulled, it will be handed to you by the person who pulled it. Place it on the ground between your feet and stand over your scarf. You are frozen in place until someone on YOUR team hands your scarf to you. This will allow you to get back into the game.

3. Your scarf can be pulled when you are rescuing.

4. You are not allowed to hold onto your scarf when you are playing.

5. Your scarf cannot be pulled when you are tucking it back in for re-entry. Getting down on one knee will signify that you are temporarily out of the game and safe from scarf pulling.

6. The game ends when one team is completely "frozen."

Reflection / Closure / Discussion

1. Did participants work well together on their teams? What happened if teams did not work well together?

2. What are some examples of teamwork that you saw?

3. How might this information influence how you play or work in teams in other settings?

Estimated Time

1 – 5 minutes

Safety

Participants may initially feel tricked and that you deceived them. You may need to discuss this.

The Elusive Shadow

Overview

An easy-to-introduce activity with a solution that usually doesn't reveal itself until participants reach their 'lowest' moment.

Group Size	1 or more!
Learning Themes	• Fun and Play
Materials / Props	None, well maybe a sunny day or high-powered spotlight!

Setup

None necessary

Framing

Say to group:

"Sometimes solutions come from shadow sides, or moments that seem like failures."

Procedure

1. Say to participants: "Try this! Attempt to tag the head of your own shadow with your actual/physical hand. Go!"

2. At this point, many participants may take off running chasing their shadows, laughing either at themselves or others, and turn to you with some perplexed

looks. The looks reveal their questions, "Is this even possible?" or "Are you tricking us, getting us to do something simply for your humor?"

3. To offer more humor and perhaps a clue, you could say, "Keep playing and sharing your ideas with each other. You are bound to trip over the solution!"

4. Some participants will likely continue a variety of bodily twists and tweaks, while others will choose to stop their own process and observe.

5. Eventually, someone or some few, will reach success at their *lowest* moment!

Reflection/Closure/Discussion

- Given the nature of this activity, it may simply be appropriate to play, laugh, and move on to the next activity.

- If you desire to process the experience, consider the following. Direct participants to:

  - Choose a few Feeling Cards that describe their experiences during this activity. (a variety of feelings and expressions cards available through PA)

  - Share with the whole group, a small group of four to six people, or in pairs.

  - Describe an experience from your life when you were at a low point only to discover a solution or realize a positive outcome.

  - Express (verbally, in writing, in a picture, etc.) how this may help to create a positive future for themselves.

Tips and Comments

The Elusive Shadow is a great filler activity for when the time and sun are right.

The Mystery Box

Overview:

A nice warm-up activity in which participants get to work both independently and with partners. Participants perform tasks assigned by cards they pick up. The Mystery Box is adaptable to any age, setting, and content matter. It is also a great activity for review and assessment. Play with it, change the cards, and see where it takes you...remember it's a mystery!

Group Size	10 persons
Learning Themes	• Physical Activity and Movement • Building Trust, Relationships, and Community
Materials / Props	• 1 Mystery Box • 1 Set of Mystery Box Cards (see end of activity write-up)

Setup

Place the mystery box in the center of the area of play. Scatter the individual task-oriented cards, including the "Go to the Mystery Box" cards, face down around the area of play. Place the partner-oriented cards inside the mystery box.

Framing

"Playing this game is like a box of chocolates...you never know what ya gonna get."

Procedure

1. Tell participants to stand next to an unoccupied card.
2. Explain and demonstrate the rules:
   a. Each card laying face down has a task on the other side.
   b. On a start signal, participants may pick up the card next to them, read it, and perform the task. Participants should place the card face down where they found it to assure a surprise for the next person who comes along.
   c. After completing the task, players travel to a different card, read it, and perform the task. Remind participants to return the cards face down.
   d. This process is repeated over and over during the allotted time.
3. Now, there are some cards that read, "Go to the Mystery Box." These should have been scattered around the area of play with other individual task-oriented cards. There is no need to mention these cards at the beginning as they should come as a surprise during the game.
   a. If a participant picks a "Go to the Mystery Box" card, he or she should do just that – go to the mystery box and select a card. The "Go to the Mystery Box" cards not only direct participants to the mystery box, but lead them to tasks that require a partner. Participants must return the card to the mystery box,

quickly find a partner, and execute the task. They then return to regular play, picking up cards from the greater area of play rather than another card from the mystery box.

Reflection/Closure/Discussion

The Mystery Box is a warm-up, an activity which typically does not require much of a debrief or reflection. It may, however, spark a few comments or reactions. Be prepared to process these if you desire and as time allows. Also, if trying some of the technical or academically-oriented variations below, consider a reflection on how well participants knew the content or associated skills. For example, invite participants to consider if they knew the content well, so-so, or not at all and respond verbally or stand in groups according to your questions.

Tips and Comments

Tip

- The actual Mystery Box should be just that, a mystery. It should be intriguing and provoke curiosity. Therefore it shouldn't be any old box. If you have the time, look for a box around your house, at a yard sale, or online that is unique and fits the criteria of a good mystery box. Perhaps it is a box that has a special life story or one that was a gift. If you are not able to acquire a special box, make one. For example, consider wrapping a shoebox like a present that can be opened and accessed without tearing the paper. Whatever it is, care about it. Because if you care, so will your participants.

- As an activity, The Mystery Box, is great for review and assessment of particular content and associated skills.

Variations

- **Create Your Own** – Have participants create their own task cards. Once participants get the concept, invite them to create a set of cards to play with themselves or share with another group. Doing so empowers your participants and provides an opportunity to see fun, challenging, and socially interactive activities through their perspective of play. Prepare to be amazed!

- **Add Technical Content** – Chris Damboise, Project Adventure's Director of Credentialing and a Technical Trainer, loves to use this activity during the technical workshops he leads, such as Technical Skills Intensive (TSI) and Advanced Skills and Standards (ASAS). In addition to traditional warm-up and stretching activities represented on the cards below, Chris includes cards associated with technical skill or content. Some cards, for example, direct participants to tie specific knots, identify particular equipment, or hardware, or demonstrate a particular technique related to the challenge course. By adding this content and maintaining the original Mystery Box concept, Chris has utilized a significant and emerging trend in education – to be physically active while learning.

  Adding technical content to the Mystery Box game has proven to be a great assessment tool for both the individual and the instructor. Furthermore, it has opened the door for other content, such as academic content, to be explored and experienced in a similar way.

- **Add Academic Content** – As noted above, there is a significant and emerging trend in education toward including more physical activity while learning. Physical activity not only makes learning fun, it makes it accessible. More and more research, such as the information presented in *Spark*, by Dr. John Ratey, is helping this idea to become more credible.

  Let's look at how adding Academic Content to The Mystery Box might work. Using Chris's example, any educator could insert any content for review and assessment purposes. For example, a Language Arts teacher could add cards that direct participants to share the meaning of particular vocabulary words or use them in a sentence with a partner. Cards could have a brief math problem to solve or a particular event in history to identify on a map. Participants could collaborate in the co-creation of a drawing or painting by being directed to do so by one or a few cards. The potential is endless and fun.

Go to the Mystery Box	Go to the Mystery Box
Go to the Mystery Box	Go to the Mystery Box
Give 1 Person a High Five	Give 1 Person a Sincere Compliment

Wiggle Waggle
With a Partner

Challenge
Someone to a
Thumb Wrestle

Tell 1 Person
They are
Awesome!

Come up with a
Secret Handshake
with Someone

Give 1 Person
a Hug

Give 1 Person
a Happy Salmon
Handshake

Challenge
Someone to
Finger Fencing

Find Someone
to do a
Windmill Stretch

Do 10
Jumping Jacks

Do 10
Torso Twists

Jog in Place
for 10 Seconds

Touch Your Toes
for 10 Seconds

Skip Around the
Perimeter of the
Room 1 Time

Power Walk
Around the
Perimeter of the
Room 1 Time

Find Someone
to Waltz With

Stretch Any
Muscle You
Choose for
10 Seconds

Tell Someone a Funny Joke	Do the Can-Can Dance with Someone
Butterfly Stretch for 10 Seconds	Reach for the Sky Stretch for 10 Seconds
Shake Your Whole Body for 10 Seconds	Stretch Any Muscle You Choose for 10 Seconds
Wild Card Your Choice	Wild Card Your Choice

Safety

Sending 'guessers' out in pairs or trios is a lower risk than solo as it diminishes the potential humiliation or pressure that a lone person can feel if they are unable to interpret the word.

Three Syllable Word

Overview

Three small groups simultaneously annunciate one syllable of the same three-syllable word while two or three other participants ('guessers') not present for word selection, try to decipher each syllable to form the word. Repeated soundings of the syllables can be requested by guessers. This seemingly straightforward task is surprisingly challenging as well as intriguing due to the mystery, the chaotic synchronous speech, dichotomy between disguising yet assisting, and the ultimate discovery which evokes congratulatory cheers.

Group Size	12 or more
Learning Themes	• Fun and Play • Relationship Skills • Responsible Decision Making
Materials / Props	Back-up list of interesting, three-syllable words

Setup

Creatively separate your group into three sub-groups. Have the groups cluster, facing each other.

Framing

Say to the group:

"Who knows what a syllable is? Someone give me an example of a word that has one syllable. How about two? How about three?"

Procedure

1. Ask for one volunteer from each group to be part of the guessing team. Once volunteers have been selected, ask that they leave the room. These three participants should not be able to hear the others. When they return to the room, their objective is to try to guess the three-syllable word chosen by the large group.

2. While the guessing team is out of earshot, the other groups work to come up with a three-syllable word. If they were to select CHIMPANZEE, each small group would take one of the three syllables. For example, group one would be the CHIM group; group two, the PAN group; and group three, the ZEE group. When the guessers return to the room, the three groups say their syllables at the same time.

3. The guessers will do their best to listen to the different syllables and assemble them like a puzzle until the sounds make sense. If they don't get it on the first try... a rarity...they can re-position themselves and ask the class to repeat the syllables. Guessers can request a 'sounding' of the word using motions of a conductor starting a symphony.

4. Play a few more rounds, giving all students the opportunity to be the guessers.

Reflection/Closure/Discussion:

Ask students:

- What strategies did you develop in order to succeed as speakers and guessers?

- What was challenging about this activity? How did it feel to not know the word?

- As speakers, what did you do to challenge or assist the guesser?

- Which were some of the easier words to guess? Which were the hardest ones?

Tips and Comments

- If three syllables are too hard, try the same activity with two-syllable words.

- If students have a hard time coming up with words, make suggestions or provide a list from which they can select.

- Send a larger group of four to eight out of the room. They can strategize while the 'word' group selects their word and develop their own strategy which may involve scattering syllables about the room

- If sending a student outside the room or to a distant location is not possible, have them cover their ears and turn away. Alternatively, challenge the group to do their planning in whispers which can heighten suspense and engagement.

Tie that Eight...

Overview

A problem-solving activity for two people. Pairs are challenged to tie a figure-eight knot in a section of rope. It's not as simple as it seems and thus leads to great dialogue and learning that can be transferred directly to actual teaching and tying of knots.

Group Size	12 or more
Learning Themes	• Self Awareness and Self Management • Relationship Skills • Responsible Decision Making
Materials / Props	One 15 – 20 ft. length of rope per participant pair

Setup

Spend about five minutes showing the group the figure-eight knot. Let them try it with their own ropes. Find a fun way to separate the group into pairs.

Framing

Holding the end of a rope in your hand, say to the group:

"Learning to tie knots is challenging and sometimes difficult. It can be even more challenging when you have to tie the knots in a specific way, with a partner, each holding one end of the rope."

Procedure

Objective: Participants, working in pairs, tie a basic figure-eight knot in the center of a rope.

Rules:

1. Participants may only hold the very end of the rope with one hand. Allowing the use of the other hand is often a decent option, still creating a challenging task.

2. Participants may not take their hands off their end of the rope until the task is completed.

Reflection / Closure / Discussion

1. What was it like working with a partner? How well did you communicate your ideas and movements? Was it easy?

2. Did anyone discover anything about giving directions and/or interpreting directions?

Safety

Encourage the group to move safely while attempting to move quickly. Moving too quickly may result in tripping over or through a hoop or webbing circle and could also result in damaged hoops.

Toll Booth Boogie

Overview:

A classic in the making, Toll Booth Boogie drives individuals and groups to collectively meet at the same destination. Participants, or teams of participants, seek efficiency as they travel from point A to Point B through a series of hula hoops. This versatile activity has a myriad of potential learning outcomes and a host of variations.

Group Size	10 or more
Learning Themes	• Self Awareness and Self Management • Relationship Skills • Responsible Decision Making
Materials / Props	• Numbered spot markers (1-30) • 30 hula hoops • 2 lengths of rope approximately 30 feet each to mark Start and Finish lines

Setup

1. Establish a start and finish line using play rope or webbing.

2. Create five rows of six hula hoops, a total of 30 hoops, between the start and finish lines. Place the hoops in each row in a straight line. The hoops represent toll booths.

3. Place a numbered spot marker, a total of 30 spot markers, face down inside each hoop.

4. Be sure that each row has at least one odd-numbered spot marker and at least one even-numbered spot marker.

Framing

Vacation Traffic

"How many of you have ever been in a car heading toward a toll booth on a weekend or vacation week? Have you noticed how the cars seem to criss-cross the lanes seeking either the open lane, lane with the shortest line, or the desired payment method? It seems problematic. Envision yourself as individual cars, yet a collective group of people hoping for a relaxing vacation. Your task is to find the most efficient way to get everyone through the toll booths, from Point A to Point B, and on to your well-deserved vacation!"

Goal Setting

"Goal setting is a relevant way for a group to go from good to great. Revising a goal is essential for fairly challenging the group. Tracking a goal helps to accurately assess progress. During this activity, you will set, revise, and track goals while working as a team toward the most efficient solution to get from point A to point B."

Procedure

1. Working as a team, participants attempt to move from Point A, the starting line, to Point B, the finish line, by passing through even-numbered hoops, or toll booths, as quickly as they can. Everyone must pass through at least one hoop in each row and may only advance to the next row after passing through an appropriate hoop in the previous row.

2. To "pass" through a toll booth, each participant must physically move their body through the hoop, which requires the hoop to be passed from head to toe, toe to head, or a participant stepping through a hoop that is lifted and held vertically off the ground. Participants may not pass through a hoop while it remains on the ground.

3. A hoop, after being used by everyone needing it, must be placed back on the ground around its original spot marker.

4. Participants may not pass through an odd-numbered toll booth. If an odd-numbered spot marker is discovered, the participant who discovered it, as well as anyone else who notices it, must move laterally to another toll booth, hoop, in that row seeking an even-numbered spot marker.

5. Spot markers, whether odd or even, may remain face up once flipped.

6. The event is timed. Time starts when the first person crosses the starting line and stops when the last person crosses the finish line.

7. Provide an opportunity to plan and prepare after the first round and before each sequential round. Play three to five rounds.

Reflection/Closure/Discussion

Vacation Traffic

1. How would you describe your communication?

2. What aspects of your communication, both as individuals and as a group, were most helpful?

3. How did these positive aspects of communication affect your decisions and ultimately your solutions?

4. Can you identify other aspects of your self – values, morals, strengths, limitations, cultural norms, etc – that may have impacted your decisions?

5. What might this tell us about how we communicate and interact with others in our everyday lives?

Goal Setting

1. How would you describe your goal setting – increasingly challenging or less challenging?

2. How many revisions were made to reach optimal efficiency? What went into making these revisions?

3. What is the value of revising a goal?

4, What are the benefits of a positive or challenging goal?

Tips and Comments

- This activity was inspired by many days of travel, especially those including at least one, if not multiple, toll booths and the fascinating driving behaviors that surround them.

- A few teachers who have tried Toll Booth Boogie early on have shared their students' experiences. The information that was shared was similar. While playing Toll Booth Boogie, students from two different sites have developed the language of "carpooling" and "toll keepers" to describe specific solutions or roles. Carpooling refers to passing more than one person through a toll booth (hoop or webbing circle) at a time. Toll keeper refers to the individual who lifts, lowers, or holds the hoop in order for others to pass safely and efficiently. Processing either or both of these concepts would offer a group the opportunity to explore the concepts of caring for self and others and creating and sustaining a healthy lifestyle through social support.

Variations

There are many ways to vary Toll Booth Boogie depending on the overall objective, size of the group, or to provide additional challenges.

- **Memory or Random Redistribution** – Before beginning the activity, determine whether the spot markers will remain in the same place for each round or if they will be randomly re-distributed. Keeping spots where they are allows the group the opportunity to memorize or become more and more familiar with the pattern of even-numbered toll booths. Random Redistribution provides novelty for each round. There is value in both options, yet the facilitator, and subsequently the group, should be clear of the challenge prior to the first attempt.

- **Odd and Even (Same Direction)** – Separate the group into two teams. Start the teams on the same side with the same objective of traveling from point A to point B and passing through the hoops as quickly as they can. However, one team may only pass through hoops with an even-numbered spot marker, while the other may only pass through hoops with an odd-numbered spot marker. Teams can either compete or work toward a collective best, depending on the desired learning outcomes.

Tips and Comments *(continued)*

- **Odd and Even (Opposite Directions)** – Similar to the odd and even variation above, divide the group into two teams. This time, however, start the teams on the opposite sides with the objective of traveling from their respective point A to point B, passing through the hoops as quickly as they can, as described in the procedure above. Again, similar to odd even (same direction) one team may only pass through hoops with an even-numbered spot marker, while the other may only pass through hoops with an odd-numbered spot marker. Teams may either compete or work toward a collective best, depending on the desired learning outcomes. Participants should be made aware of the potential for collision and should do their best to avoid contact with other people to ensure a safe passing.

- **Multi-Way Toll Booth Boogie** – Larger groups may be divided into three or four groups and attempt to pass through the tollbooths from three or four directions. Again, teams can compete or work collectively for their best time.

- **Webbing** – Replace hoops with tubular webbing tied in a circle with a water knot.

- **Pop Quiz** – Replace numbered spot markers with Quiz Questions, Riddles, Rebus Puzzles, etc.

- **Disabling** – Inviting some participants to be blindfolded, wear earplugs, or be muted are always options for varying the activity and challenge. Doing so during Toll Booth Boogie, may result in significant learning regarding communication or interaction with people of different abilities.

- **Change the Setup:**

1. **Triangle** – Instead of five rows of six hoops, place hoops and numbered spot markers in a triangle shape providing the group with many options initially and fewer as they progress.

2. **Inverted Triangle** – Similarly, an inverted triangle could present the group with fewer choices initially and more as they progress.

3. **Diamond** – A diamond shape of hoops would create a blend between the two, more choices in the middle and fewer at the beginning and end.

4. **Hourglass** – An hour glass shape would create fewer choices in the middle and more at the beginning and end.

Tollbooth Boogie Setup Diagrams

Overview

There are many ways to vary Tollbooth Boogie. One way is to change the setup and, even within this opportunity, many possibilities lie. Below are five diagrams, including the original, listed in the activity write-up.

Original

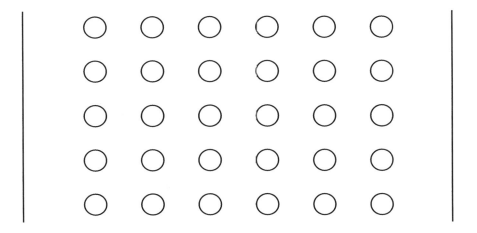

Variations

Triangle:

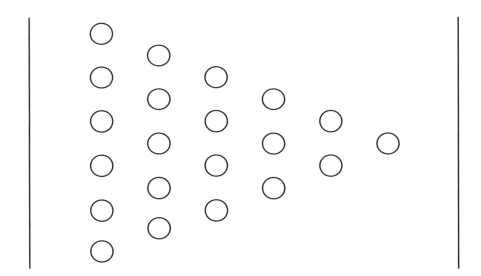

Inverted Triangle:

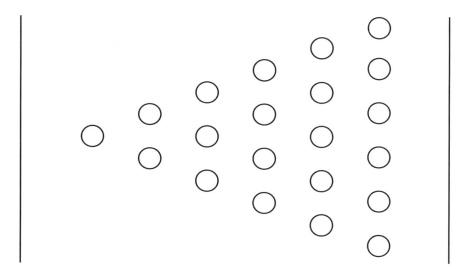

Diamond:

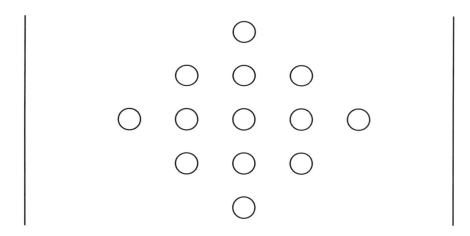

Hourglass:

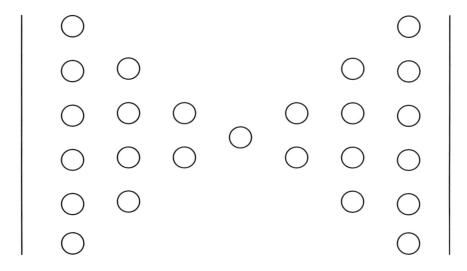

Total Eclipse of the Heart (aka Lunar Eclipse)

Overview

The group attempts to cast a shadow big enough to eclipse the heart.

Group Size	12 persons
Learning Themes	• Relationship Skills • Responsible Decision Making
Materials / Props	• A 50 ft. length of rope or webbing • Most importantly, a bright sunny day or adequate lighting for defined shadows to be cast on the ground

Setup

Using the rope, create the outline of a heart on the ground. Think about your group size as they will need to be able to cooperatively cast a shadow large enough to cover their creation. Start small. You can always increase the challenge in a second round.

Framing

Begin by asking the group:

"Have you ever seen a total eclipse of the moon? How about a total eclipse of the heart? Well, today you're going to have the opportunity not only to see one but to create it as well."

Procedure

1. Show participants the heart outline on the ground.
2. Participants may only use their bodies to cast shadows. No other props are allowed – unless you provide them.
3. The group must cover the entire inner space of the heart outline with shadow.
4. Ask the group to set a shared goal by creating the largest outline they're capable of covering.

Reflection / Closure / Discussion

1. Was it challenging to be present and active in this activity?
2. What about creating the group goal – was it challenging to be present?
3. Did you achieve your goal? What contributed to that?

In addition to typical problem-solving and relationship skills themes, the idea of who we are in relation to others may present itself. It is significant to consider how or where all people fit in with the others to accomplish a common goal or simply exist. Look for this opportunity and process accordingly.

Traffic Signs

Estimated Time

15 – 20 minutes

Overview

An activity for navigating group-generated norms. The group is challenged with establishing some broad group norms. Traffic Signs is an effective way to raise awareness of desirable and undesirable behaviors while efficiently checking in throughout the adventure together.

Group Size	4 or more
Learning Themes	• Building Trust, Relationships, and Community • Self Awareness and Self Management • Social Awareness
Materials / Props	Three pieces of flip chart paper per group and a variety of markers

Setup

Write the word *Go* at the top of one sheet of paper. Write *Yield* on another and *Stop* on the final sheet.

Framing

Say to the group:

"Traffic signs can help us to navigate out in the world. They can also help us to navigate among ourselves, as members of a working group giving us direction and an understanding of the expected."

Procedure

1. Ask participants to discuss and record behaviors that will help the group to succeed on the sheet labeled *Go* – behaviors they want to "Go" with.

2. Ask participants to discuss and record behaviors that may be distracting to progress on the sheet labeled *Yield* – the behaviors they want to be cautious of.

3. Finally, ask participants to discuss and record behaviors that hinder a group's ability to succeed and lead to disengagement and distrust on the sheet labeled *Stop* – behaviors that should "Stop" or rarely happen.

Reflection / Closure / Discussion:

1. How does exploring group behaviors and expectations provide direction for a group? Why is direction important?

2. How are these lists going to help us? How are we going to remember what we discussed?

3. Have you ever discussed norms in a group before? Is it helpful?

Tips and Comments

Post the signs in a visible location to refer to in the future. Periodically ask participants to evaluate their progress according to what is written on each sheet.

Safety

- Leaders must have proper training before doing this activity.

- You may need to add participants' names to the verbal communication so that multiple groups don't get their communications confused.

- Make sure that the ground is level and clear.

- Assess your group's readiness for this activity before beginning.

- Make sure that there is clear communication about when the activity is over.

Trust Line

Overview

Trust Line is a dynamic and collaborative version of a Three Person Trust Lean. One person puts their trust in the entire group as they lean back and forth, believing that his or her group mates will be there to spot them as the previous spotter leaves.

Group Size	10 – 15
Learning Themes	• Building Trust, Relationships, and Community
	• Self Awareness and Self Management
	• Social Awareness
	• Relationship Skills
Materials / Props	None

Setup

None

Framing

Say to the group:

"Have you heard the saying 'I've got your back'? What does that mean to you? Would you agree that it is helpful to trust many people in your life? In this activity, you will have a chance to put your trust in everyone in our group."

Or:

"What does it mean to 'be there' for someone? What skills have we developed as a group that demonstrate our readiness to be there for each other? Let's illustrate that."

Or:

"Have you ever noticed resilient trees that bend in stormy weather, but don't fall? It is usually an indication of a strong root system and nutritious soil. Consider our Full Value Contract as nutritious soil and our connectedness as a strong root system utilizing the nutrients needed to support each other should we sway."

Procedure

1. Introduce this activity after sufficient spotting practice, e.g., Two and Three Person Trust Leans (*Middle School Adventure Curriculum for Physical Education*, p. 127), has occurred.

2. Check in regarding the group's trust in each other and confidence in their spotting skills.

3. Ask for a volunteer to be the leaner.

4. Direct the group to form two lines, one facing the back of the leaner and one facing the front.

5. Explain that the activity is very similar to a Three Person Trust Lean, with the leaner leaning toward the first spotter in either line. The difference is that, after spotting, the spotters leave and progress to the end of the other line. Each time a spotter leaves, a new spotter (the next person in line) steps up to take the previous spotter's place.

6. The leaner then initiates the activity with verbal communication to ensure that everyone is ready. Verbal communication is critical:

    Leaner: "Spotters ready?"

    Spotters: "Ready."

    Leaners: "Leaning."

    Spotters: "Lean Away!"

7. After a clear verbal exchange of readiness, the leaner leans in either direction, spotted by the first spotter in that line. The spotter provides the leaner with just enough momentum to lean toward the opposing spotting line.

8. After spotting, the spotter moves to the opposite line. Direct spotters of each line to move from one line to the other on opposite sides of the leaner to avoid collisions.

9. Continue this exchange of spotters, until the leaner asks to stop or enough time has passed.

10. Complete the experience by having the current spotters place their hands on the leaners' shoulders.

Reflection/Closure/Discussion

1. What was it like to be a leaner? What was it like to be a spotter?

2. Were there ever any moments of doubt? How was that communicated? How did people respond?

3. What does trust in others feel like? How was trust demonstrated in our activity?

4. In what ways did we care for self and others?

5. How does caring for and trusting self and others help to support a healthy lifestyle?

Tips and Comments

- While adding names to the verbal communication may be necessary for safety, it also personalizes the experience adding great programming value. It reinforces the connections that participants have with one another.

- Allow the leaners to choose if they want to hear verbal cues from each new spotter or if they would prefer to trust in silence that someone is there to spot them.

Estimated Time ◔

5 – 10 minutes

Safety

Watch for hands on the floor, potential for stepping on fingers.

Tunnel Tag

Overview

A fast-paced tag game that might leave players rolling on the ground laughing. Participants play a game of tag, forming "tunnels" when tagged. A tagged player is free to move again when another player crawls through his or her tunnel. Tunnel Tag is a playful look at movement and helping others.

Group Size	10 or more
Learning Themes	• Fun and Play • Physical Activity and Movement • Self Awareness and Self Management • Social Awareness
Materials / Props	Fleece Balls (used as Tagger Identifiers)

Setup

Identify one of every ten participants as a tagger.

Framing

Say to participants:

"Helping one another is the key to keeping this game going!"

Procedure

1. The goal is for the tagger to touch anyone who is not a tagger on the shoulder with a free hand (no throwing the fleece ball).

2. If tagged, participants must freeze where they are and spread their feet wide, creating a tunnel with their legs. They may not re-enter the game until someone who is free crawls through their "tunnel."

Reflection / Closure / Discussion

1. What happened during the game? Did people help one another?
2. What would happen if people did not help one another and only worried about themselves?
3. How do you know if someone needs help? Have you ever asked for help?
4. What is the value in asking for help in this game?
5. Are there other situations in which you might find yourself "frozen" if you did not ask for help?

Tips and Comments

Variations

- To increase difficulty and provide more opportunities for helping, add more taggers to the game.

- Play an 'Everybody's It' version, where anyone can tag anyone else. Likewise, anyone can help anyone else by crawling through their tunnel. A fleece ball or tagger identifier is no longer necessary as everyone identifies as a tagger. Got it? Go play!

- Play with a variety of different tunnel forms. For example, participants may form an inverted 'V' with both hands and feet on the ground and bottom (buttocks) pointing toward the sky as in the yoga posture Down Dog. Other options might include placing both hands and knees on the ground as in the yoga posture Table or, if appropriate, and done safely, participants could position themselves in a back bend or gymnastics bridge as in the yoga posture Wheel. Most importantly, invite participants to playfully create their own tunnel shapes. Keep the door of creative possibilities open, while monitoring for safety.

Safety

- Be sure to use a ball that will not harm, especially a player's face, as it is likely to go there from time to time. Some recommendations for this are: beach balls, fleece balls, and Thumballs.

- When players are moving around the space, they should be aware of others as they will most likely be looking down.

Tweener

Overview

A silly and fun activity, great for making transitions and expending lots of energy! Players form a circle with legs hip to shoulder width apart and try to score a goal by hitting a ball through the legs of other players. Tweener can be an energizing and playful look at the empathy and compassion in the group.

Group Size	10 or more
Learning Themes	• Fun and Play • Building Trust, Relationships, and Community • Social Awareness
Materials / Props	• 1 – 2 inflatable plastic balls • Space enough for the group to stand in a circle, and/or move around slowly

Setup

Inflate the balls. Gather the group into a circle.

Framing

Say to the group:

"We are going to play a game that involves each person being able to score goals, and a person having a goal to protect."

Or:

"We are going to play a seemingly competitive game that will truly test the empathy and compassion in our group. Consider how this influences your play."

Procedure

1. Have the participants stand in a circle with their feet touching the feet of the person next to them. Each person's legs should be about two feet apart.

2. The area between each person's legs is his or her own 'goal' to protect – with the palm of their hands only. They may not bend their knees or use any other part of their bodies to guard their goals.

3. Explain that a goal is scored when the ball goes between one's legs. The ball should only be hit with the palm, and should stay on the ground as much as possible.

4. If the ball leaves the ground, anyone who can should grab it and continue playing with the ball on the ground.

5. Players may not move their feet while playing.

6. When players have a goal scored on them, they put one hand behind their backs. After a second goal is scored, the other hand is placed behind the back. If a third goal is scored, the player turns around and plays from a backward stance. (Optional).

7. When a ball is hit between two people, it is called a 'tweener.' When a tweener occurs, all players re-set (regaining the use of one or both of their arms or turn around) and play resumes. This rule provides an opportunity for everyone in the group to show compassion for others.

Reflection / Closure / Discussion

1. What strategies did you use to protect your goal? Was it difficult to focus on scoring and protecting your goal at the same time?

2. Did having an additional challenge (losing the use of an arm or two) make it more interesting for you?

3. How did you feel when someone else lost the use of an arm in the game? Did you use a different strategy with him or her?

Tips and Comments

Variations

- **Elimination** – Instead of playing in a backward stance, explain that a third goal now results in being temporarily eliminated. Temporarily, of course, because an empathetic and compassionate group will likely score a tweener. A tweener, in this instance, not only re-sets all of the players but also brings anyone who may have been eliminated back into the game.

- **Mooooove** – Occasionally, a ball, especially beach balls, will exit the group by bouncing or being hit over the heads of the players' circle, rather than in the typical fashion of a goal or tweener. When this happens, it is called an 'over' originally coined by a sixth grade class. This playful group also decided that when an 'over' occurred, the whole group would put bumpers up (hands up) and "moooooooove" their way to a new spot in the circle without bumping into or contacting anyone else. Yes, bumpers up, moving to a new spot and "mooooing" just like a cow! Now, get a "mooooooooove on" and give it a try! And be playful about it.

- **Call It Out!** – In an effort to increase the energy and fun, lead players to instantaneously call "Goooooooooal!" (loud and drawn out as in World Cup Soccer), "Tweener" (short, sweet, and high pitched), or "Over" (a joyful yell) for each appropriate occasion. Doing so initiates the development of a playful voice among the group.

- **More Action** – Introduce an additional ball or two into the game to increase the action and the fun.

- **Tweener on the Move** – To make the game more physically active, and perhaps more challenging, invite participants to play Tweener while moving around a space rather than in a stationary circle. Players still attempt to score goals between the legs of another player. Goals may now be scored from the front or back of other players. All players must do their best to keep an appropriately-sized goal, keeping feet hip to shoulder width apart, while moving around. For humorous moments and awkwardly funny movements, require players to move while maintaining a wide goal the entire time. To offer a memorable visual, envision and model the movement of an Emperor Penguin running around with a giant egg between his legs, referencing the movies *March of the Penguins* or *Happy Feet* if needed.

Safety

Provide participants with adequate time to practice, experience, and process or review spotting and leaning with traditional Trust Leans (*Adventure Curriculum for Physical Education: High School*.p.107, a PA publication). Walk and Lean is a variation of traditional Trust Leans and is intended to build upon pre-existing experiences and skills such as spotting, letting go, and trusting.

Walk and Lean

Overview

A dynamic addition or expansion to the traditional Trust Lean activity. In pairs, one participant walks randomly, followed by his or her partner. At some point, the person walking and leading stops and leans, trusting that the partner will be present. Walk and Lean is a great way to build on pre-existing trust and spotting skills as well as reinforcing the importance of self-spotting during the activity and in life.

Group Size	6 or more
Learning Themes	• Building Trust, Relationships, and Community • Self Awareness and Self Management • Social Awareness • Relationship Skills
Materials / Props	None

Setup

Provide participants with adequate time to practice, experience, and process or review spotting and leaning with traditional Trust Leans. A Trust Lean is a spotting based activity – one person leans forward or backwards into the trusting hands or spot of another person.

Framing

Say to the group:

"Now that you have experience with leaning and spotting, let's add a new dynamic to your experience. This variation provides the leaner with more directions to lean and the spotter with more realistic opportunities to respond accordingly. Ultimately, you will have an opportunity to explore the boundaries that exist within a relationship."

Procedure

1. Demonstrate. Ask for a willing volunteer to be the leaner in the demonstration. Explain to this person that he or she will walk for a bit and lean backwards while you (the facilitator) follow and spot.

2. After demonstrating a few leans in a backward direction, have participants partner up and do this activity. Remind the participants who are leaning that they should try to stay in the lean as long as they can, and for spotters to be very alert and ready.

3. Check for understanding.

4. Direct participants to determine who will lean and spot first, then begin.

5. Switch roles after a few minutes.

Reflection/Closure/Discussion

1. The transition in roles, from leaner to spotter and spotter to leaner, may be an opportune time for participants to process their experience and apply what they have learned.

2. In pairs, ask participants to discuss the following:

   a. How was your experience as a leaner? How was your experience as a spotter?

   b. On a scale of 1 to 5 (Fist to 5), how well cared for did you feel?

   c. On a scale of 1 to 5 (Fist to 5), how well did you care for yourself?

   d. If you just leaned, what leaning recommendations would you give to your partner? Similarly, if you spotted, what spotting advice would you give to your partner?

3. After the participants experience Walk and Lean in the reciprocal role, ask participants in pairs to discuss the following:

   a. How was your experience as a leaner? How was your experience as a spotter?

   b. On a scale of 1 to 5 (Fist to 5), how well cared for did you feel?

   c. On a scale of 1 to 5 (Fist to 5), how well did you care for yourself?

   d. What similarities and differences existed for you within each role?

   e. How do you typically care for others? How do you prefer to be cared for? What helps you to care for yourself?

4. After allowing adequate time for partners to process their experiences, bring the whole group together or clump into small groups. Invite participants to share significant discoveries with the whole group.

Safety

As the crossings become more challenging and require participants to be connected, encourage participants to be aware of themselves and each other. Participants should be encouraged to let go and self-spot if a fall is inevitable.

Watch Your Step

Overview

A problem-solving activity that is challenging yet provides plenty of room for choice. Participants – individually, in pairs, and collectively – attempt a series of progressively challenging, physical crossings through a mishmash of rope. Watch Your Step naturally reinforces Challenge by Choice as participants explore personal stretch zones individually and with others, make mistakes, succeed, and move creatively.

Group Size	8 or more
Learning Themes	• Physical Activity and Movement • Relationship Skills • Responsible Decision Making
Materials / Props	• Ropes, webbing, tape, or • Just the right amount of cracked pavement (there would need to be lots of cracks intersecting with one another!)

Setup

- Scatter ropes and/or webbing in a random criss-cross pattern within a start and finish line.
- Tape can be used if playing indoors.

Framing

Say to group:

"Before you is the valuable artwork of a fire-breathing dragon. Your task is to cross from one side to the other without stepping on the art work, and ultimately upsetting the dragon. Good luck and watch your step."

Or:

"Journeying through life can have its challenges. The lines before you represent pathways of unhealthy lifestyles and subsequently, the spaces between the lines represent healthy lifestyle choices. Whether you travel alone or with other people, it is helpful to identify ways you and others would like to be supported."

Procedure

1. Establish a start and finish line.
2. Round 1 – Warm-up
   a. Invite participants to cross from one side to the other without touching the ropes.
   b. Explain that if anyone touches the rope, it will be announced and the group will move on. (You could invite participants to make their best fire-breathing dragon sounds!)
   c. This round is intended to be a warm-up so allow for a few attempts of the following scenarios and encourage creativity, style, and playfulness.

    d. Invite participants to:

        i. Cross the section of rope individually.

        ii. Cross the section of rope while physically connected to a partner.

        iii. Cross the section of rope while physically connected as a whole group.

3. Round 2 – Increasing the Challenge

    a. Now that everyone has had a chance to warm up, explain that the following crossing scenarios are likely to be more challenging and require more communication, coordination, and creativity.

    b. Explain that participants will again cross the section of jumbled rope as they did before – as individuals, in pairs, and as a whole group.

    c. However, in order to move forward in this round:

        i. Participants may only contact the ground with their hands or feet.

        ii. Additionally, each participant must use both hands and both feet before repeating the use of either hand or foot.

        iii. Participants may not have more than one hand or foot in the space between the ropes at any given time. In other words, participants may only place one hand or foot in each space between the ropes at any given time.

        iv. If a player touches the rope or violates another rule, he or she must return to the starting line and attempt again if playing individually. If playing in pairs or as an entire group, the pair or whole group needs to start over.

    d. In accordance to the rules outlined in this round, invite participants to again:

        i. Cross the section of rope individually.

        ii. Cross the section of rope while physically connected to a partner.

        iii. Cross the section of rope while physically connected as a whole group.

4. Round 3 (if time allows) – Create Your Own Challenge

    a. Now that everyone has experienced crossing individually, in pairs, and as a whole group and perhaps identified what made each scenario challenging for them, explain that there is yet another twist to this story.

    b. Invite participants to again work individually, in pairs, and this time in groups of four, to create a crossing intended to challenge another person, pair, or group of four.

    c. Each Crossing Challenge should be:

        i. Something that the individual, pair, or group of four is able to do and demonstrate on their own.

        ii. Creative, fun, and challenging while also allowing for choice within the solutions or result.

Reflection/Closure/Discussion

1. What did you notice about crossing individually, in pairs, and as a whole group?

2. How did you support each other as a whole group?

3. What were the similarities and differences, in terms of support, during each crossing?

4. How did you like to be supported? How did others like to be supported?

5. Do these examples hold true in your life? What examples of support would you like to experience in your life?

Tips and Comments

- Inspired by a scene in the movie *How to Train Your Dragon* in which the main character, Hiccup (a boy destined to make many mistakes and experience eventual success) discovers and interacts with a notorious dragon. The dragon is known by two names – Night Fury or Toothless – depending on the perspective you see him from. The themes in the movie – making many mistakes, eventual success, and perspective – are also significant in the activity.

- Flowing through all three rounds and every scenario in each round – individual, pairs, small groups, and whole groups – can be time-consuming. Choose what is appropriate for the goals and interest of the group as well as the time frame you have to work within. Round 3 could be considered an optional round or an event for another day.

Variations

- Change the rule in Round 2 regarding how many hands or feet are allowed in the space between the ropes at one given time. Try allowing participants to have as many hands or feet in the space between the ropes as they need to balance themselves and move forward. This variation significantly changes the challenge, yet still offers value.

- Consider adding consequence for crossing without touching the rope. For example, for every five successful steps, the group earns the ability to disregard an incident of contact with the rope. Similarly, consequences could be introduced for touching the rope or disconnecting.

- Consider having a couple of participants, stationed outside of the rope scramble. Have one participant sighted and the other non-sighted (eyes shut or blind folded). As the rest of the participants attempt to cross the rope scramble, the sighted and non-sighted team pay close attention to anyone touching the rope. If someone does touch the rope, the sighted participant directs the non-sighted participant to throw a fleece ball at the person or line of people. If someone is contacted, the whole line must either start again or separate at that section.

- During the paired and whole group crossings, consider having some non-sighted participants accompanied by sighted guides.

What Do You See?

Overview

A centering or convening activity designed to introduce the group to the setting, each other, and the goals of the program. Participants are directed to look around and consider what they see literally and figuratively.

Group Size	10 or more
Learning Themes	• Fun and Play • Building Trust, Relationships, and Community
Materials / Props	None

Setup

Have the group stand in a circle. Find a way to get their attention.

Framing: None

Procedure

1. Point in one direction (north) and ask, "When you look over there, what do you see?" Allow for a few (sometimes simultaneous) responses.

2. Point in another direction (south) and ask again, "When you look over there, what do you see?" Again, allow for a few (sometimes simultaneous) responses.

3. Repeat this two more times, pointing in the other directions (east, west).

4. Then point to the sky and ask, "When you look up there, what do you see?" Allow for responses.

5. Point to the ground and ask, "When you look down here, what do you see?" Allow for responses.

6. Finally, point and look around at the entire group and ask, "When you look around the circle (this group), what do you see?" Allow for responses.

7. After listening to the responses, take a moment to frame the day.

Reflection/Closure/Discussion

Speak for the experience and say, "Consider who is in this group, how it looks and feels now, and what it may look and feel like at the end of the day, semester, year, etc. The goals for today are..."

Tips and Comments

- This activity seems to work best when the experience is set in a location that is new to the group; a place that is unfamiliar to them.
- This activity works well for small and large groups and can provide an opportunity for an initial assessment of the group.

Where in the World?

Overview

An icebreaking initiative that's creative and interactive. Participants create a map of the world and consequently interact with it and each other Where in the World? is a great way to build awareness among members of the group and the different parts of the world that they come from.

Group Size	4 or more
Learning Themes	• Building Trust, Relationships, and Community • Self Awareness and Self Management • Social Awareness • Relationship Skills

Materials / Props	• 7 lengths of rope
	  - One, 20 foot
	  - Four, 40 foot
	  - One, 60 foot
	  - One, 80 foot
	• Random props (e.g., beanie babies, fleece balls, processing cards, etc.)
	• Additional sections of rope

Setup

Place ropes and random props in the center of an open space.

Framing

"How familiar are you with the world we live in? Have you ever looked at a map of the world and thought 'I want to go there' or 'that's were I was born'? How familiar are you with people in this group? Have you ever wondered where they were born or where they might want to visit? We have a chance to learn about both by creating a map of the world and interacting with it and one another."

Procedure

Map Making

1. Explain to the group that they will embark on a creative process with about 5-10 minutes to create a map of the world that is oriented correctly, yet not perfectly proportioned.

2. Check in at the end of five minutes to see if the group needs more time to finalize their creation. Remind the group that the map does not need to represent perfect shapes or scale.

3. Encourage the use of additional props to make borders, islands, or places of personal significance.

4. Once the world map is created, provide opportunities for the group to briefly reflect on their process and transition to the next part of the activity.

Where in the World?

1. Say to the group, "Move to the location where you were born."

2. Once participants seem to have found their places, ask them to share out to the group.

3. If there are any unique responses, feel free to ask for more information, and encourage your participants to do the same!

4. Repeat this process with other topics such as:

   - Move to the location that represents your ethnical background. Feel free to demonstrate by moving to and from a few different locations.

   - Move to any location, for any reason. Be prepared to share where you are and why?

   - Move to:

     "…where your heart is."

     "…a place that you would like to learn more about."

     "…a place that you would like to share something about."

     "…a place where you would be scared to travel to."

     "…a place that best represents your lifestyle."

     "…a location you believe needs help or support."

5. Process responses and reactions as needed.

Reflection/Closure/Discussion

Discussions can be established throughout the activity. Many interesting conversations may be sparked by specific responses to questions or reactions to where group members place themselves on the map. Be prepared to encourage sharing, while keeping the activity moving.

Tips and Comments

- Instead of a world map, consider mapping a specific country, city, or town.
- Consider the use of this map to teach geography or social studies.

Safety

Participants should be made aware that there may be moments during the game when they or their group mates run in opposite or unexpected directions. Every effort should be made to play safely and avoid collisions. Check in as needed.

World Travelers

Overview

A quick energizer with a world of possibilities. Participants run around a map of the world demonstrating their knowledge of direction, identifying locations, and representing well-known land marks and natural features as quickly as they can. World Travelers is a great way to get your group moving and playfully test their worldly knowledge.

Group Size	10 or more
Learning Themes	• Physical Activity and Movement • Building Trust, Relationships, and Community • Responsible Decision Making

Materials / Props	• 7 lengths of rope
	  - One, 20 foot - One, 60 foot
	  - Four, 40 foot - One, 80 foot
	• Random props (e.g., beanie babies, fleece balls, processing cards, etc.)
	• Additional sections of rope

Setup

Place ropes and random props in the center of a large open space.

Framing

Say to participants:

"Have you ever wanted to travel around the world? Where would you go? Would you know where you were? Could you create a map of the world to help?"

Or:

"Some people travel all over the world for work, vacations, and to volunteer. Regardless of reason, traveling around the world can be tiring and energizing. We are going to travel the world, but first we need to create a map."

Procedure

Map Making

1. Explain to the group that they will embark in a creative process lasting about five to ten minutes to create a map of the world that is oriented correctly, yet not perfectly proportioned.

2. Check in at the end of five minutes to see if the group needs more time to finalize their creation. Remind the group that the map does not need to represent perfect shapes or scale.

3. Encourage the use of additional props to make borders, islands, or places of personal significance.

4. Once the world map is created, provide opportunities for the group to briefly reflect on their process and transition to the next part of the activity.

World Travelers

1. At this point, participants should be familiar with the map they created and the association with an actual map. With this understanding, either the facilitator, or a participant caller, could challenge the participants to find particular directions and locations on the map as quickly as they can.

2. To warm up, explain that you will call specific directions – North, South, East, and West. Participants must run to the furthest point on the map of the specific direction called. For example, if "North" were called, participants would run toward the Arctic Circle or if, "South" were called, participants would run toward Antarctica.

3. Once the group has moved around a bit and become more familiar with the map, introduce more possibilities. Now, in addition to the four directions, participants must run to the general location in response to the following options:

   - Specific locations such as a particular continent, country, state/province, capital, etc.
   - Specific geographic features, such as rivers, mountain ranges, oceans, and deserts could also be called.

4. The possibilities are endless. Choose locations that seem most appropriate for your group at the time. The goal here is to have fun, get the group moving, and increase their heart rates.

5. Players are temporarily eliminated if they:

   - Run in the wrong direction.
   - Run to the wrong location.

6. The caller may then shout, "Go help somebody!" instructing remaining players to retrieve eliminated players and bring them back into the game.

Reflection/Closure/Discussion

1. Move to a place you know very well.
2. Move to a place that you needed help getting to.
3. Move to a landmark or natural feature that you know a lot about.
4. Move to a landmark or natural feature that you needed help understanding.

Tips and Comments

- World Travelers is inspired by the joy generated from running around wildly and grouping with others while playing the game Captains Calling. If you are familiar with Captains Calling, sometimes called Captains Coming or Shipwreck, then play on, World Travelers should be familiar to you. Otherwise, if Captains Calling is unfamiliar, take a look at the descriptions found in the following publications:

  – *No Props*, Collard, 2005
  – *Adventure Curriculum for Physical Education, Elementary School*, Panicucci et al, 2003

For a version of Captains Calling with leadership as a central learning theme check out:

- *Adventure Curriculum for Physical Education, High School*, p. 179, Panicucci et al, 2003

Tips and Comments (continued)

Variation

- Invite even more possibility and creativity by welcoming the player to call a number followed by a well-known landmark or natural feature. Participants then form groups according to the number called and use their bodies or kinesthetically represent the landmark or natural feature near the correct location. For example, the caller might call "1" followed by "the Statue of Liberty." Participants would then quickly move to the part of the map where the mouth of the Hudson River or the Upper Bay of New York Harbor would be located and individually pose in their best representations of the statue of liberty. However, if the player called "2" followed by "the Eiffel Tower" or "the Gateway Arch," participants would move quickly to the appropriate location, in these cases, France or St. Louis, Missouri respectfully, and find a partner. Partners would then perhaps lean in towards each other, supporting one another's weight by pressing into the palms of the partner with outstretched arms. When playing this variation, add to procedure number 5, that if players do not find themselves in a group according to the number called, they are also temporarily eliminated.

  Other calls to get you started:

  - **1 Person** – The Statue of Liberty (New York City, NY, USA) or the Sphinx (Egypt)

  - **2 People** – The Eiffel Tower (Paris, France), Gateway Arch (St. Louis Missouri, USA), The Lincoln Memorial (Washington D.C., USA), The Leaning Tower of Pisa (Pisa, Italy), Delicate Arch (Arches National Park, Utah)

  - **3 People** – The Lighthouse of Alexandria (Alexandria, Egypt) or a lighthouse anywhere really! The Great Pyramids (El Giza, Egypt) – spotting and safety considerations apply! Old Faithful (Yellowstone National Park, Montana, USA)

  - **4 People** – Mt Rushmore (South Dakota, USA) or The Golden Gate Bridge (San Francisco, California, USA)

  - **5 People** – The Pentagon (Virginia, USA)

  - **6 People** - The Presidential Mountain Range (White Mountains, NewHampshire, USA) or The Hawaiian Islands (Pacific Ocean)

  - **Everyone!** - The Great Wall of China (China), The Amazon River (South America), The Nile (Africa), The Sahara (Africa), Victoria Falls (Africa), The Great Barrier Reef (Australia), The Rocky Mountains (USA), The Grand Canyon (USA), Stonehenge (United Kingdom), Easter Island (South Pacific Ocean), etc.

  - What ideas can you offer? Considering what your participants are interested in or studying is a good place to start. Call out whatever it may be and let the participants collectively figure out the correct location and creatively represent the feature or landmark called.

Other Ideas

- **Globe Trotting** – Incorporate basketballs and basketball-related skills into traveling the world.

  - **Dribble** – Participants dribble a basketball as they move from place to place, according to what was called.

Tips and Comments *(continued)*

- **Pass** –Participants find partners. One partner moves to a particular place on the map, according to the caller's call. The other partner who holds the basketball until his or her partner is ready will attempt to pass the basketball to his or her partner. Participants may need to decide which type of pass may be appropriate (bounce, chest, etc.) based on the distance the ball needs to travel.

  - **Harlem** – Listening to the Harlem Globetrotters' theme song, "Sweet Georgia Brown" by Brother Bones, participants attempt tricks and stunts inspired by the Harlem Globetrotters while moving to different places on the map called by the caller.

- **Planes, Trains, and Automobiles** – Incorporate movement inspired by various modes and associated speeds of travel as participants move to specific locations on the map as they are called. With this variation, the caller may call "Planes fly to Antarctica!" Participants would then stretch their arms out to the side and "fly" (run) to Antarctica. Consider these other forms of transportation:

  - **Planes** – Individually, participants stretch their arms out to the side and "fly" (run) to the destination called.

  - **Bicycles** – Individual participants move to the location called as if pedaling bicycles. Once the specific location is reached, participants lie on their backs and continue peddling.

  - **Horseback** – Two people quickly partner. One person hops on to the back of the other, as in a piggyback, and, together, make their way to the destination called.

  - **Boats** – Participants form groups of three, place and connect hands in the middle and spin, as if to form a giant propeller, to the location called.

  - **Automobiles** – Participants form groups of four and assume roles. With one driver, one front passenger, two passengers in the back, the group needs to meander their way to the destination called.

  - **Trains** – Groups of five people in a straight line place hands on the shoulders of the players in front of them and chug their way to the location called. If playing in a gym, people could be required to follow the lines on the floor, as a train would follow tracks, to get to the destination.

  - **Busses** – Participants form groups of nine, and then create two lines of four and select one driver. While moving, participants should act out a bumpy bus ride to their destination.

- **Academic Link** – The Great Migration/Animal Kingdom – Call out particular animals that participants may know of or are studying in association with their habitat locations. Participants migrate in the manner of the specified animal to the appropriate habitat location based on the season.

243

Safety

If playing "You're Going the Wrong Way" or "World Wide Key Punch Chaos Variation," inform participants of the random directions and erratic movements that can occur. Participants should be more aware of self and others to prevent collisions.

World Wide Key Punch

Overview

Here we have the classic problem-solving activity, Key Punch, played on a global scale...sort of! Participants create a map of the world and attempt to reach the furthest corners of the Earth in the most efficient way. This is measured by how quickly, over the course of a few rounds, a group of people can contact numbers 1 to 30 distributed throughout the seven continents. World Wide Key Punch is an exciting twist to the original and offers new experiences regarding communication, goal setting, and honesty.

Group Size	12 or more
Learning Themes	• Self Awareness and Self Management • Relationship Skills • Responsible Decision Making
Materials / Props	• 8 play ropes/webbing • Numbered spot markers • Stop watch • Flip chart and markers for tracking results

Setup

Once a map of the world has been created (see Map Making), randomly distribute, or ask participants to help randomly distribute, numbered spot markers (numbers facing up) among the seven continents (rope boundaries).

Framing

Say to the group:

"Consider yourselves the top international scientists seeking to discover the most efficient means to travel around the world. As more and more people continue to travel the world, it is important to seek more efficient ways of doing so. Fast and faster means of travel is essential for connecting our global community and following safety and environmental guidelines are necessary for our survival. We must continue to work together towards more efficient travel."

Or:

"Efficiency, and its correlation to sustaining life on earth, is a concept that individuals, communities, and businesses are more consciously considering. While it may be important to do something quickly, it may be equally important to do it well. Most of us understand what it means to accomplish a task quickly and are challenged to also do it well. We will be working toward our best rate of efficiency – quality with quickness."

Or:

"Is everyone familiar with 'Around the World Tickets'? It just so happens, that we have one for everyone in your group; however, according to 'Around the World Ticket' guidelines, not everyone can go everywhere. Your task is to determine who should go where and collectively contact pre-selected landmarks as quickly as you can."

Procedure

Map Making

1. Explain to the group that they will embark in a creative process and have five minutes to create a map of the world correctly oriented.

2. Check in after five minutes.

3. The map does not need to represent perfect shapes or scale.

4. Additional props could be used to make borders, islands, or places of personal significance.

5. Once the world map is created, provide opportunities for the group to interact with it and each other.

World Wide Key Punch

1. *World Wide Keypunch* is played with similar rules as traditional *Key Punch*, however there are now seven boundaries/continents for the group and facilitator to be responsible for. Participants attempt to contact the numbers in ascending order with guidelines that only one person can be in any of the seven roped boundaries at a time. Penalties occur if numbers are contacted out of order and if there is more than one person in any of the seven rope boundaries at the same time.

2. Only one player is allowed in any of the seven continents at one time.

3. Numbers must be touched in sequence.

4. The time starts when the first person crosses the starting line. Time stops when the last person crosses back over the starting/finish line.

5. Ropes and spots may not be moved.

6. Although players may talk while interacting with the map, *no planning* can occur there, only execution of a plan. Planning may only occur behind the start/finish line.

7. Players have three to five trials to achieve their best rate of efficiency, meaning quality (least number of penalties) with quickness (fastest time possible). While the group is planning, encourage them to set and communicate a goal for each trial.

8. The penalty for each rule infraction is ten seconds added to that group's time for that particular trial. For example, if a group has more than one person in a continent or continents five different times during a trial, add fifty seconds to the total time of that trial.

Reflection/Closure/Discussion

1. **Chiji Processing Dice** – Chiji Processing Dice flow in concert with the Experiential Learning Cycle. Questions are posed and customized on dice to identify facts, make meaning, and explore connections to life beyond the activity.

2. **Reflective Map Debrief** – Participants use particular countries, continents, landmarks, natural features, etc. to respond to particular questions. For example, the facilitator might say, "Move to a region on the map that best represents how your group worked together." Participants may choose to move to the Middle East if there had been a lot of conflict or to New Zealand if their process seemed peaceful (New Zealand is considered the most peaceful place on earth, according to the Institute for Economics and Peace) or the Himalayas if the group felt as though they experienced many peaks and valleys.

3. **Potential Questions:**

   a. Did you meet your goal? How does it feel to meet or not meet your goal?

   b. Describe your group's process to meet or not meet the goal? How would you describe your communication?

   c. Describe how you felt during and after each trial. Did your feelings affect your results in any way? How?

   d. Describe your goal-setting process. Were there times when a goal needed to be revised as a result of being too accessible or too difficult? What would you say are the benefits to positive and challenging goals?

   e. Where and how might you use this information in other areas of your life?

Tips and Comments

- **Planning Time** – If time is limited, consider introducing a structured planning time. For example, once rules have been communicated, ask the group to summarize the rules or ask any questions they may have. After the summary or additional questions, provide five minutes of planning time for the first trial. As each trial occurs, reduce the amount of planning time. Provide four minutes for the second trial, three minutes for the third, two minutes for the fourth, and one minute for the fifth.

- **Goal Setting** – Key Punch is an activity that seems to highlight goal setting, making it more accessible to participants' understanding of effective goal setting. During each trial, record or have the group record their goal on a Key Punch tracking sheet, so that participants may use that information for evaluating and revising a goal for the next trial.

Variations

- **Where in the World?** – When contacting a number spot, participants must also call out the specific location – continent, country, landmark, etc. – associated with the number spot location. Using pictures of a specific landmark, country map, or location would make this variation more viable.

- **You're Going the Wrong Way!** – Whether you are working with a larger group or desire to increase the activity level of your participants, splitting a group in half offers a variation of dynamic passage. Same rules apply, yet in this variation, one team would start from 1 and contact number spots in ascending numerical order to 30. The second team, playing simultaneously, would work in reverse contacting numbers in descending order from 30 to 1.

- **World Wide Key Punch (Chaos Variation)/World Wide Chaos** – Similar to "You're Going the Wrong Way," World Wide Key Punch (Chaos Variation) offers a very dynamic challenge. Again, as a way to manage larger groups or classes or increase the activity level of your participants, consider adding multiple Key Punch kits (preferably different colors). This variation also invites multiple teams, perhaps two or three, to engage in World Wide Key Punch at the same time. Adapt the rules so that multiple people can physically be in a continent at the same time, as long as they are on different teams. Additionally, if a participant from one team steps on a number spot of another team, a ten-second penalty would be added.

Given that multiple teams are playing, consider a way to monitor accomplishments and rule infringements. A few considerations might be to ask a few participants to assist the facilitator or assume the role of accountability monitor. Emphasize the need for each individual person and team to be accountable for their own and others' behaviors, or record the event with a digital camera and review as needed!

- **Where Have You Been?** – This title could inspire two additional, more individual than team, variations. Participants can individually attempt to contact number spots as quickly as they can and choose to either contact numbers in consecutive order or any order as long as they are able to demonstrate accountability or track their progress. The other variation could simply be to disregard the number of people in a continent (rope boundary) rule, and challenge the group to contact the numbers as quickly as they can from the start/finish line. Participants could then check in, not only regarding time, but also where they have been.

Yeehaw

Overview

A highly-charged energizer in which participants exchange a series of extremely energized and theatrical gestures and verbal commands. Yeehaw is a perfect choice for generating laughter, as a filler or energizer, or to playfully explore making mistakes and accountability.

Group Size	10 or more
Learning Themes	• Fun and Play • Building Trust, Relationships, and Community • Self Awareness and Self Management
Materials / Props	None

Framing

Say to the group:

"Let's have everybody gather in a circle. On the farm, we cowboys and cowgirls like to say YEEEEEHAAWW! Say it with me now! YEEEEEHAAWW!"

Or:

"Life on the farm is all about learning. There are times when things seem to go well and other times when we make mistakes. We often celebrate when something goes well and we could practice celebrating when we make mistakes. During this activity, I am sure that there will be some mistakes and we will practice appreciating and celebrating them."

Estimated Time

20 – 30 minutes; Ongoing!

Safety

Ensure participants that the sound and motion "Yeehaw" is not an opportunity to punch or hit their neighbors.

Or:

"Has anyone heard of the acronym FUNN? Functional Understanding Not Necessary. This is a FUNN game. It all begins with the sound 'YEEEEEHAAWW!'"

Or:

"The game we are about to play may be stressful for some people. As we play, be aware of how you feel and respond."

Procedure

1. Explain to the group that they will be passing a sound and motion around the group. If your group has previous experience with similar activities such as Ah So Ko, Hi Lo Yo, or Hu Ha Pako, it may be helpful to reference these activities, and then continue explaining the rules to this game.

2. Introduce and practice the first sounds and motion, "Yeehaw!" Explain that Yeehaw is the first sound and motion of many. Instruct participants to extend their right arms straight out in front of them while making a fist. Then direct them to bend their right arms 90 degrees and turn their fists to the ground, elbows facing the sky. The participants will now be in proper Yeehaw initiating position. Instruct participants to swing their fists across their chests toward their left shoulders while exclaiming, 'YEEEEEHAAWW!' Then have them try it with their left hands. Explain that Yeehaw sends the sound and motion to a player's left or right as indicated by the swinging direction of the fist.

3. Introduce the second sound and motion, "Pitchfork." Instruct participants to reach up and around their neighbor to the left or right, as if they were sending a pitchfork full of hay around them while squeaking 'pitchfork' in a high pitched voice. This motion skips the person to the immediate left or right of the caller, depending upon the direction indicated, sending the sound and motion on to the next player.

4. Practice playing with both 'Yeehaw' and 'Pitchfork.'

5. Introduce the third sound and motion, "Git down little doggie." At this point, the caller may choose either of the first two sounds and motions (Yeehaw or Pitchfork) or they could bravely step one foot out, bend their knees slightly, point both hands out to someone anywhere in the circle while wagging their pointer fingers, and wildly exclaim, "Git down lil doggie!" This sends the sound and motion call directly to the person indicated, who must immediately call and perform the next sound and motion. Practice with all three sounds and motions until ready to play an official game.

6. To play:

    a. Participants stand in a circle and exchange these highly energized and theatrical gestures and verbal commands.

    b. Play continues until a notable mistake or pause is made at which point there are a few variations. The entire community can applaud/celebrate the mistake and continue play. The person who made the mistake starts the next round of sound and motions.

    c. Alternatively, the player who made the mistake, after a celebratory round of applause, is either eliminated or transitioned. See variations below. In either case, the person to the left of the person eliminated or transitioned immediately begins another round of sound and motions. If they do not initiate activity by the count of three, they are also eliminated or transitioned! Tough we know, but it keeps everyone alert and the game moving.

7. Once your group has experienced Yeehaw at a base level, as described above, consider adding more sounds and motions from the list below or empowering the group to create their own. Either way, adding more sounds and motions will likely increase the challenge, confusion, and fun! Similarly, introduce one of the combinations, also listed below, after the group becomes very familiar with Yeehaw, including additional sounds and motion. This will be evident when participants start initiating their own games of Yeehaw. These combinations keep it fresh and add a ridiculous twist of humor!

Reflection/Closure/Discussion

Reflection #1

1. What was it like to appreciate and celebrate mistakes?
2. How might that influence/impact our time together?
3. Can you think of a time when making a mistake is okay? Are there times when mistakes are not okay?
4. How might we determine whether a mistake is okay to make or not?

Reflection #2

1. Was this activity stressful? What makes it stressful or not?
2. How do you know if it was stressful or not?
3. Is there a particular place in your body where the stress presented itself?
4. Does this happen in other stressful situations in your life?
5. What are some ways of managing stress?

Tips and Comments

There are many ways to play Yeehaw. This write-up documents one or a few of them. If you already know other rules or variations of Yeehaw, then play on. In doing so, we hope that you find something valuable to your understanding of the game that makes everyone laugh ten times as hard. Enjoy!

Variations

- **Modes of Play**

    - **Elimination** – When a player clearly makes a mistake or fails to perform the correct sound and motion in a timely manner, including a clap and jump when incorporated, they are eliminated. Eliminated players are asked to simply observe in amusement until the game ends and a new one begins. No worries, the games are typically quick and usually entertaining enough to keep players interested and present for the next game. Also, once the game has been played enough, it can make for a great instant activity for any physical education class or a way for participants to prepare themselves for a meeting, practice, lecture, etc. Simply, this game engages the heart and gets the brain ready to learn.

Tips and Comments (*continued*)

- **The Distractor** – What better way to engage participants than to provide an opportunity to distract other players? Play games in the elimination mode as described above. However, when a participant is eliminated, he or she earns the opportunity to transition to a role that they are perhaps better suited for at the moment, that of being a distractor. Distractors do their best to distract other players by making sounds and motions while remaining outside the circle. They may not visually or physically impede nor can they impair the hearing of others. This mode of play adds another dimension to the game, an opportunity to practice calm and focus amidst the confusion and chaos sure to ensue.

- **Cooperation** – The challenge or goal with this variation is for the group to keep the sounds and motions going for as long as possible, including a clap and jump when incorporated. Now, the group may develop particular strategies while working toward their personal best. This moves the game from an individually competitive game to a group cooperating towards a common goal.

- **Multiple Games** – If you are working with a group of 15 or more, it may be beneficial to create multiple games after explaining and demonstrating the rules. Doing so will create a space where two, three, four or more games are happening simultaneously. Each game could be played in the cooperative mode as described above. However, if you hope to get your participants playing and interacting with as many people as possible, play multiple games in the elimination mode. When players are eliminated, they leave their original circles and join other games already in progress. An alternative to this variation is to start one game with lots of people and invite eliminated participants to start a new game with other players who have also been eliminated. This creates opportunities for engagement, initiative, and empowerment.

- **Additional Sounds and Motions**

  - **Haybarn (a.k.a Pole Barn)** – Fourth sound and motion. Given the previous three options, the callers may choose to call "Haybarn" (*spoken very quickly*) to check the attentiveness of the last person to call "Git down lil doggie!" To do this, the caller reaches and claps his or her hands above his or her head in a triangle shape and quickly says, "Haybarn." This sends the call back to the last person who said, "Git down lil doggie!" who must immediately continue action by calling and showing any sound and motion.

  - **Ford-Four-Shifting-Gearbox** – Fifth sound and motion. Say it slowly when you introduce it so that every one can hear the words – "Ford-Four-Shifting-Gearbox" – yet explain that the phrase should be said quickly during the game. When "Ford-Four-Shifting-Gearbox" is called, everyone **extends their fists** into the center of the circle, then move their hand as if they are shifting a four speed manual transmission while yelling, "1, 2, 3, 4!" After this resounding chorus of community chimes, the person who called "Ford-Four-Shifting-Gearbox" continues action immediately with another sound and motion. As the intensity of the game builds, "Ford-Four-Shifting-Gearbox," is typically said faster and faster until the point where the phrase becomes shortened, jumbled and eventually almost unidentifiable, e.g., "Four-Shifting-Box-Gear," "Shifting-Thingy," "Four on the Floor," and "Ford-blah-ha-blah-or-whatever." Encourage and celebrate all forms as it typically adds to the fun in ridiculous ways.

Tips and Comments *(continued)*

- **Cows Out of the Barn (a.k.a. The Goose is Loose)** – Sixth sound and motion. Last but not least. On the callers' turns, they may choose to say "Cows out of the Barn" This will indicate that everyone in the circle will proceed to MOOOOOO and moooove, with bumpers up, to a new spot across the circle. The person who called "Cows out of the Barn" continues action immediately with another sound and motion.

Oops! Did we say 'Cows out of the barn' was last? There seems to be an endless flow of fun. Here are some more sounds and motions to add to the comical chaos!

- **Pitch-n-Fork** – Skips two in the reverse direction.

- **Do Se Do (a.k.a. Hoedown or Barn Dance)** – Grab a partner, link elbows and do se do for one, two, or a few spins. Everyone returns to the circle and play continues immediately with the player who called "do se do," calling the next command (sound and motion).

- **Ride the Horse** – Players hold one hand out in front of them, as if they are holding the reins to a horse, motioning their other hand as if they are whipping the horse, and galloping their feet.

- **Cow Tipping** – The person who calls "cow tipping" initiates the motion by wobbling a bit, then bumps into the person to their immediate right or left. The bump is then passed consecutively around the circle until the motion returns to the person who initially called "cow tipping." This person resumes play with another command.

- **Create Your Own** – Invite participants to create their own sounds and motions. Doing so will instill creativity and fun, while empowering them to engage further.

- **Combinations:**

- **Yeehaw/Dead Ant Tag Combination** – If the game Dead Ant Tag is known the caller could call "Dead Ant" and attempt to tag any other players according to Dead Ant Tag. The caller could call "Yeehaw" at any time to resume play with Yeehaw. The twist: players who are "dead ants" would be required to play Yeehaw in the "dead ant" position. See Dead Ant Tag in the *Elementary School Adventure Curriculum for Physical Education* (Jane Panicucci et al., Project Adventure, 2003)

- **Yeehaw/Evolution Combination** – If the game Evolution is known the caller could call "Evolution" and name four characters – Eggs, Chicken, Dinosaurs, and Apes for example – then yell, "Go!" and play according to the rules of Evolution. The caller could call "Yeehaw" at any time to resume play with Yeehaw. The twist: players would be required to play 'Yeehaw' as their current Evolution character. See Evolution in the *Middle School Adventure Curriculum for Physical Education* (Jane Panicucci et al., Project Adventure, 2003)

Game Story

I first learned Yeehaw in the field while leading trips for Alternative Youth Adventures (AYA) in Utah (2002). The story I heard regarding the history and creation of Yeehaw, was that a group of Outward Bound instructors in Florida were curious to learn how fast a game they created could pass through the (experiential education) field. I later heard this same story from another wilderness therapy guide at Summit Achievement who did not have any association with AYA! Could it be true? Does anyone know? On a different note a special thanks to Sarah Jorgenson who passed along a write-up of Yeehaw which was modified to create this version. Thanks Sarah!

Safety

Play on a level surface and point out any environmental concerns (e.g., dips in the ground, wet grass, etc.)

You, You, Me

Overview:

A fast-paced name reinforcement game suitable for groups who are somewhat familiar with one another's names

Group Size	10 or more
Learning Themes	• Fun and Play • Physical Activity and Movement • Building Trust, Relationships, and Community
Materials / Props	None

Setup

This activity requires a clear play space large enough for the entire group to stand comfortably in a circle with additional room to move around outside of the circle.

Framing

Say to the group:

"How many people are familiar with the old game called Duck, Duck, Goose? We're going to play a similar but slightly more complicated game that will test your ability to remember one another's names."

Procedure

1. Instruct the group to stand comfortably in a circle.

2. Ask for a volunteer to be It.

3. The volunteer begins by walking around the outside of the circle patting the shoulder and stating the name of each participant.

4. At any moment, or when the volunteer cannot remember the name of the person he or she is about to pass/pat, the volunteer pats the participant and yells out his or her own name instead.

5. This signifies the beginning of the chase between the volunteer and the last participant patted by the volunteer.

6. The most recently patted participant attempts to tag the volunteer running around the outside of the circle in order to make it safely back to the newly-opened spot in the circle.

7. If the volunteer is successful and returns to the open spot without being tagged, he or she is safe and the round ends. The chasing participant is now the volunteer who begins a new round of circling, naming and running.

8. If the volunteer is tagged, he or she is It again.

9. Between rounds, anyone can request a 'name refresh' which means that everyone re-states their names.

Your Add

Overview:

A fast-paced energizer that gets the group interacting and wakes up the math-oriented brain cells. Players mingle about challenging each other to be the quickest to add a total number of digits (fingers) shown. Your Add is a playful approach to reviewing basic math skills socially and is sure to get a few laughs!

Group Size	10 or more
Learning Themes	• Fun and Play • Building Trust, Relationships, and Community
Materials / Props	None

Setup

None

Framing

Say to the group:

  "We are going to play a game that will wake up our math brains while we interact with one another."

Or:

  "In this activity, you will have a chance to put your addition skills to the test. You will have to be speedy, trying to find the sum of four numbers as quickly as possible!"

Procedure

1. Direct participants to find partners.
2. Explain that pairs will begin with their hands behind their backs. Using a three count (i.e., one, two, three – show!), partners show any number from 1 to 10, using their fingers.

3. As soon as the fingers are displayed, both players try to be the first person to total all of the fingers and say the correct sum.

4. Offer a few demonstrations to make sure that everyone understands the rules It is usually helpful if the facilitator demonstrates a few combinations of one to ten using different fingers while playing a willing volunteer. Invite other participants to watch or shout out answers for understanding and practice.

5. Play best out of ten or try to win as many times as possible in 45 seconds.

6. Switch partners and play again!

Reflection/Closure/Discussion

Your Add is typically used as a warm-up or energizer and does not require much reflection. If desired, however, there may be opportunities to explore Self Awareness and Self Management concepts such as stress management, accepting success or failure, and initiating interaction. Topics such as Creativity and Risk Taking related to Responsible Decision Making may come up as well.

Debrief

Say to the participants:

1. Were you present during this activity? How did being present or not present affect the results of your interactions? How did you feel about these results?

2. What strategies emerged? Were any strategies more effective then others?

3. How did you feel about the strategies being used against you? How did that affect your ability to play or focus?

4. Did you try any strategies that you learned from another player?

5. How might your experience with this activity be helpful in your life?

Tips and Comments

If playing in a space with furniture, such as a classroom or meeting room, clear the furniture to create a more open space. An open space is more effective for this activity as it makes the quick exchanges of partners more feasible.

Variations

*   Invite players to mingle about and challenge other players. Regardless of who says the correct sum first, partners say good bye to one another and find new partners. Play for several minutes. Playfully offer a protocol to guide the interactions and even as a way to subtly reinforce Challenge by Choice. For example, invite the challenger to approach another participant and playfully shout, "Challenge." The participant challenged may choose to "Accept" or "Decline." If the player accepts, the challenge may continue. If the player declines, the challenger must respectfully move on to someone else. This variation allows for more playful interaction among group members.

*   Instead of addition, change the operation to either subtraction or multiplication. Division can be a bit tricky but feel free to play with it too!

Yup Boing

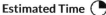

Estimated Time

10 – 15 minutes

Overview

Yup Boing is a fun game in the legacy of sound and motion activities. The group sends a sound and motion around the circle with a twist guaranteed to get them smiling, even when they try hard not to.

Group Size	10 – 15
Learning Themes	• Fun and Play • Building Trust, Relationships, and Community
Materials / Props	None

Setup

Start with the group standing or sitting in a circle.

Framing

"Imagine yourself a bit older than you are now. You know, as a wise denture-wearing elder who occasionally flashes a toothless grin while experiencing the joy of playing games with friends! This game challenges you to keep your smiles to a minimum and your teeth hidden behind your lips."

Procedure

1. Explain that Yup Boing passes a sound and motion around the circle, similar to games such as Hi Lo Yo and Yee-haw, but with a twist. The twist is to play the game without showing your teeth. Have participants practice covering all of their

teeth with their lips. Then have them try to keep it that way with a 37.4 second conversation with their neighbors.

2. Demonstrate and practice the first sound and motion with your group. Start by sending the sound "Yup" with a head nod to the left. Let it travel all the way around the circle. Practice again with a "Yup" and head nod to the right.

3. State that a "Yup" can be sent in any direction to start then must follow that direction unless someone says, "Boing." "Boing" reverses the direction of the "Yup."

4. Play with just Yup and Boing for a while. If anyone shows their teeth, delays, or does anything other than what they should have done, celebrate. Celebrate mistakes, delays, or any sign of tooth flashing with laughter and applause, and then play on.

5. Ready for more? When the time is right, add additional sounds and motions. You may have also noticed at this point Yup Boing could be exclusively played among only half the circle. To be more inclusive, add the following sounds and motions.

   a. Participants can send the sound and motion to anyone in the circle by saying "Doing," as in "Boing" with a "D," followed by any participant's name, still without showing their teeth. The person whose name was called must respond with a "Yup" in either direction or "Doing..." to another person.

   b. Saying "Do-op" skips the person next to them.

   c. Send a "Zoom!" Saying "Zoom" initiates the group to send the sound, "Zoom," around the group as quickly as they can, each person saying "Zoom" when it's their turn. When the "Zoom" returns to the person who originally called it, they must say "Yup" and indicate a direction of travel with a head nod.

Reflection/Closure/Discussion

None needed.

Tips and Comments

Variations of Play

- **Elimination** – Play the game as described above. If a player makes a mistake, he or she is eliminated. Eliminated players step out of the circle and observe in amusement. Play continues until the game ends with two victors, and then a new game begins.

- **New Circle, New Game** – If there are enough players, those who were eliminated from the original game can gather with other eliminated players and start a new game just for fun!

- **Multiple Games** – With larger groups, any group with more than 20 people, it can be effective to play multiple games simultaneously. When players are eliminated from one game, they may move on and join another game in progress. Players can then simply bounce from game to game trying to remain in one game for as long as they can.

Tips and Comments (continued)

- **Transition** – Transitions allow players, who would be otherwise eliminated, to assume a new role in the game, that of being distracters. Distracters may do their best to heckle and distract other players by making sounds and motions outside of the circle. Distracters may not enter the circle, cover the eyes of another player, yell in someone's ear, or physically disrupt another player's ability to perform particular motions needed for the game. Beyond this, distractors can be as obnoxious as they like!

Additional Sounds and Motions

- After playing with a "Zoom" for a while. Introduce a "Ding." A participant may say "Ding" immediately followed by "Yup" interrupting the "Zoom," and moving the game forward.

- If "Mingle" is called, participants point their index fingers to the sky and say, "Mingle, Mingle, Mingle," still without showing their teeth as they Mingle Dance their way to a new spot in the circle. The person who called "Mingle" resumes play with a "Yup" in either direction.

Quick Review of Sounds and Motions

- "Yup" sends the sound and motion either left or right.

- "Boing" reverses direction.

- "Doing" and someone's name sends the sound and motion to the person whose name was called. They must follow with either a "Yup" or "Doing".

- "Do-op" skips the next person.

- "Zoom" sends a "Zoom" as fast as it can around the circle.

- "Ding" interrupts "Zoom" and must be immediately followed by a "Yup".

- "Mingle" gets participants to Mingle Dance their way to a new spot in the circle.

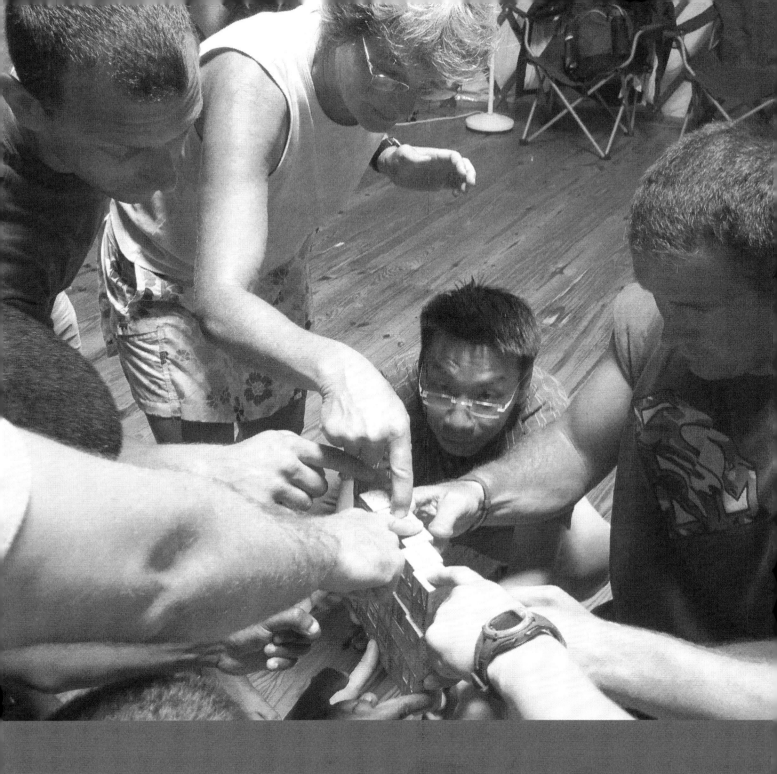

Activities Sequences

Introduction to Activity Sequences

As mentioned in the introduction of this book, this section presents a concept newer to our activity books. Project Adventure has a rich history of developing, leading, and training practitioners in the use of innovative activities. This section of the book focuses on the importance of sequencing activities in order to meet specific results. The importance and value of properly sequencing cannot be emphasized enough. In this section, we offer five activity sequences with activities directly from *The Hundredth Monkey*. Our hope in sharing these sequences is to encourage you to consider how activities connect to each other and the over all goal – physically, socially, emotionally, etc. Additionally, the use of the sequencing model – ice breakers, de-inhibitizers, and peak experiences – described in the foundational concepts section should be clearly evident. Finally, we hope this affirms a practice you have already developed or provides enough information to inspire you to craft your own playful and effective sequences.

One key to linking a sequence of activities is the language used to segue or transition from one activity to another. Each activity sequence includes a sample segue or transitional framing that we believe inspires a playful and effective flow. It is the framing of each activity, essentially preparing your group for what is next, that will likely lead to the most participant engagement and optimal experience. Use the segues and transitional framings as a guide and feel free to develop your own voice and flow. Okay, go play!

Activity Sequencing (in order by time)

1. A Mess of Handshakes   (30 minutes)
2. Full Value Flow   (45 minutes)
3. Building Blocks   (60-90 minutes)
4. World Wide Wonder   (120 minutes)
5. Spotting Sequence – Enhanced (120-180 minutes)

NOTE: Unless otherwise referenced, activities can be found in *The Hundredth Monkey*.

1. A Mess of Handshakes

Overview

A great opening sequence for almost any program or experience. Participants experience the familiar to the bizarre as they journey through a series of greeting- or handshake-based activities. A Mess of Handshakes is fun, interactive, and quickly gets to the heart of building an effective learning community.

Group Size	12 or more
Playlist/Sequence	• Stationary Handshake • 5 Handshakes, 5 Minutes • Log Pile
Learning Themes	• Fun and Play • Physical Activity and Movement • Building Trust, Relationships, and Community • Relationship Skills • Responsible Decision Making
Materials / Props	None

Opening Activity: Stationary Handshake

An excellent tone-setter, full of subtle challenges and whispers of Challenge by Choice

Learning Themes	• Physical Activity and Movement • Building Trust, Relationships, and Community

Setup

Gather your group into a circle. Have participants casually greet their neighbors, the participants to their immediate right and left with a resounding "Hello!", "Good Morning!", "Buenos Dias!", or the like.

Framing

Say to participants:

"Challenge by Choice is an opportunity to challenge or stretch your self. How much are you willing to stretch? How far are you willing to reach out to others to build your community and help each other grow? Try this."

Procedure

1. Engage participants in multiple rounds of interaction and challenge.

2. First, challenge participants to shake hands with as many people as they can, providing the use of one pivot foot.

3. Again, challenge participants to shake hands with as many people as they can. This time however, they may not move their feet from the spot where they are standing. Many people will try bending awkwardly at the waist only to reach a few people and often miss opportunities to greet more people. One possible solution is to crouch down and extend into a push-up or plank (from yoga) position without moving their feet from their spots, and then reach one arm out to shake hands with another. Another solution is to rely on the support and spotting of other people nearby as participants may lean on or hang off of their neighbors. No need to explicitly tell participants that they can do this; however, asking a simple question such as "Can you think of other ways to greet more people without moving your feet from their spots?" usually triggers the creativity of enough participants to reveal the behaviors described above.

4. Invite participants to leave their spots and greet, yet again, as many people as possible. Provide some signal indicating when to return to the circle.

   How you describe the interaction in this round can create subtle connections to Challenge by Choice and our typical desires as humans for comfort and routine. For example, you might say, "This time you can leave your spot and greet as many people as possible. When you see my hand raised, return to the circle." Given these words, most people will return to the exact spot in the circle from which they started. However, the directions were to "return to the circle" not "return to your spot in the circle." Survey the group to see how many people returned to their original spot. It is likely that most people will have returned to their original spots, yet be entirely convinced they heard the latter. You can anticipate the typical argument to be something like, "You told us to return to our spots..." or "You said 'return to your spots'...", which, of course, you did not say. This is a great time to speak to Challenge by Choice, comfort zones, and patterns of behavior and how perhaps we as people might stretch ourselves.

5. Allow for one final round. Ask the participants to scan the group and determine whom they have not yet greeted. Allow 37.7 seconds or some obscure amount of time to greet these remaining people and return to the circle. If it seems right, survey the group one more time to see how many people found a new spot to stand in or returned to their original spot. Celebrate everyone for making a choice that was right for them in that moment.

6. Transition to the next activity, 5 Handshakes, 5 Minutes.

Say to the group:

"While we greeted each other using a standard handshake, we may have discovered new ways to connect with others, stretching us out of normal routines. Connecting with others, stretching out of normal routines, and trying something new or different are all part of an adventure. Let's try some different handshakes. I would like to share 5 unique handshakes with you in 5 minutes. That's 5 handshakes in 5 minutes. Here's how it works."

Estimated Time ◗

10 minutes

Next Activity: 5 Handshakes, 5 Minutes

A playful exchange of bizarre handshakes

Learning Themes	• Fun and Play
	• Physical Activity and Movement
	• Building Trust, Relationships, and Community

Procedure

1. Explain how 5 handshakes in 5 minutes will work, then play.

    a. Ask for a volunteer.

    b. Demonstrate a handshake.

    c. Say, "Go!" Participants attempt the handshake with as many people as possible before you display a signal to return to the circle.

    d. Display a signal to return to the circle.

    e. Ask for another volunteer and repeat four more times.

2. Choose 5 handshakes from the list of descriptions on page 21 or pages 292–298, but finish with the Logger Handshake page 22.

3. Transition to the culminating activity, Log Pile.

Segue/Transitional Framing

Say to the group:

"So I've heard that loggers were once challenged at an annual lumberjack competition to perform their handshake, the Logger Handshake, typically involving only two people, with as many people as they could. Can you think of any solutions to this challenge? Try each solution as it is shared, then seek other solutions."

Culminating Activity: Log Pile

An introductory problem-solving activity that is all thumbs!

Estimated Time

10 minutes

> **Learning Themes**
> - Building Trust, Relationships, and Community
> - Relationship Skills
> - Responsible Decision Making

Safety

Heightened awareness of safety may be necessary when playing Log Pile, especially with larger groups. In general, participants should be gentle when grabbing one another's thumbs and moving toward whatever solution has shown up.

Procedure

1. Explain to the group that unlike more traditional handshaking techniques, the Logger Handshake is not limited to two people. Ask the group to explore how many people they can involve in a single logger handshake.

2. Ask participants if there is any way to involve the entire group in one logger handshake. There are many possible solutions. Encourage participants to share and try their ideas.

3. When it seems that most ideas have been exhausted, briefly process the experience or move on.

Reflection/Closure/Discussion

1. Did you think that there could be that many solutions to this challenge? What helped to bring forth these solutions?

2. What is the value of sharing and listening to ideas in a problem-solving setting?

3. What lessons from our experience might be helpful as we encounter future challenges?

> **Tips and Comments**
> - This sequence is a great tone setter for creative problem solving and looking at a situation from every angle.
> - Consider using Crosstown Connection instead of 5 Handshakes, 5 Minutes.

Safety

- Emphasize tagging below the knee, and not tagging too hard.
- Be sure the ground area is level.
- Remind participants of the collision potential during the boffer exchanges in the middle.

2. Full Value Flow

Overview

A playful way to generate a group's Full Value Contract. Participants flow through a few similarly-formatted activities and variations getting to know each other, generating group norms, and practicing their Full Value Contract during a game of tag.

Group Size	8 – 12
Playlist/Sequence	• Whampum • FVC Cards • Swat Tag • FVC Cards Debrief/Check-in
Learning Themes	• Fun and Play • Physical Activity and Movement • Building Trust, Relationships, and Community • Self Awareness and Self Management • Social Awareness • Responsible Decision Making
Materials / Props	• Spot Markers (1 per person) • 1 Hula Hoop • 1 Boffer • Index Cards • Markers

Opening Activity: Whampum

Playfully engaging the group while generating group norms

Learning Themes	• Fun and Play • Building Trust, Relationships, and Community • Social Awareness

Setup

Ask the group to stand in a circle, each person on a spot marker.

Framing

Say to the group:

"This game is about rapid recall and quick reactions. You'll need to know one another's names and eventually remember what is valued."

Procedure

1. Have each person say his or her name.

2. After everyone in the circle has spoken, stand in the middle of the circle with a boffer and explain the basic rules of Whampum.

   a. Have someone start by saying another player's name. You, as the middle person, try to "whack" the named person on the foot before he or she can name another person.

   b. When you finally whack someone before that player says another's name, he or she must take your place in the circle.

   c. If anyone flinches without due cause, that player must move to the center position.

   d. If a name is said other than that of someone in the circle (e.g., the person in the middle or someone who is not present), the person who said the incorrect name moves to the center position.

3. After playing for a while and once everyone seems to have good recollection of one another's names, add a new spin on the game.

   a. Invite players to think of one value/behavior that they believe is important for their group's success or to create a safe and respectful learning environment. Values/behaviors should be easily communicated using one word or a brief phrase.

   b. Once everyone has determined their one value/behavior, have them say their names and their values/behaviors.

   c. Play Whampum as described above and add that in order to avoid a tag now, both the name *and the value/behavior* must be called. Of course, values/behaviors must be accurately called in association with the correct person for tags to count or be avoided.

4. Again, play for a while then introduce a third twist on the game.

   a. Play Whampum as described above, however this time only an accurate value/behavior needs to be called to avoid a tag.

5. When it seems right to move on, do so. The final variation highlights the values/behaviors selected by the group and sets them up well to establish FVC Cards, which is the next activity in the sequence. Transition when ready.

Segue/Transitional Framing

Say to the group:

"Can anyone recall any of the values/behaviors they heard while playing this game? Would you say these values might help the success of our group or create a safe and respectful learning environment? Let's write down what we have shared so far and see if anything is missing as we consider what we can do to create a positive experience."

Next Activity: FVC Cards

Recording the FVC (group norms) on index cards and growing the community

> **Learning Themes**
> - Building Trust, Relationships, and Community
> - Self Awareness and Self Management
> - Social Awareness

Procedure

1. Hand out one index card to each person and have them record the value/behavior they contributed during Whampum. Let everyone know that it's okay to have duplicates.

2. Once everyone has recorded their initial value/behavior on an index card, facilitate an investigation to see if any other values/behaviors should be added.

3. Record additional values/behaviors on index cards as they arise.

4. After the cards have been created, state that the cards will represent the group's Full Value Contract. Explain what a Full Value Contract is as needed and ask for the group to commit to their FVC in some way, e.g., thumb-o-meter, thumb prints on yet another index card, or verbal affirmation, etc.

5. Transition to the next activity.

Segue/Transitional Framing

Say to the group:

> "The values/behaviors on these cards are significant, however, they are not helpful to our group unless we bring them to life and demonstrate them as we play. Let's practice these values/behaviors as we play another game. We will reflect, using these cards as we play."

Next Activity: Swat Tag

Practicing the Full Value Contract while playing an ever intensifying game of tag

> **Learning Themes**
> - Physical Activity and Movement
> - Self Awareness and Self Management
> - Social Awareness
> - Responsible Decision Making

Procedure

1. Add a hula hoop and boffer to the center of the circle.

2. Explain and demonstrate the rules of the base version of Swat Tag.

   a. One person, the SWATTER, begins in the center of the circle with the boffer.

b. The SWATTER may move freely inside the circle while he or she chooses another person to tag.

c. Tapping someone below the knee with the boffer constitutes a tag. Do not try to avoid this tag.

d. Once a person is tagged, the SWATTER races back to the hoop and drops the boffer in the hoop. At the same time, the tagged person goes into the middle of the circle.

e. Once the boffer lands on the ground, the tagged person picks it up and attempts to tag the SWATTER with the boffer before he or she runs back to the spot vacated by the first person tagged.

f. If the SWATTER successfully makes it to the vacant spot in the circle, he or she remains there and the tagged person becomes the SWATTER.

g. If the original SWATTER gets tagged on the way to the vacated spot, he or she remains in the middle and rule 'd' above continues until he or she successfully gets back to a spot marker.

h. There can be a series of tag exchanges that occur between the original SWATTER and the person he or she tagged, before one person returns to the circle and the other moves on.

3. Play the base version for a while, and then add any one of the following variations, typically in the order listed. All of the variations increase participation, movement, and fun by providing more challenge and choice. Anyone who chooses to move to an empty spot or hoop in the following variations, however, may be tagged whenever they are not standing on a spot.

a. **Commit to Switch** – Allow anyone to switch spots with another person at any time as long as he or she makes a commitment to switch before moving. This means there must be some communication – verbal, non-verbal, overt, covert, etc. – in which two people agree to switch spots. There is no turning back once a person leaves his or her spot.

b. **Side Step** – Allow anyone, at any time, to side step to any open spot on his or her immediate left or right.

c. **Challenge Yourself** – Allow anyone, at any time, to move to an empty spot. This means that anyone can move at any time, free of commitment from another person.

d. **Ultimate Challenge** – Allow players to run into the middle, touch the inside of the hoop and yell a phrase such as "I love this game" three times, attempting to then return to an empty spot before being tagged.

4. Play with any of the variations above, facilitate a FVC check-in at any time and/or transition to a final debrief.

Segue/Transitional Framing

Say to the group:

"Let's take a minute to check in with our Full Value Contract."

Reflection/Closure/Discussion

FVC Cards Debrief – Use the FVC Cards created earlier in the sequence as a processing tool. There are many ways to do this. Here are a few suggestions:

1. **FVC Check-in** – Spread the FVC Cards out in front of the group. Ask everyone to choose one card that is resonating with them for some reason. Remind participants that cards may be shared if more than one person reaches for the same card. Have participants share their cards and tell why they chose them.

2. **FVC Affirmations** – Instruct everyone to hold one FVC Card. Once everyone has a card, ask them to think about one person in the group who best demonstrated the behavior on the card during the activity. Invite participants to mingle and share this affirmation, then the actual card, with that specific person. As participants receive a FVC Card, they should immediately think of another person who also embodied the behavior represented on the card, find that person, share the affirmation, and then the card. Continue mingling in this mode, until it seems right to move on.

3. **FVC Take a Stand** – Scatter the Full Value Cards face up on the ground or floor. Invite participants to stand near a card that:

   a. Best represents their behavior during the activity.

   b. Best represents someone else's behavior during the activity.

   c. Represented a behavior the group demonstrated well.

   d. Represented a behavior the group could make some improvements with.

   e. Depicts what the group used to create a playful and safe learning environment.

Tips and Comments

- Whampum can be played while participants are seated or standing. Either way is fun. Determine which is most appropriate for your group and setting.

- For larger groups, consider explaining and demonstrating the rules of Whampum with a sample group of people, and then separate the group into smaller groups of 8-10 to play.

- When transitioning to Swat Tag, consider playing in the same small groups, recreating groups of 10-15, or playing a large game with three or so SWATTERS in the center of the circle. This last option is usually appropriate for up to about 40 people. Monitor for safety, as the involvement of more people usually increases the potential for incidents.

- Consider duplicating FVC Cards generated in the sequence above to use in FVC Marketplace. FVC Marketplace can be found on page 86.

Whampum was published in *Adventure Curriculum for Physical Education: Elementary and Middle School* (Panicucci et al., 2003) and Swat Tag was published in *Adventure Curriculum for Physical Education: Elementary and High School* (Panicucci et al., 2003)

3. Building Blocks

Overview

A skill building sequence of warm-ups, ice breakers, problem-solving activities, and debrief using one prop – blocks! Players make a connection with each other, learn to move together, create strong bonds, and then continue connecting with others. They then work collaboratively in partners, and eventually, as a whole group. The Building Blocks sequence is seamless and rich with teachable moments around the themes of collaboration, leadership, communication, resiliency and perseverance, to name a few.

Estimated Time ●
60 – 90 minutes

Group Size	8 or more
Playlist/Sequence	• Mingle and Match • Bust A Move • Don't Break the Ice • Ice Breakers • Bridging the Gap • Block Party • Crossword Debrief
Learning Themes	• Fun and Play • Physical Activity and Movement • Building Trust, Relationships, and Community • Self Awareness and Self Management • Social Awareness • Relationship Skills • Responsible Decision Making
Materials / Props	• Plastic or wooden blocks – At least two blocks per person 1-2 inch ABC/123 blocks work best

Opening Activity: Mingle and Match

A simple get-to-know-you pairing activity using blocks

Estimated Time ◔
10 minutes

Learning Themes	• Fun and Play • Building Trust, Relationships, and Community • Relationship Skills

Setup

Scatter blocks on the floor or ground in the center of an open space.

Framing

Say to the group, "According to Wikipedia, collaboration is a process in which two or more people or organizations work together at an intersection of common goals by sharing knowledge, learning and building consensus. Most collaboration requires leadership, which can take many forms. In particular, teams who work collaboratively generally experience greater success. We will have the opportunity to collaborate, develop common goals, and work with the intersection of those goals."

Procedure

1. Invite participants to pick up two blocks from the pile.

2. Have them then find someone with whom they share a common block – same letters, numbers, colors, symbols, similar symbols, etc. Exact matches are bonuses worthy of grand celebration, but finding some connection is the key! Add that once a connection is found, everyone should take a moment to find a personal connection, or commonality, beyond their blocks, and then move on.

3. Allow your group to mingle and match for a few minutes. Stop them at some point and have them stand with the person with whom they currently match. Help others find a partner as needed.

4. Transition to the next activity.

Segue/Transitional Framing

Say to the group:

> "Okay, now that we have made a few connections, let's connect in a different way and see how it moves us."

Estimated Time

5 – 10 minutes

Next Activity: Bust a Move

Playful movement exploration and confidence building

Learning Themes	• Fun and Play
	• Physical Activity and Movement
	• Building Trust, Relationships, and Community

Procedure

1. Tell participants to suspend four blocks in a straight horizontal line between them using only the tips of their index fingers. In other words, participants position two blocks on the tips of their index fingers and connect their blocks directly to their partners' in a straight horizontal line – to start anyway!

2. Invite participants to then play and explore, moving creatively with their partners. Encourage participants to discover different ways of moving together while challenging themselves to move beyond their comfort zones. You will know if this is happening if blocks are crashing to the floor! At this point, participants should know what to do – pick 'em up and play on! If not, a little gentle coaching should get people and blocks up and moving again.

3. Consider introducing additional movement ideas from the list of Block Stunts on page 48.

4. After playing around for a bit, transition to the next activity.

Segue/Transitional Framing

Say to the group:

"Now that you have been moving around a bit, let's make this more interesting and interactive."

Next Activity: Don't Break the Ice

Working as a team to stay connected

Learning Themes	• Fun and Play
	• Physical Activity and Movement
	• Building Trust, Relationships, and Community

Procedure

1. Announce to your group that they will now move about the space attempting to maintain their connections through the four suspended blocks while trying to break the connections of others using only their free index fingers.

2. Explain and demonstrate the rules:

   a. Players may break the connection of others only if they are connected to their partners.

   b. Physical contact should be kept to a minimum. This is a game of finesse and positioning, not asserting oneself physically. Everyone should refrain from pushing, blocking, swatting, etc.

   c. Players may box out (as in basketball), move, and position themselves to protect their blocks.

   d. Players may only use the tips of their index fingers to connect through their blocks. In other words, participants may not link hands, fingers, or thumbs in an attempt to better secure their blocks.

   e. If your blocks fall to the ground, pick them up, reconnect with your partner and continue playing.

3. Play for a while, then transition to the next activity.

Segue/Transitional Framing

Say to the group"

"Have you noticed that once we make a connection with someone, we typically like to stay connected? So perhaps we could agree to practice connecting with other people."

Next Activity: Ice Breakers

Playing the game, connecting with different people

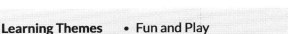

Learning Themes	• Fun and Play
	• Physical Activity and Movement
	• Relationship Skills

Procedure

1. Play using the same rules as "Don't Break the Ice," however, once a connection is broken, add one rule change – each individual player picks up their blocks and finds a new partner.

2. Continue playing, then pause the play and ask a few reflective questions "So, how did it go? What was it like to play with other people? Did you learn different strategies or techniques by playing with different people?

3. Ask everyone to stand with their most current partner, and then transition to the next activity.

Segue/Transitional Framing

Say to the group:

"Let's explore a little further what it takes to really collaborate with another person. We will also take a look at the effort it takes to achieve a goal."

Next Activity: Bridging the Gap

Setting goals and bridging the gap

Learning Themes	• Self Awareness and Self Management
	• Relationship Skills
	• Responsible Decision Making

Procedure

Say to the group:

1. Your goal is to suspend as many blocks between you and your partner as possible.

2. Each person may use one index finger on one hand.

3. Blocks must be in a straight line and single plane.

4. Blocks must start on the ground and be lifted to standing height for a successful bridging of the gap.

5. Be aware of how others are doing and what their goals are while continuing to work toward your personal best.

Segue/Transitional Framing

Say to the group:

"Let's take what you are learning and build with it."

Culminating Activity: Block Party

Bringing it together – the blocks, the learning, the people

Learning Themes
- Self Awareness and Self Management
- Relationship Skills
- Responsible Decision Making

Procedure

1. Say to the group:
   a. Your goal now, as an entire group, is to lift or suspend as many blocks as you can.
   b. Each person may use one or two index fingers only.
   c. All blocks must be connected to each other in a single plane. Blocks may not be lifted in separate disconnected sections.
   d. Blocks must be on the ground and then lifted to standing height for an attempt to be considered successful. Even more challenging and perhaps fun, would be to lift the blocks overhead!
2. Allow time for many attempts and facilitate the trial of many solutions or strategies sure to arise.
3. After a sufficient number of attempts, move on to the closing activity to reflect.

Segue/Transitional Activity

Say to the group:

"Wow, you've put a lot of energy and thought into this challenge. Let's take a moment to reflect on our entire experience."

Reflection/Closure/Discussion

Crossword Debrief

1. Facilitate a discussion regarding any reactions or comments as needed.
2. Then invite participants to create an intersection of words that summarize their experience or the most significant part of the building blocks progression. The crossword could focus on the general experience or particular themes such as collaboration, leadership, communication, perseverance, etc.

Tips and Comments

- Don't Break the Ice and Ice Breakers seem to bring out the best, and sometimes the worst in people, as both activities seem to ignite charged emotional reactions ranging from joy to retaliation. Monitor for safety, especially when engaging larger groups and process as needed. Great learning opportunities are likely to present themselves!

- Block Party seems most effective with groups of 8-12. It may be helpful to separate your group into smaller groups if they are larger than this. While there is an acceptable solution, given the parameters, larger groups often prefer to explore solutions that require everyone to huddle tightly around their masterfully designed shape.

Safety

Bring awareness to the playing area, especially as activity increases. Inform participants of the terrain, the conditions, and any potential hazards.

4. World Wide Wonder

Overview

An interactive way to get to know each other and the world. Participants create a map of the world using ropes and other random props, and then interact with the map and each other. Throughout the progression, the group will build community, be physically active, and explore goal setting and collaboration. Ultimately, World Wide Wonder is a whirlwind tour of the world designed to increase group cohesion and perhaps make the world a better place.

Group Size	6 or more
Playlist/Sequence	• Map Making • Where in the World? • World Travelers • World Wide Key Punch • Reflective Map Debrief
Learning Themes	• Physical Activity and Movement • Building Trust, Relationships, and Community • Self Awareness and Self Management • Social Awareness • Relationship Skills • Responsible Decision Making

Materials / Props	• 8 ropes or tubular webbing ranging in lengths
	  – 2 20 feet – 1 60 feet
	  – 4 40 feet – 1 80 feet
	• Random props such as tossables, spot markers, debrief cards, etc.
	• Numbered Spot Markers
	• Stop Watch

Opening Activity: Map Making

Informally learning about one another while making the map

Learning Theme	• Building Trust, Relationships, and Community

Setup

Place 7 ropes and random props in the center of an open space. Leave one 20-foot rope and the numbered spot markers to the side, as they will be needed for World Wide Key Punch later in the flow of activities.

Framing

"With all of the concerns expressed about the current state of our world, have you ever wondered what you can do about it? We are about to embark on one of the greatest journeys this world has ever known. While I hope it is fun, we will be doing some serious work along the way. We will learn about each other and the world, explore how best to work with each other throughout the world, and perhaps consider how we can use what we learn to help our world. This sequence of activities is designed to help us explore the challenging question – 'what can I or we do?' – and hopefully enable us to discover solutions applicable to improving our reality. Ready!"

Procedure

1. Say to the group: "First we need to work together to create a map of our world."

2. Explain to the group that they will embark on a creative process and have five minutes to create a map of the world that is oriented correctly, yet not perfectly proportioned.

3. Check in at the end of five minutes to see if the group needs a few more minutes to finalize their creation. However, do not allow this process to go on forever. Remind the group that the map does not need to represent perfect shapes or scales.

4. Encourage the use of additional props to make borders, islands, or places of personal significance.

5. Once the map of the world is created, take a moment to briefly explore how the group feels about their creation and the process of its creation.

6. Transition to the next activity which provides opportunities for the group to interact with the map and each other.

Segue/Transitional Framing

Say to the group:

"You may have learned a bit about each other while making the map. Let's expand that learning by interacting with the map and each other."

Next Activity: Where in the World?

Interacting with the map, getting to know one another

Estimated Time

15 minutes

Learning Themes	• Building Trust, Relationships, and Community • Self Awareness and Self Management • Social Awareness

Procedure

1. Say to the group, "Move to the location where you were born."

2. Once participants seem to have found their places, ask them to share with the group.

3. If there are any unique responses, feel free to ask for more information, and encourage your participants to do the same!

4. Repeat this process with other topics such as:

- Move to the location that represents your ethnical background. Feel free to demonstrate by moving to and from a few different locations.

- Move to any location, for any reason, be prepared to share where you are and why?

- Move to:

  "...where your heart is."

  "...a place that you would like to learn more about."

  "...a place that you would like to share something about."

  "...a place where you would be scared to travel to."

  "...a place that best represents your lifestyle."

  "...a location you believe needs help or support."

5. Process responses and reactions as needed.

6. Transition to the next activity to get the group moving and playfully test how familiar they are with each other and the map.

Segue/Transitional Framing

Say to the group:

"All right, let's move around a bit more and see what we remember about each other and our map."

Estimated Time 🌓

20 minutes

Next Activity: World Travelers

Getting better acquainted with our world while testing what we have learned about one another

Learning Themes	• Physical Activity and Movement
	• Self Awareness and Self Management
	• Social Awareness

Procedure

1. At this point, participants should be familiar with the map they created and the association with an actual map. With this understanding, either the facilitator, or a participant caller, could challenge the participants to find particular directions and locations on the map as quickly as they can.

2. To warm up, explain that you will call specific directions – North, South, East, and West. Participants must run to the furthest point on the map of the specific direction called. For example, if North was called, participants would run towards the Arctic Circle or if South was called, participants would run towards Antarctica.

3. Once the group has moved around a bit and has become more familiar with the map, introduce more possibilities. Now, in addition to the four directions, the caller may call:

- Specific locations such as a continent, country, state/province, capital, etc.
- Specific locations associated with the response from the group, such as "Move to where Peter was born," "Move to the place that best represented Paul's lifestyle," or "Move to where Larry's heart is."
- Specific geographic features, such as rivers, mountain ranges, oceans, and deserts could also be called.

4. The possibilities seem endless. Choose locations that seem most appropriate for your group at the time. The goal here is to have fun, get them moving around, and increase the heart rate.

5. Just before the group loses interest, transition to the next activity.

Segue/Transitional Framing

Say to the group:

"Hopefully you became more familiar with the map and each other. The world needs your help. It has been determined that in the next few years, more and more natural disasters are destined to occur. More wild fires, tornadoes, floods, earthquakes, and tsunamis mean more disaster relief will be needed. We need to be prepared to provide support at a global scale. Not just support, but efficient and effective support. You, as the world's most compassionate and sympathetic disaster relief providers have been selected to identify a solution to an enormous challenge. Your goal is to access multiple sites around the world in the most efficient and effective way, while demonstrating respect and compassion for each other."

Culminating Activity: World Wide Key Punch

Estimated Time

45 minutes

Exploring the most efficient and effective ways to collaborate with each other throughout the world

| **Learning Themes** | • Relationship Skills |
| | • Responsible Decision Making |

Procedure

1. Additional Setup: Randomly distribute number spot markers throughout the seven rope boundaries. Create a start/finish line by placing a piece of rope or webbing about 20-30 feet away from the map.

2. Highlight the map that the group created, reinforcing that there are seven rope boundaries depicting each of the seven continents. In addition, indicate that there are now numbered spot markers distributed throughout each of the continents.

3. State the goal:

   a. Contact the numbered spot markers as quickly as you can, with the fewest violations possible.

4. Explain and demonstrate the rules:

   a. Everyone must contact at least one number.

b. Numbers must be touched in sequence.

c. Ropes and spots may not be moved.

d. Only one person may be in any of the seven roped boundaries at a time.

e. Penalties (typically ten seconds added to the overall time) occur if:

    i. There is more than one person in any of the seven rope boundaries at the same time.

    ii. Numbers are contacted out of order.

f. The time starts when the first person crosses the start/finish line. Time stops when the last person crosses back over the start/finish line.

g. Although players may talk while interacting with the map, *no planning* may occur there, only execution of a plan. Planning may only occur behind the start/finish line.

h. There will be three to five trials for the group to demonstrate their most efficient and effective solution, meaning the fastest time with the least possible number of penalties.

5. Check for understanding regarding the rules, and then begin.

6. While the group is planning, encourage them to set and communicate a goal for each trial.

7. Process after each round as needed.

8. After performing three to five trials, conduct a debrief appropriate for the group and experience. Below are a couple of ideas.

Reflection/Closure/Discussion

Debrief #1

Reflective Map Debrief – Participants use particular countries, continents, landmarks, natural features, etc. to respond to debrief prompts. For example, the facilitator might say, "Move to a region on the map that best represents how your group worked together." Participants may choose to move to the Middle East if there had been a lot of conflict or to New Zealand if their process seemed peaceful (New Zealand is considered the most peaceful place on earth, according to the Institute for Economics and Peace) or the Himalayas if the group felt as though they experienced many peaks and valleys. Other prompts the facilitator might give:

1. Move to a location on the map that indicates the efficiency of your group.

2. Move to a location on the map that depicts your efforts toward goals set by the group.

3. Move to a location that depicts the level of respect you demonstrated.

4. Move to a spot that represents how you feel about the world today.

5. Move to a spot that represents how you feel when part of a solution.

6. Move to a spot that represents the type of action you would like to demonstrate tomorrow to make the world a better place.

Debrief #2
The More You Learn the Less You Know

1. Many well-known people have been quoted as saying something similar to "The more you learn, the less you know."

   a. "The more I learn the less I know." – George Harrison

   b. "The more I see the less I know for sure." – John Lennon

   c. "The more I learn, the more I learn how little I know." – Socrates

   d. "The more you know, the less you understand." – Lao Tse

   e. "The more you learn, the more you know. The more you know, the more you forget. The more you forget, the less you know. So why bother to learn?" – George Bernard Shaw

2. So why bother? We just learned a lot about each other, how to work together, and maybe even a bit about our world. We learn more about our broader world every day through our connections with others and media. Why bother to learn more about each other and about our world?

3. What are some of the things you have learned about other people and the world that it seems you know less about?

4. What can we do about some of the concerns for these people and the broader world? What from our experience will help?

5. What is one thing you will do tomorrow to address one of your concerns? Is there anything that you would like to propose as a long-term goal or project?

Tips and Comments

- **Debrief #1:** The Reflective Map Debrief offers the opportunity to keep moving and interacting with the map while reflecting on the experience. Most effective for groups that desire to move, prefer an informal setting for sharing, and can make metaphorical connections.

- **Debrief #2:** The More You Learn, the Less You Know, offers a deeper reflection opportunity. If a group seems ready and able to discuss these questions, consider a traditional debrief circle for your setting and get comfortable. Otherwise, the questions offered may be better suited as a journal assignment.

Variations

- Instead of a world map, consider mapping a specific country, city, or town. Provide resources and references as needed.

- Scan the write-ups of each individual activity for other framing, debriefing, and playing variations.

  – Map Making – page 134

  – Where in the World? – page 238

  – World Travelers – page 240

  – World Wide Key Punch – page 244

Safety

• Make sure you have proper training before facilitating this sequence.

• It's okay to have different-sized people spotting each other, within reason.

• Make sure the ground is level and clear.

• Assess your group's readiness for these activities, especially the spotting activities, before beginning.

5. Spotting Sequence Enhanced

Overview:

A playful enhancement of a traditional spotting sequence. Participants flow through a series of activities designed to playfully introduce spotting while developing the physical, social, and emotional skills necessary to be present and effective.

Playlist/Sequence	• People to People
	• Palm Off
	• Spotting Stance
	• Super Spotters Social
	• 2-Person Trust Leans
	• 3-Person Trust Leans
	• Wind in the Willows
	• Can You Levitate?
	• Levitation
Learning Themes	• Fun and Play
	• Physical Activity and Movement
	• Building Trust, Relationships, and Community
	• Self Awareness and Self Management
	• Social Awareness
	• Relationship Skills
Materials / Props	None

Opening Activity: People to People

Warming up physically, socially, and emotionally while introducing physical contact, moving the body, and playing with different people

Learning Themes	• Fun and Play
	• Physical Activity and Movement
	• Building Trust, Relationships, and Community

Setup

None

Framing

"We are about to engage in a sequence of activities that provide an opportunity to explore our physical, social, and emotional limits. We'll start by connecting with each other in a variety of ways and progress to a place where we really lift each other up. Really!"

Procedure

Say to the participants:

1. Here's an opportunity to connect with each other.

2. When I say, "people to people," quickly find a partner.

3. You will then hear me say two body parts. For example, back to back. Your task is to stand back to back with your partner (demonstrate). Elbow to elbow; connect elbows to elbows. Or elbow to shoulder; connect elbow to shoulder.

4. I will then call, "people to people" again. Each time you hear, "people to people," find a new partner and be prepared to connect again.

5. Play for a while, and then transition to the next activity.

Segue/Transitional Framing

Say to the group:

"People to People. (Make sure everyone has a partner) All right, new partner, new game."

Next Activity: Palm Off (Multiple Stances)

Estimated Time 🕐

10 minutes

Playfully introducing the spotting stance and self spotting with a competitive classic

Learning Themes
- Fun and Play
- Physical Activity and Movement
- Building Trust, Relationships, and Community

1. Get ready to play. "Face your current partner and stand heel to toe, with your own feet, a foot or two away from your partner. Raise your hands with elbows bent and in by your rib cage, and palms facing your partner."

2. Introduce the game. "Your task is to cause your partner to go off balance. The only way that you may contact your partner is touching their palms with your palms, essentially clapping. No grip and grapple, just clapping or avoiding the clap (demonstrate)."

3. Check for clarity and begin. "Questions? Go!"

4. After participants play for a bit, ask them to freeze. Say, "Same partner, same game, new stance. Introduce and demonstrate the new stance. New stance – standing on one foot. Go!"

5. Again, after a bit more play, introduce a third new stance. Call "People to people!" Or interrupt and call, "People to people!" At this point, most everyone should find a partner. A few may need a reminder that "People to people" means to find a new partner. Then say, "Same game, new partner, new stance. New stance – feet together. Go!"

6. Introduce yet another new stance in the same way. Call "People to people" to have them find new partners. Then introduce and demonstrate the next new stance. "New stance – feet hip to shoulder width apart. Go!"

7. Introduce the last stance. "Same partner, same game, new stance. New stance – feet hip to shoulder width apart and staggered, one foot forward, one foot back. Go!"

8. After allowing a sufficient amount of play, bring the group back to a circle to explore which stance was most fun and which felt the most stable. Say, "We played this game with five stances. Review them with me."

9. State and demonstrate the five stances. Have the group demonstrate them with you. "Number one was feet heel to toe. Number two – one foot, Number three – feet together, Number four – hip to shoulder width apart, and Number five was hip to shoulder width apart with one foot forward and one foot back."

10. Discover which stance was most fun for them. "I am going to say 'Set show.' When you hear 'Show,' jump into the stance in which you had the most fun. 'Set show.' Look around at each other's stances. What do you notice? Would anyone be interested in sharing why they chose the stance they chose?' Often times participants will display a variety of stances. Do not judge one stance over another; people are entitled to their own perceptions.

11. Discover which stance felt the most stable. "Again I will say, 'Set show.' This time, jump into the stance you felt the most stable in. 'Set show.' Take another look around. What do you notice? Would anyone be interested in sharing why they chose the stance they chose this time?' During this check-in, most people will demonstrate stance number 4 or 5, feet hip to shoulder width apart or feet hip to shoulder width apart with one foot forward and one foot back, respectively. Occasionally, a participant will either jokingly or seriously show that they felt most stable on one foot. Roll with the jokesters and seek to understand the serious ones. Again, do not judge the stances. Affirm their different perceptions and explain that they will play with the last stance, feet hip to shoulder width apart with one foot forward and one foot back, as they learn to trust and spot one another.

12. Transition to a brief lesson regarding a proper spotting stance.

Segue/Transitional Framing

Say to the group:

"We are going to play with the last stance some more and will use it as a way to develop trust in our group and prepare ourselves for some of the activities and low elements to come."

Next Activity: Spotting Stance

Understanding the spotting stance

| Learning Themes | • Physical Activity and Movement |
| | • Self Awareness and Self Management |

Procedure

1. Describe, demonstrate, and discuss the spotting stance and the spotter's responsibilities. "Let's clarify a good spotting stance. Hands up and elbows bent like Palm Off, head up, straight back, and bent knees. Eyes ready to focus on

another person's head, neck, shoulders, and back. Stand firm and flexible, yet not as firm as a wall and not as flexible as a cooked noodle, firm and flexible like a spring. Joints ready to articulate."

2. Transition to the next activity – Super Spotters Social.

Segue/Transitional Framing

Say to the group:

"Now, I'm not sure if you noticed, but you just experienced a special transformation. By discussing, reviewing and demonstrating the spotting stance, you have been accepted into the secret society of super spotters. And you have been invited to a Super Spotters' Social!"

Next Activity: Super Spotters' Social (aka Cocktail Party)

Estimated Time

5 minutes

A Secret Society of Super Spotters

Learning Themes	• Fun and Play
	• Building Trust, Relationships, and Community
	• Social Awareness

Procedure

1. Invite participants to mingle with each other as if they were attending a social gathering or, if appropriate, a cocktail party. "We will be mingling about as if we were attending a cocktail party. Following the norms of a social gathering, you should engage others in conversation, and not spend too much time with any one person. I will provide three different topics to discuss. Everything seems normal until you hear, "Spotters ready!"

2. Introduce the intent of the activity, responding to the 'Spotters' ready!' call. "When you hear 'Spotters ready!', immediately stop your conversations, jump into the spotting stance and respond with a resounding 'Ready!'"

3. Introduce the first topic. "The first topic of discussion: If you were to hit Play on your iPod, mp3 player, CD player, radio, etc., what would we hear? "Mingle, go!"

4. Once participants are engaged in good conversation, check their super spotter response time. Say, "Spotters ready!"

5. Observe how they respond and share a second topic. "Next topic for discussion, if you could have any vehicle, known or created, what would it be? Mingle, Go!"

6. Once again, when participants are engaged in good conversation, call out, "Spotters ready!"

7. Continue this sequence of mingling conversations and "Spotters ready!" calls one or two more times, then prepare the group for Trust Leans.

Segue/Transitional Framing

Say to the group:

"Have you ever wondered how far you could lean backwards before you needed to catch yourself? Likewise have you ever wondered what it would be like to let someone else catch your lean? We have the opportunity to explore our boundaries by trusting another person to catch us. In other words, one person will prevent the fall."

Estimated Time

15 – 25 minutes

Next Activity: 2-Person Trust Lean

Exploring physical, social, and emotional boundaries with one person

Learning Themes	• Self Awareness and Self Management
	• Social Awareness
	• Relationship Skills

Procedure

1. Playfully explore self-spotting. Say to the group, "Let's see what it's like to lean without anyone spotting us, except ourselves. To do this, bring your feet together, cross your arms across your chest, and flex your legs, especially your gluteus maximus (rear end). Keep your body as straight as you can and lean back as far as you can without completely falling to the ground. At some point, one of your legs should kick backwards to catch you. This is called self-spotting. Give yourself some room and try this going forward as well."

2. Demonstrate each step of the sequence, asking a participant to be the leaner/faller so that you can teach proper spotting. Say to the group, "I need a volunteer who is willing to lean while I spot so that we can demonstrate what is involved with a trust lean. Any volunteers? Thanks."

3. Ask the faller to stand with arms crossed in front of his or her chest, keeping elbows from flying out. The faller must also keep feet still and body stiff.

4. The spotter stands about a foot behind the leaner/faller, with one foot in front of the other, hips to shoulder width apart. The spotter's knees are bent, and arms and hands are up. Remind the group that this is the proper spotting stance.

5. Make sure that the group understands the concept of spotting. The critical areas to protect are the head, neck and back of the faller. This may mean that you can only break a fall rather than actually catch a fall.

6. The object of the activity is for the faller/leaner to fall backward against the spotter's hands. After properly spotting the faller, the spotter pushes the faller back to an upright stance.

7. Demonstrate a series of leans spotting close to the faller/leaner, then moving further and further away. Verbal communication is critical here:

    Faller: "Spotter Ready?"

    Spotter: "Ready."

    Faller: "Falling."

    Spotter: "Fall Away"

8. After each fall, the spotter can ask if the faller would like to step further away. Model check-ins that explore the boundaries and limits of both the leaner and spotter.

9. Check for understanding, and then direct participants to practice Trust Leans. Say to the group, "Do you have any questions or comments regarding leaning or spotting? All right, practice with your partners and discuss how it felt after each attempt, explore your boundaries as both leaners and spotters."

10. If time allows, invite participants to try a Trust Lean with other partners.

11. Transition to 3-Person Trust Leans, which introduces two spotters for one leaner.

Segue/Transitional Framing

Say to the group,

> "Let's take this a bit further and see what it's like to fall backwards and forward. This time, two people will spot one person."

Next Activity: 3-Person Trust Lean

Exploring physical, social, and emotional boundaries with two people

Learning Themes	• Self Awareness and Self Management
	• Social Awareness
	• Relationship Skills

Estimated Time

15 – 25 minutes

Safety

• During 3-Person Trust Leans, be sure the spotters don't pass the faller aggressively back and forth.

Procedure

1. Again, demonstrate proper spotting technique and communication. "This time I need two volunteers. One who is willing to spot in the back and the other willing to lean while I spot in the front so that we can demonstrate what is involved with a 3-Person Trust Lean. Any volunteers? Thanks."

2. Ask the faller to use the same posture and arm position as they did in the Trust Lean.

3. Both spotters should stand equi-distant from the faller – only a short step away to begin with.

4. Remind the group that the faller initiates communication, as in the Trust Lean. Both spotters need to respond.

   a. *Faller: "Spotters Ready?"*

   b. *Spotters: "Ready."*

   c. *Faller: "Ready to Fall."*

   d. *Spotters: "Fall Away."*

5. Demonstrate a series of leans with the spotters close to the leaner at first then moving further and further away as the lean advances. Spotters gently pass the faller back and forth between them. Emphasize a slow and gentle pace. For example, you might say, "Now, our goal as spotters is not to see how fast we can get our faller to move back and forth, but to maintain a pace that we can all manage."

6. Model in the moment check-ins regarding the boundaries and limits of both the faller and spotters.

7. Check for understanding and then direct participants to practice 3-Person Trust Leans. Say to the group, "Do you have any questions or comments regarding falling or spotting in this scenario? All right, practice with your partners and discuss how it went and felt after each attempt. Continue to explore your boundaries as both fallers and spotters."

8. If time allows, invite participants to try a 3-Person Trust Lean with other partners.

9. Transition to Wind in the Willows.

Segue/Transitional Framing

Say to the group,

"At this point, you have demonstrated the skills necessary to support one another. Let's use those skills and explore what it means for one person to be supported by their entire community."

Safety

• With Wind in the Willows, 12-15 people is about the largest each circle should be. Divide your group accordingly.

Next Activity: Wind in the Willows

An entire community supporting one individual

Learning Themes
- Physical Activity and Movement
- Building Trust, Relationships, and Community
- Self Awareness and Self Management
- Social Awareness

Procedure

1. Demonstrate with one group of 8-10 people.

2. Ask a volunteer to stand in the middle. This person, as the faller, must do everything the faller did in the leaning activities: arms crossed across the chest, feet planted solidly on the ground, body stiff.

3. The spotters around the circle need to stand close together, shoulder to shoulder. There should be no gaps in the circle that the faller could slip through.

4. The group should use the same commands as those used in the leans.

5. This time, the faller may fall in any direction. The group is to pass the faller gently around in a random pattern.

6. Stress that no one person should ever be the only one holding the faller; there should always be multiple people with hands on the faller.

7. Process each experience as needed, and then move on.

Segue/Transitional Framing

Say to the group:

"Okay, let's move on."

Next Activity: Can You Levitate?

A brief, healthily distractive stunt

> **Learning Themes**
> - Fun and Play
> - Physical Activity and Movement

Procedure

1. Playfully inquire about the group's skill associated with this stunt. Say, "Can anyone levitate?" Some people may be aware of this stunt or trick, while others will not, and still others may think you are talking about Levitation, the activity you are setting up for.

2. If someone does say they can levitate, provide a moment for them to demonstrate. Then review and explain the stunt. If no one knows the stunt, perform it and then explain it, so others can try.

3. Explain the stunt. Say to the group, "Face side ways to your partner or audience with your feet side by side. Attempt to create the illusion of levitation by slowly raising the front foot and heel of the back foot, while gently standing on the rear toes. Gently wave your hands as a distraction. Slow and steady is the way to amaze your friends, family, and co-workers!"

4. Allow a few minutes for practice, and then transition into Levitation.

Segue/Transitional Framing

Say to the group:

> "All right, let's levitate a different way. This time the group will provide an unforgettable experience for those who choose to try it."

287

Safety

• During Levitation, make sure the volunteer's head stays even with the rest of his or her body and that the body stays level. Also, remind people that a person's torso is heavier than the legs. Position more people to lift the torso area.

Culminating Activity: Levitation

A community that lifts each other up

Learning Themes	• Building Trust, Relationships, and Community
	• Self Awareness and Self Management
	• Social Awareness
	• Relationship Skills

Procedure

1. Ask for a volunteer to lay on the ground face up.

2. Direct the rest of the group to place their hands under the volunteer's body. Someone should tend exclusively to the person's head.

3. Select a leader (who should be you for the first round). The leader is the voice who calls out the commands for each round of the activity. The leader asks if the volunteer is ready. If the volunteer answers, "Yes," then the leader asks, "Lifters, ready?" The group responds accordingly.

4. When everyone is ready, on the leader's count, the group lifts the volunteer to waist level. It is important that the volunteer remains straight and still.

5. Depending on the group and the comfort of the volunteer, he or she can be raised higher, even going as high as head level.

6. On the leader's signal, the volunteer is then slowly lowered, with a gentle head to toe rocking motion added to the descent, until he or she is safely on the ground.

Reflection/Closure/Discussion

Typically, this sequence is significant enough to inspire reactions and comments along the way. Process as needed, and then highlight important themes that have emerged. One way to do this is to set up a Graffiti Wall Debrief. To create a "graffiti wall", hang large sheets of paper on a wall (or lay them on the ground). Provide participants with markers and invite them to write, draw, doodle about their experience during the Spotting Sequence – Enhanced. Encourage them to play off of each other's art work as most graffiti walls would depict. Once an appropriate amount of time has passed, allow your group members to mingle and observe their expressive art work and process any reactions and comments as they arise or simply let it be.

Tips and Comments

Trust Leans, 3-Person Trust Leans, and Wind in the Willows

• You cannot emphasize enough the need for all participants to focus during these activities.

• Adding the participant's name to the verbal communication helps personalize the experience and is especially helpful for clear communication with multiple groups.

• Make sure that there is clear communication about when the activity is over. We suggest the spotter or spotters put both hands on the faller's shoulders to designate that they have completed that series of falls.

Tips and Comments (*continued*)

Wind in the Willows

- Allow participants to choose the experience they would like from the following options. Help monitor safety, yet allow for some fun as well.
  - **Silent** – Provides a peaceful experience, helps the group focus, and typically reduces any unwanted comments.
  - **Sing a Song** – Ask participants to announce a song they would like the group to sing or hum during the activity. Participants may also choose a song they would consider their theme song. You know the one that plays as they enter an arena or event. Remind the group of their primary responsibilities, as singing can be distracting.
  - **Eyes Shut** – Another peaceful or adventurous way to experience Wind in the Willows!

Levitation

- Only let the group lift the volunteer higher if they give permission.
- You may allow the group to turn 360 degrees or walk around after the person is raised.
- Invite the person being lifted to close his or her eyes.
- Doing this in silence typically makes for a peaceful experience.
- Levitation can be combined with Wind in the Willows. Designate a person in the Wind in the Willows circle to be the head person for the levitation. After the volunteer in the middle has been passed around the circle a few times, the group should lean the volunteer toward the head person. Everyone should then gently lower the volunteer into a levitation position. The volunteer will not ever lie on the ground, but rather should be lowered into the arms of the people in the circle and picked up entirely. Then levitation continues as already described.

Sequence Enhancements and Alternatives – You may further increase the fun, engagement, and effectiveness of the flow described above by adding the following activities.

- People to People Twister (*Stepping Stones*)
- Walk and Lean (*The Hundredth Monkey*)
- Stationary Foot Tag (aka Top It) (*The Hundredth Monkey*)

Sequence Continuation – Spotting Sequenced – Enhanced can help prepare a group for the following low elements.

- Spider's Web
- The Beam
- Porthole
- The Wall

People to People was published in *Adventure Curriculum for Physical Education: Elementary* (Panicucci et al., 2003)

Palm Off was published in *No Props* (Collard, 2005)

2-Person Trust Leans, 3-Person Trust Leans, and Wind in the Willows were all published in *Adventure Curriculum for Physical Education: Middle and High School* (Panicucci et al., 2003)

Levitation was published in *Adventure Curriculum for Physical Education: Middle School* (Panicucci et al., 2003)

Appendix

Afterword

Hopefully you have enjoyed *The Hundredth Monkey* and found it to be a useful collection of activities and ideas. We hope that PA's foundational concepts and the importance of leading activities in a playfully adventurous way was effectively communicated and inspiring...and that you are enthused to give this approach along with the activities and sequences a go. In doing so, perhaps you and your participants have had a lot of fun, become more engaged, and experienced significant learning and growth. With all the potential between the covers of this book, one question (well, two) may still remain.

What will inspire a "tipping point" of positive change among the individuals, groups, institutions and communities whom you work with? For the pioneers of Project Adventure, it was fun and play. As the project evolved, the foundational concepts have played a significant role (as well). Perhaps, it may be developing your self personally and professionally. Whatever it may be, we hope you have found it here. Furthermore, we hope all of the ideas presented have reached way beyond the pages of this book and our trainings, as the ideas of Project Adventure have always done. In other words, our hope is that the contents of this book and the ever-evolving practice of adventure and experiential education continues to jump from one community to the next, as it phenomenally occurred in Ken Keyes, Jr.'s story, influencing the change that's meant to happen.

There are many ways to interpret and apply the hundredth monkey phenomenon to the work we do. Let's suppose that the sweet potatoes represent the activities and ideas in this activity guide, as well as many others that came before it. The act of washing the sweet potatoes then could represent the way in which to facilitate these activities – the practice and craft of adventure and experiential education. When a practitioner in any setting experiments with the playfully adventurous use of activities for particular outcomes – fun or otherwise – practitioners and participants alike, taste a bit of success. The experience, like tasting the freshly washed sweet potatoes, becomes "more palatable." Each time an activity is used effectively, a practitioner develops his or her craft, and the fun ensues, the (taste of) success becomes sweeter and sweeter; participants enjoyably engage in a way that genuinely leads to learning and growth. Most practitioners, the monkeys in this case, can hardly keep this success to themselves. They gladly share it with others who are ready and interested, paralleling the inspirational actions of the younger monkeys and the openness of the older monkeys. The ideas and actions are then picked up by almost everyone!

So maybe, just maybe, the big question is what will move YOU to inspire the hundredth monkey phenomenon in your tribe – the one that empowers people to build on the ideas and actions of others before them to reach the critical tipping point that inspires playful learning?

"Be the change that you wish to see in the world."
— Mahatma Gandhi

40 Handshakes for PA's 40 Years

Celebrating 40 Years of Innovative People and Powerful Relationships

The following are 40 (silly) Handshakes to celebrate PA's 40 years of innovation which would not exist without the creative dedication of so many amazing people. We are including them here in hopes that they may add delight to a day of activity.

1. **Happy Salmon (a.k.a. Ice Fishing)**
   - Happy What? Happy Salmon, a favorite for ice fishing fanatics!
   - Two people face one another and extend arms and hands as if to perform a regular handshake.
   - Instead of shaking hands, they slap each other's forearms like a fish's tail and say, "ey, ey, ey..."
   - Variations:
     - Introduce the Happy Salmon with a story of where the handshake originated perhaps Minnesota, Maine, New Hampshire, Vermont, Alaska, but not Florida or California. There is a phenomenon that occurs in (insert ice fishing state) when it gets really cold and the lakes and ponds freeze over. People push little boxes out onto the ice, drill holes, sit on a crate, and wait. Much excitement comes when a fish is caught and here's how people in the ice fishing community celebrate."
     - Here's a story specific to Minnesota. "During the winter, the people in Minnesota wear a brilliant pair of mitts called choppers – genuine moose or deer hide leather outers with rag wool liner. They are great at keeping your hands warm and connecting you with the Minnesotan way of life. The challenge, though, is that it is difficult to shake hands when wearing them. Here's the solution our friends in Minnesota came up with."

2. **Dairy Farmer (a.k.a. Milking the Cow)**
   - A greeting that mooooooooooooooves people.

   - Two people face one another.
   - One person creates the cow's utter by interlacing fingers with thumbs pointing up. Keeping fingers interlaced, he or she then rotates wrists and extends arms to turn thumbs pointing down.
   - The other person, then performs the duties of the dairy farmer by gripping the utters, their partner's thumbs, with both hands and begins milking by gently pulling downward on each thumb.
   - During the exchange, the cow "mooooooos..." and the dairy farmer makes the sounds of milking, "squirt, squirt, squirt..."

3. **Logger (a.k.a. The Lumberjack)**
   - Create a thumb on thumb stack.
   - One person extends the "thumbs up" gesture.
   - The other person grabs their partner's thumb and extends their thumb.
   - Repeat until all four hands are stacked on top of one another.
   - Participants move this handshake with a push and pull motion, back and forth, with the deep repetitive sound of "hey, hey, hey..." that gets louder and louder and faster and faster.
   - Variations:
     - Use names instead of the "hey, hey, hey..." sound. Participants either say their own name or their partners'.

4. **Witch's Brew (a.k.a. Human Mixer)**
   - Three or four participants create a thumb on thumb stack as in The Logger Handshake.
   - One person extends the "thumbs up" gesture.
   - The other person grabs his or her partner's thumb and extends their thumb.
   - Repeat until all hands are stacked on top of one another.
   - Participants move their hands in a circular stirring motion rather than back and forth and verbalize their best witch's cackle!

5. **Full Value Contract (FVC) Handshakes**
   - A great way to bring a Full Value Contract to life!

- In pairs or small groups, two or a few people create handshakes to represent each or one of the components from their Full Value Contract.

6. **Popcorn Handshake**
   - A new sizzling sensation with an explosive ending.
   - Two or a few people face one another, hold hands, stand close, and crouch down.
   - They make a sizzling sound by exhaling slowly and pressing their tongue against their top front teeth.
   - Participants "pop" or jump up and away from their group and into the air at any random time (e.g., they could try to exhale as long as they can, then pop or pop when they feel the time is right), extending both arms and legs forming an X or starfish shape with their bodies. Really, they can and perhaps should pop using any creative style they can muster.
   - Participants yell, "pop," as they jump away from their partners.
   - Variations:
     - Instead of saying "pop," participants could yell their own name or the names of their partners.
     - Small groups of kernels, participants, could attempt to pop at exactly the same time. Heck, large groups of kernels could attempt to pop at exactly the same time. Some people call this a group jump — the whole group attempts to jump and land simultaneously, with or without communication.

7. **Wind-up Toy Handshake**
   - A greeting of unpredictable wound-up wonder.
   - Two people face each other, hold hands, and wind-up three times.
   - The wind-up is performed by simultaneously moving arms and bending legs. While arms and hands roll down toward the ground, participants move towards a squatting position. As arms roll up towards the head, participants stand tall.
   - After three wind-ups, participants detach from their partners and move in their most inspired and unique wind-up toy manners.

- Encourage a variety of unique and fun wind-up toys. Some ideas, if participants are stuck, might be:
  - The Energizer Bunny
  - The Cymbal Clanging Monkey
  - The Penguin
  - The Hopper
  - The Forward Roller
  - The Spinner
  - The Robot
  - The Break Dancer
  - The Curly Shuffle
  - The Chattering Teeth
  - The Inchworm
  - Additionally, the idea here is to move playfully and have some fun, so encourage unique movements. Random, spontaneous movements add to the fun!
  - Need more ideas? Google: Wind-up Toys and filter through images!

8. **Butterfly**
   - A greeting of transformative beauty.
   - This was shared during a 2007 Youth & College Program by a group of 4th and 5th graders from Atrium School, Watertown, MA.
   - Begin with a traditional handshake, but keep the arms loose.
   - Shake hands three times allowing the arms to move in a wave-like motion (caterpillar).
   - Grip thumbs (cocoon) and extend fingers (butterfly wings).
   - Flap fingers and fly hands away (butterfly).

9. **Suffern Shuffle**
   - The handshake for pro-athletes to non-athletes.
   - Introduced by a group of PE Teachers from Suffern, NY.
   - Slap right hand to right hand, left to left, right to right again, and left to left again.
   - Turn to the side, jump, and gently – gently – bump shoulders.
   - Including a fun sound, "ding," when bumping shoulders adds to the fun. Encourage unique sounds.

10. **High 5**
    - A classic handshake that inspired many others.
    - Two people face one another, extend an open hand in front of them and slightly above their heads, and then slap their hands together.
    - Variations:
      - Jumping High 5 – Jump and High 5 while in the air!
      - Jumping High 5 Personal Best – execute a Jumping High 5, however, while in the air, complete as many High 5s as you can.
      - Soap Suds High 5 – If soap suds are available to you, then you are in for a sudsational treat. Each person scoops up some soap suds in his/her hand and High 5s their partner causing the suds to squirt sporadically through the air.

11. **High 5 Hug**
    - For the affectionate ones among us.
    - Perform a High 5 as it is typically done, however on contact keep hands connected.
    - Each person then wraps their thumb around the hand of their partner and "hugs."

12. **Wild Turkey (a.k.a Turkey Handshake)**
    - Inspired by a community of wild friends residing on Moraine Farm.
    - Two people set up as if to give each other a High 5.
    - However, one person spreads their fingers wide, making the feathers of the turkey, while the other makes a fist and extends their thumb, making the body and head of the turkey.
    - They then connect these turkey parts, making a whole turkey complete with commonly associated turkey noises or not, "gobble, gobble, gobble…"
    - Variations:
      - Consider introducing the double-fisted turkey. Two people, two turkeys, one on each hand.
      - A whole group turkey can be unifying, fun, and a way to celebrate. In a circle, each person brings their right hand up and extends their feathers (fingers) toward the neighbor on their right. Then, with their left hand, they make the head and body (fist and thumb). In a unifying moment they connect and sound off, "Gobble, gobble, gobble… meeooooow…gobble, gobble…"
    - Tips:
      - Encourage creativity, goofy, and fun noises!
      - Be prepared for the two-feathered or double-headed turkey, as well as the Are you the head? or am I? or are you the feathers? (mostly demonstrated by flickering hand movements), as it seems that not everyone is comfortable with these findings. This moment is teachable, as it provides the opportunity to briefly highlight any uncomfortable feeling or awkwardness that comes with trying something new or stepping outside of the comfort zone. It also provides the opportunity to introduce the idea that mistakes and confusion are part of learning.

13. **Top Gun**
    - Actor Tom Cruise couldn't get any cooler in Top Gun, but you might by doing this handshake more often!
    - Two people, walking toward each other, set up as if they are going to High 5.
    - However, they miss or pass through the High 5 at the height of their extension and rotate their hands forward and down at roughly the same speed.
    - They slap hands, or catch the five, just as each person reaches the lowest point of their rotation.

14. **Ankle Shake**
    - Two people, walking toward each other, set up as if they are going to High 5.
    - However, they miss or pass through the High 5 at the height of their extension and rotate their hands forward and down at roughly the same speed.
    - At the same time, they are bending and lifting one of their legs.
    - They then, with the hand that had missed the High 5 up top, grab and shake each other's ankle.

15. **Whippi Dip**
    - Two people, walking toward each other, set up as if they are holding an ice cream cone and preparing to give each other a High 5.
    - However, they miss or pass through the High 5 at the height of their extension and rotate their hands forward and down at roughly the same speed.
    - At the same time, they are bending and lifting one of their legs.
    - They then, with the hand that had missed the High 5 up top, grab and shake each other's ankle.
    - Remind everyone to mind their ice cream cone, assuring that it doesn't end up on the ground or floor.
    - Variations:
      - Replace the ice cream cone with a favorite morning beverage.

16. **New Yorker**
    - New Yorkers were multi-tasking long before the iPhone 4.
    - Participants envision themselves walking through the busy streets of New York with a newspaper (The New York Times) under one arm and a brief case in the hand of the same arm, a cell phone held by the head and shoulder on the other side, and a coffee in the other hand.
    - Participants greet their partners with either an elbow bump on the cell phone and coffee side, a tap of the feet on either side, or both.

17. **Under the Leg Five**
    - Is this stretching it?
    - Facing each other, yet slightly to the side, two people lift the leg closest to their partner and attempt to High 5 under their legs.
    - Tips:
      - This seems to be a bit of a stretch for some, so inform your participants of this potential to reduce the risk of tweaked backs and strained legs, etc.

18. **High Ten**
    - A variation of a classic only twice as cool.
    - Two people face one another, extend two open hands in front of them and slightly above their heads, and then slap their hands together.
    - Variations:
      - High 10 Sweep – After connecting at the height of the greeting, High 10 partners maintain contact through their hands and sweep them down toward the sides of their bodies, then in front of them, culminating by disengaging from their partners and clapping their own hands.
      - 2 Times the Fun – If you can do it with 5 why not 10?
        - Jumping High 10 – Jump and High 10 while in the air!
        - Jumping High 10 Personal Best – execute a Jumping High 10, however, while in the air, complete as many High 10s as you can.
        - Soap Suds High 10 – If soap suds are available to you, then you are in for an even more sudsational treat. Each person scoops up some soap suds in their hands and high 10s their partners causing the suds to squirt sporadically through the air.

19. **360**
    - A challenging spin on a classic High 10.
    - While in the air, two people attempt to complete an entire 360 then High 10, before landing on the ground or floor.

20. **Low**
    - One person sets up by extending one of his or her hands palm up towards a partner.
    - The other person raises one of his or her hands and lowers it back down, palm down, slapping the open hand of their partner.
    - Variations:
      - Give Me Some Skin (a.k.a. the Slide) – Even smoother than the original. Same setup and execution as the Low 5; however, upon contact, both partners slowly slide their hands against their partner's and out of contact.
      - Flip Flop – Reciprocating the exchange. Upon contact of the Low 5 or after the slide has occurred in Give Me Some Skin, participants flip their hands and

repeat the exchange from the other position.

– Too Slow – A trickster/prankster version of smooth. Just as the partner is about to make Low 5 contact with his or her partner, the person who initiated the exchange pulls it out of the way or even smoother, pulls their hand out of the way and up to the side of his or her head to brush the hair back. Now that's smooth!

21. **Fresh Prince**
- Who's cooler than the Fresh Prince? You are!
- Two people slap right hands.
- They then, immediately bring their right hands back to their right sides while turning their head looking over their right shoulders, snap their fingers ending with casually extended fingers and make the sound "psshhhhhht."
- Variations
  - What Up? – Include the full verbal greeting of, "Hey, what up (name)?"
  - Hug – After the snap and "psshhhhhht," include a hug.
  - From behind – While standing in front of another person, a player may initiate the Fresh Prince Handshake, by extending his or her right hand back to the person behind them. They then perform the look over the right shoulder, right arm back, snap, and "psshhhhhht" in unison.
  - Shhhh – Engage in the Fresh Prince handshake in the usual way. When it is time to look back and snap, one participant waves a hand in the face of the other and says, "sshhhhhhhh."
  - Back At You – Same Fresh Prince handshake with a thumb up finger point return.
  - Point First – Prior to engaging in the Fresh Prince, participants playfully point at each other saying "woooooo," then continue in the usual way.

22. **Fist Bump (a.k.a. Pound or DAPS)**
- Firm acknowledgement
- Two people face one another, extend one of their arms and a closed fist toward their partner, until they gently bump fists.

23. **Potato & French Fries (a.k.a. Blow It Up)**
- A fun variation to the classic Fist Bump.
- As in the Fist Bump, two people face one another, extend their arms and closed fists towards each other, until they gently bump fists.
- Upon bumping fists, each person simultaneously opens their fist and spreads their fingers in an explosive manner.

24. **Let It Rain**
- Another fun variation to the Fist Bump and perfect for introducing a water cycle or weather unit!
- As in the Fist Bump, two people face one another, extend their arms and closed fists towards each other, until they gently bump fists.
- Upon bumping fists, players simultaneously open their fists and flutter their fingers dropping down towards the ground or floor indicating rain.

25. **Jellyfish**
- Still another variation of the Fist Bump. Why not? It's classic!
- As in the Fist Bump, two people face one another, extend their arm and closed fist towards each other, until they gently bump fists.
- Upon bumping fists, players simultaneously open their fists, extend their fingers and draw their arms back in a wave-like motion as if flowing through the ocean. Fingers also demonstrate a similar wave-like flow.

26. **The Snail**
- Yes, another variation of the Fist Bump, but this one's different!
- As in the Fist Bump, two people face one another, extend their arms and closed fists towards each other. This is where it's different from the rest of the Fist Bump family of handshakes.
- Just as the fists are about to bump, one person dips under the other, stopping under the partner's fist, and extends and slowly wiggles his or her index and middle fingers, as in a moving peace sign. These fingers create the antennae, while the fist of the other person creates the shell.

27. Ti Fighter

- For the Star Wars fans among us.
- One person invites another to engage in what appears to be a classic fist bump.
- Just before the bump, the initiator of this handshake sandwiches the fist of his or her partner with two hands, fingers close together, yet pointing to the sky.
- In good form, the initiator moves his or her hands and, incorporating his or her partner's sandwiched fist in the flight pattern (up, down, around, etc.) of a Ti Fighter from the popular movie, Star Wars, while making Ti Fighter shooting noises.

28. Captain Hook

- Two people facing each other make a fist then extend and hook their index or pointer fingers on the right hand.
- They then hook each other's fingers and exclaim a classic pirate greeting, "Argh!"

29. Politician's Handshake (a.k.a. Glove, Sandwich, or Double Handed Handshake)

- Two players engage in a traditional or typical handshake.
- One or both then cover their partner's hand and shake.
- Encourage greetings such as "It's very nice to meet you" and "Wonderful, wasn't it."

30. Between the Legs

- As seen on the TV show, the Simpsons, and reminiscent of Bug Tug (a game from the New Games Foundation), this simple handshake is sure to be awkward and maybe fun!
- Two people turn their backs to one another, bend over and reach through their legs to shake hands, by pulling gently back and forth.

31. Bash Brothers

- Remember the Bash Brothers? Jose Canseco and Mark McGuire of the Oakland As, the 1990 MLB World Champions. They were so great!
- This handshake can be as simple as a forearm bash or a full and complex re-enactment, pretending to hit a home run, imaginary swing for the fences, a quick jaunt around a mini baseball diamond, culminating with the legendary forearm bash.

32. Skydiver

- A new low-flying simulation of high fun!
- Two people each balance on one foot, extending the other behind them and lift arms out to the side, creating wings like an airplane.
- They then bring one of their arms toward one another and grasp hands while shaking and raising a fist on the other arm, all the while making a face depicting that of a skydiver's excitement or concern during the free fall.
- Variations:
  - As skydiving goes, consider two or more people to perform the handshake.
  - One or two hands, spinning!

33. 3 Stooges Bop

- Stooping to the 3 Stooges level.
- One person extends a fist for the other person to bop.
- Once the bop occurs, the participant who extended the original fist carries the momentum of the bop around and gently bops the top of his or her head.
- Variation:
  - The original bopper may join and follow the momentum of his or her own fist and also gently bop his or her head as well!

34. Sumo Wrestler

- Two people face one another.
- Each person establishes a solid base by stomping the right foot then the left foot into the semi-squatting position of a sumo wrestler.
- They then make fists with both hands and extend their arms out to the sides, yet low at waist level and slightly in front of the body.
- Displaying their best sumo wrestler faces accompanied with their best sumo grunt confirms the greeting.

35. Weasel (Pauley Shore)

- Inspired by an MTV has-been.
- Two participants face one another.
- One person extends his or her arms, holds his or her hands palms up, fingers bent, as if to grip an object, and wiggles them randomly.

- Simultaneously, the other person extends arms, holding palms facing down, fingers bent and wiggling.
- While the fingers of each person's hand are wiggling just out of reach of one another, they each make a weasel-like face and sounds by bucking their teeth and quivering their teeth and lips.

36. Do-se-do
- A square dance spin-off
- Two people face one another, interlock elbows, and satisfyingly spin without bumping into any other people.

37. Fishing
- A dance move that's just as valuable as a greeting
- One person initiates this greeting by pretending to cast a line from an imaginary fishing pole toward someone with whom they make eye contact.
- The other person is hooked and in a fish-faced, flip-flopping frenzy, fins and all, acts out the fish on the line. The fish face is executed by puckering the lips and sucking in the cheeks. Typically, fins are displayed by both hands fingers up fluttering on the associated cheek. The flip-flopping frenzy is portrayed best by randomly jumping and wiggling the head back and forth while in the air.

38. Lawn Mower
- A go-to dance move and hilarious handshake
- Two people grip left hands by gripping each other's thumbs.
- With their right hands, they make a pulling motion, as in pulling the imaginary fly wheel tab to start the lawn mower. To do so, each person should make a fist as if they were gripping around a handle, extend their arms, and then pull back towards their bodies bending at the elbows.
- Once the imaginary mower has started, partners release their grips and move on pretending to mow the lawn.

39. Pinky Swear
- One of the strongest commitments ever made between two people.
- Two people face each other, make a fist then extend their pinky fingers.
- Just before greeting, they ask, "Pinky swear?" or "Do you swear?"
- They then hook each other's pinkies and exclaim, "I pinky swear!"

40. Best Handshake Ever (Create Your Own)
- A mesmerizing phenomenon sure to challenge or amaze your friends.
- Two people establish a handshake linking a flowing sequence of handshaking exchanges and interactions.

Grouping Ideas

There are many ways to creatively form partnerships or small groups. The list below is a representation of that although it is not an exhaustive list whatsoever. There are plenty of other ideas out there and plenty more to discover. There are three general categories:

- **Partnering Ideas** – Simple and quick stand-alone activities for pairing.
- **Activities that Form Partners or Small Groups** – More substantial activities, activities found in this activity guide and others, that naturally create pairs or small groups.
- **Using Props to Form Partners or Small Groups** – Many props lend themselves well to seamless partnering or small group forming. Bonus: these techniques usually double as an efficient way to clean up your props and move on to whatever comes next!

Glance through the selection below and find the right pairing or grouping activity for you and your group. Look for ideas that appear to flow seamlessly into the activity you plan to lead. Ultimately, we hope these ideas inspire more creative partnering and grouping ideas from you!

Partnering Ideas

Sole Mate – Playfully invite your participants to find their "*soul mate*" as it would be implied at first. Allow a moment of shock, excitement, and wonder to set in and with perfect comedic timing deliver the punch line, "Yes, I am inviting you to find your *sole mate*, right here, right now," as you lift your foot and examine the sole of your shoe. Invite participants to look at the soles of their shoes and find partners who have similar colors, styles, tread patterns, or even wear patterns. Explain that not every sole will match perfectly, but participants should do their best to find a connection. For fun, have participants place the ankle of one leg on the knee of the other which helps others to see their soles. Keeping the foot resting on the knee, encourage everyone to hop around until they find their partners. Assist anyone who needs help finding a partner. Sole Mate works well for most partner activities as well as forming goal partners for goal setting activities like GPS-E.

What Foot Do You Hop On? – Another pairing technique is to direct participants to hop on one foot, acknowledge which foot they are hopping on, hop to someone who either is hopping on the same or different foot, which ever you choose, to form a partnership. What Foot Do You Hop On? is a great lead-up for Pogo Stick Tag, found in *The Hundredth Monkey* or any other paired activities.

Psychic Hopping – Ask partners to think of a number 1-5 without sharing it with anyone in the group. Invite participants to mill about until they meet up with another person. Upon the meeting, participants say, "Set, Go!" and hop the amount of times indicated by the number they were thinking of. People who hop the same number of times become partners. If the hops are different, participants simply mill about some more until they meet up with someone else and attempt to hop the same number of times without saying anything. Got it? Psychic Hopping is a hopping variation of an activity called Psychic Handshake in *No Props*, and is also ideal for Pogo Stick Tag, and other paired activities.

Total Letters – Ask participants to think of a response to a particular topic, e.g., their favorite human powered vehicle – a bike, scooter, skateboard, canoe, feet, etc. Then have them total the number of letters in the word of their response. Instruct each person to find a partner with the same, or roughly the same number, of letters used to spell their word. Once partnerships have formed, provide a moment for participants to share their responses with their partners, and then move on to frame the activity and explain how to play. This works with names as well, however, names do not typically lead to the conversation related to a particular topic. Using names may be a great choice when a group needs to learn or reinforce the names of each person in the group.

Snappy Partners – If you are still looking for more ideas to form partners, check out Snappy Partners in *No Props* (Collard, 2005). This fun list of partnering techniques was mentioned a few times in this activity guide. If you haven't picked up *No Props* yet, you should; you will not be disappointed!

Activities that Form Partners or Small Groups

Crosstown Connection – Crosstown Connection (*The Hundredth Monkey*) is ideal for forming partners. By the end of the activity, each participant typically has three to five different partners associated with unique handshakes. Use these handshake partners later in the day as a way to form pairs.

Name Trains (Trains of 2, 3, or 4) – Name Trains (*The Hundredth Monkey*) offers a unique way to form partners or small groups by using the first and last letters in each person's name. For a more detailed explanation, see the activity description.

Icebreakers – By its very nature, Icebreakers (*The Hundredth Monkey*), mixes people up. It gets people to connect, at different times, with nearly everyone in the group. At some point, the game will end, resulting in participants being paired with different players than they started with. This provides a great opportunity to transition to another partner-based activity, move on to a paired debrief, form groups of four, or divide the group in half.

Knot Again – Knot Again (*The Hundredth Monkey*) typically ends with two people holding the ends of one small rope. Simply, it's another opportunity for pairing. Prepare for it and use it when appropriate.

Line-up or Spectrum Splits – Line-ups or spectrum splits are a way to divide any group because they are simple and offer many options once your group is standing in a line. There are many activities - Name Trains (*The Hundredth Monkey*), Spectrums (*No Props*), Silent Line-Up (*No Props*), etc. – that end with your group in a line. With your group in a line, you could:

- Split the line in half to form two groups.
- Fold the line in half resulting in each person facing another person from the other half of the line. With each person facing another person, partnering is now simple. Have the two people, now facing one another on the ends of each side of the line form partners. Instruct each subsequent pair of people facing one another to pair off as well. If there is an odd number of people, jump in to join the remaining person or invite that person to join a pair (forming a group of 3) depending on the needs of the next activity.
- Divide the line into quarters to form four groups.
- Start at the end of the line and invite two, three or four people to form pairs or small groups. Work your way down the line and move on to your next activity.

Clumps or Grouplets – A fun and efficient way to get your larger group into pairs or smaller groups is with an activity called Clumps or Grouplets. What you have to do is simple. Explain to your group that you will call out a number and that they need to group according to the number called. So if 3 has been called, the participants quickly form groups of 3. When 7 is called, participants form groups of 7. Call multiple numbers and play the game for a while and end with the number that would match your desired group size. Yes, there are moments when participants do not find a group. It's part of the game. Call another number and move on. When it comes time to end with your desired group size, find a fun way to help those who went astray into a group. For a more detailed description of this activity, see *No Props* (Collard, 2006)

Captains Calling – Similar to Clumps or Grouplets, Captains Calling is another game that is helpful for grouping. Basically, a captain, typically the facilitator calls out either specific areas on a boat, e.g., bow, stern, starboard, port, or a specific task requiring a certain number of people, e.g., Swab the Deck (1 person), Captain's Ball (2 people), Life Boats (3 People), Captain's Table (4 people), Starfish (5 People), etc. Participants then quickly either run to the specific location called or form groups required and perform the task. As with Clumps and Grouplets, as you near the end of the game, call a task that would result in a group that matches your desired group size. For a more detailed description of Captains Calling look in the Elementary or High School Version of the *Adventure Curriculum for Physical Education* (Panicucci et al., Project Adventure, 2003).

From One Group to Another – This heading represents a type of grouping that involves a similar idea and a little math. Simply, there is a way to go magically from groups of a specific number of participants to a specific number of groups. A theme has been added to each example below for fun, enhancement, and possibly a connection to an activity with a similar theme.

- **Groups of 3 to 3 Groups** – Think of all of the things that come in 3. The 3 Stooges; The Star Wars Trilogy; Rock-Paper-Scissors; Igneous, Sedimentary, and Metamorphic Rocks; Caterpillar, Cocoon, Butterfly…the list goes on. Divide your group into groups of three people. Have them briefly discuss whatever list of three things you suggested; then have one person in each group choose one of the three headings. For example, if you chose the three basic types of rock, you might suggest that the participants engage in any number of conversations – noting which types they can identify, explaining which type they are most like, or which type they like most. After a brief exchange, ask that each participant in each group chose one of the three types of rock. Each group should have one person who chose igneous, one who chose sedimentary, and yet another who chose metamorphic. From here, all that is left to do is to have the participants form groups with other people who chose the same item, or in this case, rock type.

- **Groups of 4 to 4 Groups** – As with Groups of 3 to 3 Groups, the gist is to go from groups of four people to forming four groups of people, typically setting your group up for whatever activity is next. Following is a nautically-themed version that works well for the activity Armada (page 29). Separate your group into smaller groups of four people. Once the groups have formed, explain that they are about to venture out to sea and that roles need to be defined. Ask each group to identify one captain, one crew member, one passenger, and one stowaway within their group of four. There are many ways to do this. It can be done randomly or group members can determine and identify the roles that would suit them best if venturing out to sea. Regardless, there should be one captain, one crew member, one passenger, and one stowaway represented in each group. As soon as all groups have sorted this out, explain that you will be creating four teams – one team of captains, one team of crew members, one team of passengers, and

– you've got it – one team of stowaways. Direct the newly-formed groups to their own triangle – the captains to one triangle, the group of crew members to another, and so on. Now, this could lead to an interesting study of sociological perspectives as the game is played; feel free to explore the dynamics of each group and how it impacts the overall game at any time.

- **Groups of 5 to 5 Groups** – Following the patterns established above, also works well when forming groups of five or more for that matter. When forming groups of five, a favorite group-splitting topic has been music and, more specifically, the people who make the music often referred to as a band. This splitting technique is often called Band Split. Find a fun way to get your group into groups of five and then have them discuss their favorite type of music. Following this brief conversation, have each person in each group choose one of three roles in a band – lead guitar, lead singer, drummer, bass guitar, rhythm guitar – and form groups as explained above. This one is fun to watch. The dynamic of each group may or may not represent the personalities of the group members, though often it does! For example the, drummers are often people who actively keep the rhythm of the group going, the lead guitarists can be creative and technical, and the lead singers are, well, vocal! Keep an eye or ear out as much more is likely to show up. And of course, there are many other roles – DJ, keyboardists, random dancer, etc. – to insert or exchange for variety and changing numbers. Play with it and have fun!

- **Others?** At this point, you should be able to do the math and find different things in our world that correlate to the number desired. Okay, I'll get you started with a little sports-themed rant. Basketball (5 players), Hockey (6 players), Ultimate Frisbee (7 players), Baseball (9 players), Lacrosse (10 players), and Soccer, Football, and Field Hockey all call for 11 players. Okay, off you go.

From 2 to 4 to 8… – This title indicates a little more math; can you handle it? It is a simple equation to form even groups of any size. Use any partnering technique to form pairs. Once pairs are formed, ask two sets of pairs to join one another forming a group of four. If a small group is what you need, then go no further. However, if you need a group with a few more people, clump two groups of four to get a group of eight. There, you should have it by now.

From 3 to 6 or 3 to 9 – How about starting with three? Of course, a group of three easily becomes a group of six. Or, three groups of three become a group of nine. Bam!

From 2 to 4 to 2 – There may even be times when mixing people from one partner to another, or one sharing to another, is desired. A seamless flow to make that happen works like this. Find a fun way to form pairs and do whatever you plan to do with those pairings whether it is a partner activity, game, or debrief. After whatever event has occurred, invite one pair to group with another pair forming a group of four. At this point, you may want to do something – a game or a debrief – requiring four people to be together. Regardless, from a group of four it is easy enough to split back to two pairs with people new to each other; people who haven't partnered yet.

Using Props to Form Partners or Small Groups

Fleece Balls – Fleece balls are typically red, yellow, green, blue, and sometimes multi-colored. Clearly, one technique is to partner by color either matching the same color or grouping in diverse groups. Fleece Ball Sort is a little adventure, using these props as a partnering or grouping technique.

- **Fleece Ball Sort** – Gather four colors of fleece balls, say, red, yellow, green, and blue. Make sure that you have the same number of each color (i.e., for 60 participants, there should be 15 of each color). These colors will be used to create the four teams. Begin randomly tossing the fleece balls into the air and encouraging your participants to catch one. You may then need to coach some people who have already acquired a fleece ball to step aside or share with other players who have not yet received one. Once all of the fleece balls have been distributed, direct the participants to group according to color and voila – four small groups from your one larger group! Additional ideas:
  - Use to create two, three or four groups. To do so, match the number of colors of fleece balls with the desired number of groups, then make sure you have an even number of each color.
  - Use to create pairings or groups of three to four people. To do so, direct participants to form pairings or groups with one of each color fleece ball represented, rather than directing participants to group by like color.
  - The timing of the catch could also be used to create pairings or groups. As participants catch a fleece ball, direct them to pair with another person, regardless of fleece ball color, to form pairs. Similarly, as three people catch a fleece ball, form a group of three; as four people catch, form groups of four, and so on. Likewise, after half the group has caught a fleece ball, direct them to form a group and then throw the remaining fleece balls all at the same time for the rest of the participants to catch or at least attempt to catch!

Poppers – Most poppers also come in four colors – red, yellow, green and blue – or whatever color pool noodles you have cut up! Having a set of multi-colored poppers enables you to form partners or small groups in much the same way described with Fleece Balls. Enjoy!

Wooden Blocks – The use of wooden blocks shows up in many activities found in this activity guide, e.g., Bust a Move, Don't Break the Ice, Block Party, etc. Whether the blocks are a variety of solid colors or the classic ABC/123 block, there are many partnering or grouping opportunities. Below are a few to try:

- **Find Your Match** – Have participants partner with someone who has the exact same or similar block. This can be achieved by matching the same color, letter, number, or symbol.
- **3-Letter Word** – Form Groups of three by having participants use the letters on their blocks to from three-letter words.
- **4-Letter Word** – Form Groups of four, by having participants use the letters on their blocks to form four-letter words.
- **Acronyms** – Have participants form small groups by using the letters on their blocks to form commonly known acronyms or text messages.

- **Initials** – Have two people form partners by using the letters on their blocks to indicate the initials of someone famous or well known.
- **Numbers** – For blocks that have numbers on them, see the ideas offered under Numbered Spot Markers.

Numbered Spot Markers – Numbered Spot Markers often associated with the activity Key Punch and now Tollbooth Boogie, are great for what they offer these activities. However, they also offer unique partnering or grouping opportunities. Consequently, most of these lead to a simple way of helping with the clean-up of the activity as well! Enjoy the following ideas:

- **Odd and Even** – Direct participants to pick up a spot marker, determine if it is an odd or even, and find a partner who either has the same or different number type. Or invite participants to find their group, odd or even, given that there is roughly the same number of each type of number.
- **Add 'em Up** – Have participants find a partner by whose number when totaled or added with theirs equals either an odd or even number. Same concept works when forming groups of three or four as well.
- **Any Connection** – Invite participants to pair by finding their own connection between numbered spots. Some connections that might come up are participants who hold their favorite numbers, sharing the same digit, i.e., 2 and 12, or when totaled form either an odd or even number.

Bandanas – There are many ways to creatively form partnerships or small groups using bandanas. Use bandanas to form partners for activities requiring, yet not limited to, the use of bandanas or for a debrief afterward.

- **Bandana Match** – Give each participant a bandana. Invite them to find either a partner or a small group of people who share either the same color bandana or a bandana with the same pattern on it. Clearly, your bandana collection must have either matching colors or patterns for this technique to be effective.
- **Color Match** – Place colored bandanas around the space and invite participants to stand near a color that matches, or nearly matches, something they are wearing. Allow only two people per bandana.

Exchange or provide additional bandanas as necessary. People who are standing near the same bandana are now partners.

- **Bandana Bouquet** – Grab a bunch of different colored bandanas, one for every two participants. Create a "bandana bouquet" by folding the bandanas in half, holding the fold of the bandanas in your hand, and allowing the ends of the bandanas to emerge from your hand like a bouquet of flowers. Invite participants to hold the end of one of the bandanas in your hand. Once everyone has connected to a bandana, ask him or her to hold on to his or her bandana as you let go. Every participant will soon discover who is holding the same bandana and subsequently, who is partnering with whom.
- **Guess the Color** – Provided that your bandanas are in a bag, invite your participants to a brief game of anticipation and surprise. Explain that you will be randomly picking bandanas of different colors from the bag. The participants are to guess the color. People who guess correctly are welcome to find a partner of their choice. Those who were incorrect guess again. You could always flip this by allowing the incorrect guessers to choose their partners while challenging those who respond correctly an opportunity to press their luck!

Spoons – In the case of a game with spoons, such as Spoon Jousting Tag (*The Hundredth Monkey*) or even a classic "Egg and Spoon Relay", the following may be useful:

- **Spooning** – Have participants pair with someone who has the same or entirely different spoon.
- **Playing the Spoons** – If all of the spoons are the same or similar, invite participants to "play the spoons" discovering their favorite way to make noise or even lay down a specially crafted rhythm. Direct each participant to partner with someone who plays the spoons similarly or someone they find a connection or can jam with.
- **Find Your Match** – Similarly, if the collection of spoons has two of each type, participants may find partners who have matching spoons.
- **Colored Tape** – Using colored tape to mark the ends of your spoon collection enables pairing to happen according to the tape color.

Debriefs Found In
The Hundredth Monkey
(In alphabetical order)

On the following page is a list of 25 debrief ideas found throughout *The Hundredth Monkey*. The debriefs are listed alphabetically so that you can easily locate and return to your favorites, whether you plan to use them with the suggested activity, sequence, or another. The debriefs are here to add variety and spark creativity in your own processing techniques. Use them as you see fit.

DEBRIEF	ACTIVITY OR SEQUENCE	PAGE NUMBER
Balloon Propulsion Debrief	Balloon Tag	38
Chiji Processing Dice	World Wide Key Punch	245
Crossword Debrief	Building Blocks	273
Feelings Cards	The Elusive Shadow	209
Fist to Five	Circle Call	50
	Foot Tag	78
	Longest Shadow	128
	Pogo Stick Tag	162
	Walk and Lean	233
Full Value Check-in	Don't Break the Ice	73
	Foot Tag	78
	Sonic 2	184
	Full Value Flow	268
FVC Affirmations	Full Value Flow	268
FVC Origami Check-in/Debrief	FVC Origami	89
FVC Take a Stand	Full Value Flow	268
Gift Giving/Affirmations	FVC Origami	89
Graffiti Wall	Spotting Sequence – Enhanced	288
Pair Share	Don't Break the Ice	73
	Icebreakers	98
Pass the Knot Debrief	Knot Race	121
Pi Chart	Sonic 2	183
Press Conference Debrief	Press Conference	167
Quadraphonic Debrief	Don't Break the Ice	73
	Icebreakers	98
Reflective Map Debrief	World Travelers	241
	World Wide Key Punch	245
	World Wide Wonder	278
Remote Control	Armada	32
Rope Sculpt	Knot Again	117
Static Cling Affirmations	Balloon Tag	38
Survey	Foot Tag	78
Take a Stand Debrief	Armada	31
Traffic Light/Take a Stand Debrief	Armada	31
Spectrum Debrief	Jump Tag	110
	Pitball	158
Thumb-o-meter	Merge	137

Activities and Learning Themes

ACTIVITIES	Fun and Play	Physical Activity and Movement	Building Trust, Relationships and Community	Self Awareness and Self Management	Social Awareness	Relationship Skills	Responsible Decision Making
5 Handshakes 5 Minutes	X	X	X				
52 Card Pick-up			X	X	X		
Altershake						X	X
Armada	X	X	X	X	X	X	X
Balloon Tag	X	X	X	X			
Behavioral Settings				X	X		
Block Party			X			X	X
Brain Buckets	X			X	X		X
Bridging the Gap			X	X		X	
Bust a Move	X	X				X	X
Circle Call	X	X	X				
Circle Tag	X	X	X				
Circle Up	X	X	X				
Collaborative Numbers (aka Key Punch Jr.)				X		X	X
Community Celebration			X			X	X
Concentric Circles			X	X	X	X	
Copy Claps	X		X				
Cross the Line				X	X	X	X
Crosstown Connection	X		X				
Dinosour Game	X		X				
Disguised Voice	X		X	X	X		
Don't Break the Ice		X	X			X	
Falls Ball	X	X				X	
Foot Tag	X	X	X				
Frogger (Revisted)	X	X		X		X	X
From My Perspective						X	X
Full Value Stock Market			X	X	X		
FVC Origami			X	X	X		
GPS-E				X			X
Hu Ha Pako	X	X	X	X			
I'm a starfish	X	X					
Ice Breakers		X	X			X	
Identification Numbers			X	X	X		

ACTIVITIES	Fun and Play	Physical Activity and Movement	Building Trust, Relationships and Community	Self Awareness and Self Management	Social Awareness	Relationship Skills	Responsible Decision Making
Indiana Jones	X	X	X				
Juggle Moves	X	X	X				X
Jump In Jump Out (aka Front Back)			X	X	X		
Jump Tag	X	X		X	X		
Knee Tag		X	X	X			X
Knot Again						X	X
Knot My Problem					X	X	X
Knot Race (aka NASCAR)						X	X
Lean & Walk		X	X	X	X		
Left & Right Pairs Tag	X	X	X				
Little Green Straw	X		X				X
Log Pile			X			X	X
Longest Shadow						X	X
Macrowave Popcorn	X					X	X
Magic Spells			X	X	X		
Map Making			X			X	X
Merge		X				X	X
Missle Command	X	X					X
Name Stock Market	X		X			X	
Name Trains			X	X	X	X	X
Ninja	X	X	X				
ONE WORD	X						X
Partner Get-up				X	X	X	
Phonetically Speaking			X			X	X
Pitball	X	X	X				
Playing with Poppers	X		X				X
Pogo Stick Tag	X	X	X				X
Power Ball	X	X	X				X
Press Conference			X	X	X		
Quick Math	X		X	X			X
Rock Paper Scissors Baseball	X	X	X				
Rock Paper Scissors Championship	X		X				

ACTIVITIES	Fun and Play	Physical Activity and Movement	Building Trust, Relationships and Community	Self Awareness and Self Management	Social Awareness	Relationship Skills	Responsible Decision Making
Shake It Up				X		X	X
Sneak Attack	X			X		X	X
Sonic 1	X	X		X			
Sonic 2 (aka Sonic and Tails)		X	X	X			X
Sonic 3 (aka Sonic and Knuckles)		X	X			X	
Space Invaders	X	X	X			X	
Spoon Jousting Tag	X	X	X				
Stationary Foot Tag (aka Top It)	X	X	X				
Stationay Handshakes		X	X				X
Step Tag	X	X	X				
Sticky Snakes						X	X
Stomp Clap Groove	X	X				X	X
Super Smile			X	X	X		
Tail Tag		X			X	X	X
Team Tail Tag	X	X	X				
The Elusive Shadow	X						
The Mystery Box		X	X				
Three Syllable Word	X					X	X
Tie that Eight				X		X	X
Tollbooth Boogie				X		X	X
Total Eclipse of the Heart						X	X
Traffic Signs			X	X	X		
Trust Line			X	X	X	X	
Tunnel Tag	X	X		X	X		
Tweener	X		X		X		
Walk & Lean			X	X	X	X	
Watch Your Step		X				X	X
What Do You See?	X		X				
Where in the World			X	X	X	X	
World Travelers		X	X				X
World Wide Key Punch				X		X	X
Yeehaw!	X		X	X			

ACTIVITIES	Fun and Play	Physical Activity and Movement	Building Trust, Relationships and Community	Self Awareness and Self Management	Social Awareness	Relationship Skills	Responsible Decision Making
You, You, Me	X	X	X				
Your Add	X		X				
Yup Boing	X		X				

ACTIVITY SEQUENCES							
A Mess of Handshakes	X	X	X			X	X
Full Value Flow	X	X	X	X	X		X
Building Blocks	X	X	X	X	X	X	X
World Wide Wonder		X	X	X	X	X	X
Spotting Sequence - Enhanced	X	X	X	X	X	X	

Inspiring Resources

Resources that influenced and inspired *The Hundredth Monkey*.

Books and other written sources:

- *A Return to Love: Reflections on the Principles of A Course in Miracles*. Marianne Williamson. Harper Collins, 1992.
- *A Whole New Mind*. Dan Pink. Riverheadbooks, 2006.
- *Achieving Fitness*. Jane Panicucci et al. Project Adventure, 2007.
- *Adventure Curriculum for Physical Education*. Jane Panicucci et al. Project Adventure, 2003.
- *Adventures in Business*. Ann Smolowe, Steve Butler, and Mark Murray. Project Adventure, 2001.
- *Count Me In*. Mark Collard. Project Adventure. 2008.
- *Creating Healthy Habits*. Dr. Katie Kilty. Project Adventure, 2006.
- "Developmental sequence in small groups". Psychological Bulletin. Bruce Tuckman. 1965.
- *Drive*. Dan Pink. Riverhead Books, 2009.
- *Effective Leadership in Adventure Programming*. Simon Priest and Mike Gass. Human Kinetics, 1997.
- *Experiential Learning: Experience As the Source of Learning and Development*. David A. Kolb. Prentice Hall, 1984.
- *Exploring Islands of Healing*. Jim Schoel and Rich Maizell. Project Adventure, 2007
- *Flow*. Mihaly Csikszentmihalyi. Harper and Row, 1990
- *Gold Nuggets*. Jim Schoel and Mike Stratton. Kendall/Hunt Publishing, 1995.
- *Have You Filled a Bucket Today*. By Carol McCloud and Illustrated by David Messing. Nelson Publishing and Marketing, 2007
- *Islands of Healing*. Jim Schoel, Dick Prouty, and Paul Radcliffe. Kendall/Hunt Publishing Company, 1995.
- *Journey to the Caring Classroom*. Luarie S. Frank. Woods 'N' Barnes, 2004.
- *Lynchpin*. Seth Godin. Penguin Group USA, 2011.
- *No Props*. Mark Collard. Project Adventure , 2005.
- *Play*. Stuart Brown. Avery, 2010.
- *The Art of Living*. Erich Fromm. Harper and Row, 1956.
- *The Element*. Sir Ken Robinson. Viking Adult, 2009.
- *Quicksilver*. Karl Rohnke and Steve Butler. Kendall/Hunt Publishing Company, 1995.
- *Raptor and other Teambuilding Activities*. Sam Sikes. Learning Unlimited Corporation, 2003.
- *Reality is Broken*. Jane McGonigal. Penguin Press, 2011.
- *Silver Bullets, 2nd Edition*. Karl Rohnke. Project Adventure, 2009.
- *Spark*. John Ratey. Little, Brown and Company, 2008.
- *Stepping Stones*. Peter Aubry. Project Adventure, 2008.
- *The Tipping Point*. Malcolm Gladwell. Back Bay Books, 2002
- *Tribes*. Seth Godin. Portfolio, 2008.

Websites:

Ted.com
    Sir Ken Robinson
    Stuart Brown
    Benjamin Zander
    Stefon Harris
    Evelyn Glennie
theRSA.org
Playmeo.com
Sethgodin.typepad.com
Bucketfillers101.com
nifplay.org

Activity List

5 Handshakes 5 Minutes, 21
52 Card Pick-up, 24
Altershake, 26
Armada , 29
Balloon Tag, 37
Behavioral Settings, 39
Block Party, 42
Brain Buckets, 43
Bridging the Gap, 45
Bust a Move, 47
Circle Call , 49
Circle Tag , 52
Circle Up , 54
Collaborative Numbers (aka Key Punch Jr.), 56
Community Celebration, 58
Concentric Circles, 60
Copy Claps, 62
Cross the Line, 64
Crosstown Connections, 67
Dinosaur Game, 69
Disguised Voice, 70
Don't Break the Ice, 72
Falls Ball, 74
Foot Tag, 77
Frogger (Revisted), 79
From My Perspective, 84
Full Value Stock Market, 86
FVC Origami, 88
GPS-E, 91
Hu Ha Pako, 92
I'm a Starfish, 96
Ice Breakers, 97
Identification Numbers, 100
Indiana Jones, 102
Juggle Moves, 103
Jump In Jump Out (aka Front Back), 105
Jump Tag, 109
Knee Tag, 112
Knot Again, 116
Knot My Problem, 118
Knot Race (aka NASCAR), 120
Lean and Walk, 122
Left and Right Pairs Tag, 123
Little Green Straw, 124
Log Pile, 126
Longest Shadow, 127
Macrowave Popcorn, 129
Magic Spells, 131

Map Making, 134
Merge, 136
Missile Command, 139
Name Stock Market, 142
Name Trains, 145
Ninja, 149
ONE WORD, 150
Partner Get-up, 152
Phonetically Speaking, 154
Pitball, 157
Playing with Poppers, 159
Pogo Stick Tag, 161
Power Ball, 163
Press Conference, 166
Quick Math, 167
Rock Paper Scissors Baseball, 170
Rock Paper Scissors Championship, 173
Shake It Up, 175
Sneak Attack, 177
Sonic 1, 180
Sonic 2 (aka Sonic and Tails), 182
Sonic 3 (aka Sonic and Knuckles), 185
Space Invaders, 187
Spoon Jousting Tag, 192
Stationary Foot Tag (aka Top It), 194
Stationary Handshakes, 197
Step Tag, 199
Sticky Snakes, 200
Stomp Clap Groove, 201
Super Smile, 203
Tail Tag, 205
Team Tail Tag, 207
The Elusive Shadow, 208
The Mystery Box, 210
Three Syllable Word, 216
Tie that Eight, 217
Tollbooth Boogie, 218
Total Eclipse of the Heart, 224
Traffic Signs, 225
Trust Line, 226
Tunnel Tag, 228
Tweener, 230
Walk and Lean, 232
Watch Your Step, 234
What Do You See?, 237
Where in the World?, 238
World Travelers, 240
World Wide Key Punch, 244

Yeehaw, 247
You, You, Me, 252
Your Add, 253
Yup Boing, 255

Activity Sequences (in order by time)

A Mess of Handshakes (30 Minutes), 260
    Stationary Handshake, 260
    5 Handshakes, 5 Minutes, 262
    Log Pile, 263

Full Value Flow (45-60 minutes), 264
    Whampum, 264
    FVC Cards, 266
    Swat Tag, 266
    FVC Cards Debrief/Check-in, 268

Building Blocks (60-90 minutes), 269
    Mingle and Match, 269
    Bust A Move, 270
    Don't Break the Ice, 271
    Ice Breakers, 272
    Bridging the Gap, 272
    Block Party, 273
    Crossword Debrief, 273

World Wide Wonder (120 minutes), 274
    Map Making, 274
    Where in the World, 275
    World Travelers, 276
    World Wide Keypunch, 277
    Reflective Map Debrief, 278

Spotting Sequence – Enhanced (120-180 minutes), 280
    People to People, 280
    Palm Off (Multiple Stances), 281
    Spotting Stance, 282
    Super Spotters Social, 283
    2-Person Trust Leans, 284
    3-Person Trust Leans, 285
    Wind in the Willows, 286
    Can You Levitate?, 287
    Levitation, 288

About Project Adventure

Project Adventure Books and Publications

Project Adventure has been publishing books and materials for the field of Adventure Education since 1974. Our titles cover all aspects of Adventure – from games and initiatives to specific school-based curricula, from Challenge Ropes Course use to program safety, theory and practices.

Some of our most popular titles include:

Physical Education Curriculum – Elementary, Middle & High Schools by Jane Panicucci, with Alison Rheingold, Amy Kohut, Nancy Stratton and Lisa Faulkingham–Hunt.

Achieving Fitness: An Adventure Activity Guide (Middle School to Adult) by Jane Panicucci with Lisa Faulkingham–Hunt, Ila Sahai Prouty and Carol Masterson.

Creating Healthy Habits: An Adventure Guide to Teaching Health and Wellness (Middle School) by Katie Kilty

Stepping Stones: A Therapeutic Adventure Activity Guide - Activities to Enhance Outcomes With Alternative Populations Edited by Peter Aubry

Count Me In: Large Activities That Work by Mark Collard

Silver Bullets by Karl Rohnke

Quick Silver by Karl Rohnke and Steve Butler

No Props: Great Games with No Equipment by Mark Collard

The Guide for Challenge Course Operations by Bob Ryan

Exploring Islands of Healing by Jim Schoel and Richard Maizell

Cowstails & Cobras II by Karl Rohnke

Islands of Healing by Jim Schoel, Dick Prouty and Paul Radcliffe

Gold Nuggets: Readings for Experiential Education edited by Jin Schoel and Mike Stratton

Program Resources

Adventure programs, both with and without a Challenge Course, need accessories that can often be difficult to find or adapt. The Project Adventure resource catalog provides an extensive range of innovative Adventure accessories to help you administer your program. For a complete listing of books, games and gear, visit our website at www.pa.org.

Training Workshops & Services

Open Enrollment workshops, conducted throughout the USA aim to help you to learn the skills to present safe and valuable adventure-based programs.

Project Adventure also provides a wide range of services, including:

Program Consultation

Custom Trainings

Challenge Ropes Course Design and Installation

For a complete listing of workshop types and dates, visit our website at www.pa.org

PA International Network

Project Adventure, Inc.
719 Cabot Street
Beverly, MA 01915 – 1027 USA

Phone (978)-524-4500 or (800)-468-8898
Fax (978)-524-4600
Web www.pa.org
Email info@pa.org

For more information on our licensed affiliates in Japan, New Zealand, Australia and Singapore, email info@pa.org.

Project Adventure has offices / partnerships in several southeast Asian, South American and European countries.

Contact Project Adventure at 800-468-8898 or info@pa.org for current contact details.

About the Author

Nate Folan grew up in the close knit community of North Attleboro, Massachusetts, the middle child of three and son of hardworking parents and restaurant owners/operators. During his late teens and early twenties, Nate's employment at the family restaurant helped him to develop a healthy work ethic and an initial understanding of group dynamics. His years of experience with the North Attleboro Park and Recreation Department opened a world of possibilities that he is still exploring. It was here that Nate developed a love for play, hard work, nature, and people.

Nate is a full-time Project Adventure trainer who is passionate about playful experiences and the opportunities they provide. He believes that authentic relationships and play are essential to living well. Nate leads a variety of adventure-based experiential workshops and trainings annually with professionals at camps, schools, and therapeutic agencies throughout the United States and, occasionally, other countries.

Prior to joining the PA staff in May 2006, Nate led therapeutic wilderness trips with both at-risk and adjudicated teens, where he learned important tips, techniques, and skills from some of the greatest teachers on earth – the students. For more than 15 years, Nate has delivered significant and relevant experiences for people of all ages in a variety of settings including camps, schools, after-school programs, teen-centers, ski and snowboard schools, wilderness therapy and training and professional development programs. Throughout the years, he has continued to value the effectiveness of authentic relationships and the power of play.

Nate lives on a friend's farm in Hollis, NH with his wife, Michelle. He enjoys finding meaning and inspiration in playful moments, music, nature, sea kayaking, photography, and sharing time with family.

Notes:

Notes:

Notes: